GRADING EDUCATION

Getting Accountability Right

RICHARD ROTHSTEIN

Rebecca Jacobsen • Tamara Wilder

Economic
Policy
Institute

TEACHERS
COLLEGE
PRESS

Recommended citation for this book is as follows:
Rothstein, Richard, Rebecca Jacobsen, and Tamara Wilder. 2008. *Grading Education: Getting Accountability Right*. Washington, D.C. and New York, N.Y.: Economic Policy Institute and Teachers College Press.
Published simultaneously by EPI and TCP.

1333 H Street, NW
Suite 300, East Tower
Washington, DC 20005-4707
www.epi.org
ISBN: 1-932066-36-5

TEACHERS COLLEGE PRESS
1234 Amsterdam Avenue
New York, New York 10027
www.tcpress.com
ISBN: 978-0-8077-4939-5

Printed on acid-free paper

Manufactured in the United States of America

15   14   13   12   11   10   09   08   1   2   3   4   5   6   7   8

Table of contents

Introduction

Except for the military, Americans devote more resources to elementary and secondary education than to any other activity we undertake in common. Nearly 15% of all tax dollars go to support public schools.[1] We depend on public schools to narrow social and economic inequalities and to ensure that all youth contribute to the health of our democracy and to the productivity of the economy. We expect educators to pursue these ambitions competently.

So it is entirely reasonable, indeed necessary, that citizens should hold educators accountable for effectively spending the funds with which they've been entrusted. In this book, we use the term "accountability" to describe the techniques by which citizens and their elected representatives control the activities of those who administer, teach, and serve in public schools and other institutions of youth development. It is not sufficient to insist that spending of public funds is honest and properly reported. It is not sufficient to insist that all the inputs – the resources – be adequate to the task. Nor is it sufficient to insist that educators profess good intentions, or that parents be satisfied with their children's schools. In education, "accountability," as described here, requires schools and other public institutions that prepare our youth to pursue the goals established by the people and their representatives through democratic processes, and to achieve these goals to the extent possible by using the most effective strategies available. During the last two decades, the design of such accountability has become the focus of public debates about education.[2]

We've wound up, however, adopting accountability policies based almost exclusively on standardized test scores for reading and mathematics. This book demonstrates why such narrow test-based accountability plans cannot possibly accomplish their stated intent, which is to tell the states and nation whether schools and related public institutions are performing satisfactorily and to support interventions that ensure improvement. To hold schools and other institutions of youth development accountable, information from tests of basic skills must be combined with a wide array of information from other sources, including tests of reasoning and critical thinking and evaluations by experienced and qualified experts who observe schools, child care centers, health clinics, and after-school and summer programs, to determine if they are performing satisfactorily.

In 2002, the federal government adopted an accountability system for public schools, the *No Child Left Behind Act* (NCLB). It defined the result for which schools should be held accountable as student proficiency in math and reading, and gave states a dozen years to improve their school systems so that all students, including those from disadvantaged minorities, could achieve such proficiency. States revised or adopted their own accountability systems to conform to the federal requirements.

NCLB demanded that schools bring all students to proficiency regardless of how well families and other socioeconomic institutions prepared children to learn. The law required states to test all third to eighth graders annually in math and reading to demonstrate that they were making consistent progress toward full proficiency by 2014. It also required testing once in students' high school years. In cases where any subgroup – including minority students, low-income students, or those with disabilities – failed to make such progress, the law required districts to permit students to transfer to schools where adequate progress was being made, and it required districts to spend some of their federal aid on tutoring, often provided by private contractors. If subgroups still failed to make sufficient progress, the law required states to intervene in more drastic ways, including closing the schools involved and re-opening them with new teachers and administrators.

No Child Left Behind was an utter failure, and in 2007 and 2008 Congress refused to reauthorize it in anything like its original form. Parents, teachers, school administrators, school board members, and state legislators were vocal about their contempt for NCLB's consequences. Although many policy activists admired the law's requirement that schools be held accountable for the performance of minority as well as middle-class white students, few believed that the law succeeded in improving American education – and many concluded that the law did great harm.

Yet despite widespread dissatisfaction with NCLB, Congress has been unable to devise a reasonable alternative and so, as of September 2008, NCLB remains on the books. There have been many proposals for tinkering with the law's provisions – extending the deadline for reaching proficiency, measuring progress by the change in scores of the same group of students from one year to the next (instead of comparing scores of this year's students with scores of those in the same grade in the previous year), adding a few other requirements (like graduation rates, or parent satisfaction) to the accountability regime, or standardizing the definitions of proficiency among the states. Yet none of these proposals commanded sufficient support because none addressed NCLB's most fundamental problem – although tests, properly interpreted, can contribute some important information about school quality, testing alone is a poor way to measure whether schools, or their students, perform adequately.

Many critics have denounced NCLB and similar state accountability policies that are based exclusively on quantitative measures (test scores) of a narrow set of school outcomes (basic math and reading skills). Critics have described how accountability for math and reading scores has inaccurately identified good and bad schools, narrowed the curriculum by creating perverse incentives for schools to ignore many important purposes of schools beyond math and reading test scores, caused teachers to focus on some students at the expense of others, and created opportunities for educators to substitute gamesmanship for quality instruction. And the critics have described why conventional proposals to "fix" NCLB perpetuate these problems. But some who hear these critiques, while acknowledging their merit, respond: "Do you mean that schools should not be held accountable? What do you think we should do about failing schools? If you don't like narrow test-based accountability, what is your alternative?"

These are appropriate questions, and this book endeavors to answer them by describing how the public should hold schools and other institutions of youth development accountable for adequate performance.

In one sense, we've always had democratic accountability in education. Communities elect school boards, or mayors, who appoint superintendents and who, in turn, appoint other staff and teachers to carry out policies set by the elected officials. Voters can and do re-elect or replace board members and mayors. But we've become dissatisfied with this form of accountability, skeptical that elected school boards are capable of raising performance for all students in all states and localities. Sometimes, even within districts under the supervision of a single school board, some schools are left to struggle while others continue to shine.

Partly, the dissatisfaction is unavoidable. As school districts grew, it became more difficult for elected board members to make judgments about whether schools they supervised were performing well. Most superintendents now supervise such large organizations that they cannot themselves evaluate principals' or teachers' effectiveness.

Elected board members, especially those on the first step of a political career ladder, may be more interested in burying bad news about schools than in correcting problems, and so they defer to educators' interests in preserving established ways of doing things. Low voter participation in school board or municipal elections sometimes gives disproportionate influence to teachers' unions, other employee organizations, or advocacy groups with narrow agendas, because such groups can contribute campaign funds to board members and municipal officials and then turn out their members to vote.

The mere fact that school board members must seek a mandate from voters in elections has provided an inadequate assurance that boards will hold educators accountable for high student achievement.

This book proposes to supplement school board governance with a public accountability system that avoids both the haphazard and undisciplined oversight of elected board members and the simplistic and corrupting accountability of predominantly test-based systems. A well-designed accountability system can forestall unproductive practice by schools and other institutions of youth development. It can also spur higher-quality practice when expert evaluators advise well-intentioned educators and other youth service professionals about how to improve student outcomes.

The accountability system proposed in this volume has these principles:

- Accountability properly conceived has roles for both federal and state government. The federal government should ensure that states have the means to generate adequate outcomes and should provide sophisticated testing and survey data of representative state-level samples of youth and young adults to show the extent to which schools and supporting institutions have been successful. State leaders can then use this information to identify areas in which the achievement of youth in their state is lacking and, using tests as well as qualitative inspections and evaluations, hold school districts, schools, and other local institutions of youth development accountable for appropriate improvements in performance.

- Because student outcomes are the joint product of families, schools, and other institutions – such as public health agencies, early childhood services, community development, after-school and summer programming – an accountability system should be designed to ensure that all public institutions make appropriate contributions to youth development. When schools are integrated with supporting services, they can substantially narrow the achievement gap between disadvantaged and middle-class children.

- No experts can yet say with assurance how much of a narrowing in the achievement gap is feasible, even with a coordinated effort by schools and their supporting institutions. Thus, an accountability system should avoid establishing absolute outcome goals that the children of all subgroups should meet. Rather, with appropriate supporting services, schools should be expected to improve their outcomes so that students achieve as well as better-performing students elsewhere who have similar background characteristics. Such aspiration ensures continuing improvement, because few schools are so good that they cannot improve to the level of comparable but better-performing schools.

- Adolescents should enter young adulthood with many cognitive skills and non-cognitive qualities – not only strong academic knowledge and skills, but also the ability to reason and think critically, an appreciation of the arts and literature, preparation for skilled work, social skills and a strong work ethic, good citizenship, and habits leading to good physical and emotional health. State accountability systems should ensure that schools and supporting institutions promote all these traits in a balanced fashion, because accountability for only some outcomes will create incentives to ignore others.

- The federal government is too distant from the provision of educational services to be primarily responsible for holding schools and other institutions of youth development accountable. State governments can and should be the vehicles for doing so.

- The federal government nevertheless has an essential role in making accountability for high achievement feasible. It is unreasonable to expect adequate outcomes for youth if their states do not have the funds to provide good schools and other high-quality youth development institutions. Appropriate funds are no guarantee of adequate outcomes; funds can be spent foolishly or inefficiently – that's one reason why accountability is needed. But appropriate funding is a necessary if not sufficient requirement. For those states that have too few taxable resources to properly support schools and other institutions of youth development, the federal government should provide subsidies so that accountability can be effective.

- The federal government should also develop the capacity to measure the degree to which students and young adults in each state achieve competence in all of the important cognitive and non-cognitive domains. This measurement does not require a federal assessment of every student; rather, it requires a sophisticated sampling system that can generate accurate state-level results, including disaggregated results for minorities and disadvantaged youth. Appropriate state-by-state comparisons of subgroup performance require data on important demographic characteristics so that, for example, states can know whether low-income children whose parents did not finish high school perform better or worse than similar children in other states. With information on how their states perform relative to others, governors and state legislatures can design systems that enable schools and other institutions of youth development to improve, and then hold them accountable for doing so.

- The federal government's state-by-state measurement of youth outcomes in all important cognitive and non-cognitive domains should be widely publicized. Voters and advocacy organizations in each state require information on the relative performance of their state institutions. With such information, they can fulfill their responsibility to hold state leaders – governors and legislatures – accountable for improvement where performance is inadequate. And these state leaders can then likewise hold school districts, schools, and other youth institutions similarly accountable. Although the federal government has the unique ability to collect comparative information on the performance of schools and other services across the states, only state leaders can effectively implement the policies needed to improve that performance. There is no practical way for the federal government to ensure standardization of outcomes across states, and there is no reason to believe that Congress or the president are more highly motivated to improve education and youth development than are state leaders. If there was one lesson to be learned from *No Child Left Behind*, this was it.

- High-quality standardized tests of academic skills could provide necessary information to states about student performance. But not all traits for which schools should be held accountable can be measured by paper-and-pencil tests. A proper accountability system must also have ways to review the total body of student work by, for example, observing young people demonstrating their skills and surveying the extent to which young people engage in the behaviors – good citizenship, for example – for which they are being trained.

- Although an accountability system should ideally be concerned only with outcomes – whether, upon entering young adulthood, adolescents have developed the knowledge, skills, and traits upon which their success as well as the nation's depends – such accountability for outcomes alone is impractical. If, for example, state leaders discover that young adults have emerged from schools with poor academic knowledge and skills, or poor health and citizenship habits, it will be too late to correct the early childhood or elementary schools that failed, many years earlier, to lay a proper foundation for these young adults' outcomes. Therefore, state accountability systems must have ways to assess whether teachers and other youth development professionals are engaged in practices that are likely to lead to adequate outcomes many years later. Like the observation of student performance, such assessment requires a corps of expert evaluators who can judge, on behalf of the public, whether schools and other institutions of youth development are embarked upon strategies that are likely to succeed in their missions.

One reason, perhaps the most important, why *No Child Left Behind* and similar testing systems in the states got accountability so wrong is that we've wanted to do accountability on the cheap. Standardized tests that assess only low-level skills and that can be scored electronically cost very little to administer – although their hidden costs are enormous in the lost opportunities to develop young people's broader knowledge, traits, and skills. A successful accountability system, such as this book proposes, will initially be more expensive, requiring a sophisticated national assessment of a broad range of outcomes, and a corps of professional evaluators in each state that can devote the time necessary to determine if schools and other institutions of youth development – early childhood programs, health and social service clinics, for example – are following practices likely to lead to adult success. But while such accountability will be expensive, it is not prohibitively so. Sophisticated school accountability could cost up to 1% of what we now spend on elementary and secondary education. If we want to do accountability right, and we should, this level of spending is worthwhile.

In the long run, accountability is cost-effective. We now waste billions of dollars by continuing to operate low-quality schools, because narrow test-based accountability can neither accurately identify them nor guide those it identifies to improve. And we waste billions by forcing good schools to abandon high-quality programs to comply with the government's test obsession. We cannot know how much money could be saved by more intelligent accountability, but it is probably considerable.

In developing these proposals and writing this book, I enjoyed the collaboration of two talented students who, in the course of the project, became valued colleagues. Rebecca Jacobsen is now an assistant professor of education at Michigan State University, and Tamara Wilder is a postdoctoral fellow at the University of Michigan. They each assisted with the entire project, and provided me with important advice and counsel regarding its major themes. Without question, their collaboration rose to the level of co-authorship.

With their assistance, this volume proceeds as follows:

Chapter 1 recognizes that a successful accountability system must first define the outcomes that schools and other institutions of youth development should achieve. It reviews how American leaders have historically thought about educational goals, and it summarizes these traditions by defining eight broad goal areas for which accountability is necessary: basic academic knowledge and skills, critical thinking, appreciation of the arts and literature, preparation for skilled work, social skills and work ethic, citizenship and community responsibility, physical health, and emotional health.

Chapter 2 reports on surveys we have commissioned to determine how the American public and elected representatives today value each of the goals that have been part of our national consensus. These surveys allow us to estimate how relatively important each of the eight broad goal areas should be in a well-designed accountability system. Our conclusion is that a little more than half of the weight of an accountability system should be devoted to matters that might broadly be termed academic – basic knowledge and skills, critical thinking, appreciation of the arts and literature, and the acquisition of occupation-specific technical skills – while the balance should be devoted to citizenship, social skills, and other physical and emotional health behaviors that we expect young adults to exhibit.

Some policy makers acknowledge that schools should turn out youth with this broad range of knowledge, traits, and skills, but they also say that we are now in a temporary crisis that requires putting all else aside to rapidly develop the math and literacy competence of our youth. This crisis, they say, is one of international competitiveness and, unless Americans' math and reading test scores improve, we will lose out in a race for economic survival with nations whose test scores are higher. Therefore, they conclude, we should hold schools exclusively accountable for math and reading scores, and wait until later to develop more sophisticated accountability.

This argument has little foundation in economic reality, despite its widespread acceptance. Yet until Americans understand how little foundation it has, there is little hope of mobilizing their support for the kind of accountability system that this book proposes. After all, if the nation is about to be defeated economically because of a basic skills crisis, holding schools accountable for developing social skills, good citizenship, or an appreciation for the arts can only be considered a luxury. So Appendix 1 describes why school performance, however inadequate it may be, is not responsible for the nation's economic woes.

Chapters 3 and 4 describe why narrow test-based accountability systems (such as state testing programs required by NCLB) have not only failed to improve American education but have caused great harm. Readers who have been immersed in debates about education will find some material in these two chapters familiar, and may choose to skim or skip them. Chapter 3 describes how holding schools accountable for math and reading test scores has created incentives for educators to pay less attention to curricular areas for which they are not held accountable – other academic subjects such as science and social studies, as well as physical and health education, the arts and music, character development, cooperative behavior, and civic responsibility. To confirm and illustrate the pervasiveness of this goal distortion, I asked a New York City schoolteacher (and former student, Jessica Salute) to interview teachers from around the country about how accountability policies have affected their instructional practices.[3] Appendix 4 includes excerpts from many of these interviews.

Chapter 4 analyzes other flaws in test-based accountability. It describes the false hope that achieving "proficiency" can simultaneously be a challenge and a minimum standard for all students. The chapter demonstrates that the normal range of student abilities, even with the best of instruction, will inevitably result in a wide range of cognitive and non-cognitive outcomes. By ignoring this inevitability of human variation, the designers of contemporary accountability policies have developed such fanciful proficiency definitions that even the highest-scoring countries in the world don't come close to realizing them. The chapter describes how an accountability system organized around achieving a fixed proficiency point leads to excessive concentration on students whose performance is slightly below that point and ignores students who are either above or far below it. Test-based accountability also creates incentives for educators to game the system, for example by manipulating suspension policies or special education assignments for the sole purpose of demonstrating artificial gains on accountability tests.

Chapter 5 shows why we should not have been surprised that test-based accountability plans have corrupted education. Social scientists and business theorists have long argued that public and private enterprises should avoid accountability systems that are based solely or largely on easily measured short-term outcomes like test scores. Certainly, exclusively quantitative incentive and evaluation plans in other sectors have sometimes improved outcomes, but these improvements have usually been offset by more serious adverse impacts. The chapter reviews accountability plans in public and private fields – health care, job training, welfare, criminal justice, and others –and concludes that an accountability plan in any institution will corrupt that institution if the plan relies primarily on quantitative short-term measures without substantial qualitative evaluation. Many errors in the design of test-based accountability plans at the state level, and of NCLB at the federal level, could easily have been avoided if education policy makers had considered the experiences of these other sectors.

Chapter 6 shows that other errors might have been avoided if policy makers had recalled how, 45 years ago, the federal government first designed its measurement of student performance, the National Assessment of Educational Progress (NAEP). In its early years, NAEP focused on long-term outcomes by assessing young adults as well as schoolchildren, and it measured behavioral as well as cognitive results of schooling. The model of early NAEP suggests some elements of a sophisticated accountability system. But because NAEP's complex sampling methodology can only generate results at the state level (or for very large urban districts), its value is in the information it provides to each state's governor, legislators, and other policy makers about how young people in that state perform relative to young people in other, comparable states. NAEP cannot tell these policy makers how individual schools, child care centers, public health programs, or after-school programs are contributing to these results. Standardized test scores at the school level provide some information, but only on basic academic skills; supplementing this information requires actual inspection of schools and other institutions of youth development. Easily accessible inspectorate models are available from which to draw.

Chapter 7 begins by recounting the evolution of American school boards and argues that they have lost sight of their obligation to hold schools accountable for outcomes defined by the public through democratic procedures. The chapter then describes some existing arrangements from which elements of a democratic school accountability system can be adapted. Most important is the system of school accreditation that exists today in much of the country. The system is based on school inspections, but it does not presently provide an adequate means of accountability. Those conducting accreditation visits are volunteers with inadequate training and experience, accreditation agencies have no clearly defined expectation of youth outcomes, and accreditation's mostly voluntary nature is inconsistent with the authority needed for accountability. Accreditation is a reasonably successful peer-review system leading to school improvement, but it falls short of an accountability mission.

Some other nations more successfully use school visitations for accountability purposes. Chapter 7 describes how inspection works in England, where

Her Majesty's Inspectors oversee comprehensive visitation that is focused on a broad range of outcomes, that supplements standardized testing in academic subjects, and that evaluates whether schools, early childhood centers, and other community institutions are making appropriate contributions to young people's success.

Chapter 8 summarizes by proposing the outlines of an accountability system for American schools and other institutions of youth development. The federal government's role in this system should include a funding distribution mechanism to ensure that states with limited fiscal capacity and relatively large numbers of disadvantaged children have the resources to generate the youth outcomes for which institutions in those states should be held accountable. It should also include a vastly expanded NAEP that could give state leaders the information they need to determine if their youth demonstrate balanced achievement in each of the eight broad goal areas. Chapter 8 then describes how state leaders, armed with this information, could supplement scores from well-designed tests with a professional visitation system to hold school districts, schools, and other institutions of youth development accountable for producing these balanced outcomes.

Schools have an important but not exclusive influence on student achievement; the gap in performance of schools with advantaged and disadvantaged children is due in large part to differences in the social and economic conditions from which schoolchildren come.[4] For this reason, schools can best improve youth outcomes if they are part of an integrated system of youth development and family support services that also includes, at a minimum, high-quality early childhood care, health services, and after-school and summer programs. The understanding of such an integrated system's importance is widespread – recently, a group of experts with diverse political, academic, and organizational backgrounds began a campaign to convince policy makers of its necessity. Their analysis is reproduced as Appendix 2.

If the expanded NAEP proposed in Chapter 8 were to report that a state's youth outcomes in any key cognitive or non-cognitive domain were inadequate, state policy makers would then have to decide whether the fault lies in the shortcomings of schools or of other institutions subject to state influence or control. The visitation system proposed in Chapter 8 should be designed to hold schools as well as supporting institutions accountable for high performance.

But first things first. Before detailing this accountability program, we have to ask, "accountable for what?" What are the goals of American public education? Certainly, good test scores are part of the answer, but should schools be accountable for more – say, good citizenship, or good judgment? If so, is it possible to measure these broader school outcomes to know whether educators are performing satisfactorily? It is to these questions that we now turn.

– Richard Rothstein
September 2, 2008

CHAPTER 1

The outcome goals of American public education

Federal and state policies now seek to evaluate school quality by whether students are proficient in math and reading, as measured by standardized tests.[5] An accountability policy that bases rewards or punishments for schools and teachers on their students' math and reading scores creates incentives for teachers to devote more time and attention to math and reading and less to other curricular areas for which there are no consequences for poor performance.[6]

Some supporters of contemporary accountability systems say that if students improve their basic skills, other skills will follow naturally. This seems plausible: after all, children can't understand history if they can't read about it. But children also won't learn to read well unless they are interested in stories, events, and facts that reading can uncover. An excessive focus on passing tests in basic skills can weaken students' interest, and thus their achievement, in the natural and social sciences and in the arts. Making reading drills a chore can destroy children's potential to love literature or to understand and interpret history. And if too much time is devoted to math and reading, too little may be devoted to physical education, to the development of character traits and interpersonal skills (the peaceful resolution of conflicts, for example), and to other behaviors that also flow from a well-rounded education.

From our nation's beginnings, Americans have mostly embraced a balanced curriculum to fulfill public education's mission. The following pages review a small sample of the many statements by policy makers and educators over the course of 250 years, statements that define a range of knowledge, skills, and character traits that Americans have always wanted schools to develop in our youth. It is striking how similar the goals of public education have remained during this history. Although some differences of emphasis have emerged during different eras, our national leaders seem consistently to have wanted public education to produce satisfactory outcomes in eight broad categories; it is for outcomes in these eight categories that we should hold public schools and other institutions of youth development accountable:

1. *Basic academic knowledge and skills:* basic skills in reading, writing, and math, and knowledge of science and history.

2. *Critical thinking and problem solving:* the ability to analyze information, apply ideas to new situations, and develop knowledge using computers.

3. *Appreciation of the arts and literature:* participation in and appreciation of musical, visual, and performing arts as well as a love of literature.

4. *Preparation for skilled employment:* workplace qualification for students not pursuing college education.

5. *Social skills and work ethic:* communication skills, personal responsibility, and the ability to get along with others from varied backgrounds.

6. *Citizenship and community responsibility:* public ethics; a knowledge of how government works; and participation by voting, volunteering, and becoming active in community life.

7. *Physical health:* good habits of exercise and nutrition.

8. *Emotional health:* self-confidence, respect for others, and the ability to resist peer pressure to engage in irresponsible personal behavior.

If these are, indeed, the outcomes that Americans have wanted and still want from our schools and other youth institutions, then we must devise ways of holding those institutions accountable for producing all of them in a balanced fashion.

Colonial and revolutionary eras

When the founding fathers urged public education, their motives were mostly civic. Reading was thought to teach good political judgment, allow learning from prior generations' mistakes and successes, and inculcate honesty, integrity, and compassion. While the teaching of basic academic skills was valued by early political and educational leaders, greater emphasis was placed on developing citizens who would protect and nurture the new democracy.

In colonial times, Benjamin Franklin pioneered American thinking on public education, as he did on so much else, by proposing in 1749 that Pennsylvania establish a public academy for the education of adolescents. He expected it to place as much emphasis on physical fitness as on academics: "exercise invigorates the soul as well as the body," Franklin said. "[L]et one be kept closely to reading without allowing him any respite from thinking or exercise to his body, and ... we should soon find such [a] one become no less soft in his mind than in his [body]."[7]

Schools today that cut back on physical education to make more time for math and reading would not have met with Franklin's approval.

As for academic subjects themselves, Franklin thought history was particularly important, because students will learn temperance, order, frugality, and perseverance from studying the moral character of historical figures. "[Q]uestions of right and wrong, justice and injustice, will naturally arise."[8] Franklin also proposed that students be expected to read newspapers and debate current issues to develop their abilities to use logic and reasoning.[9] He took pains to distinguish his view from those who would establish schools solely for academic purposes, writing that "it is certainly of more Consequence to a Man that he has learnt to govern his Passions...than to be a Master of all the Arts and Sciences in the World...."[10]

Of course, Franklin thought schools should require competence in reading, arithmetic, and science. Without this, students could not read texts in which virtue was modeled. But what would not have occurred to Franklin was that the quality of a school could be judged solely, or even primarily, by students' basic skills. These were but means to an end.

The American Revolution established a representative government that, the founders were aware, was experimental, taking sovereignty for the first time from a heritable monarchy and placing it in the hands of voters. It gave rise to two somewhat conflicting motivations for universal education. Some founders, mostly Jeffersonian Democrats,[11] emphasized having public schools that would create the capacity for ordinary citizens' intelligent democratic choice. Other founders, mostly Federalists, accepted democratic governance (though with less enthusiasm), hoping that universal education could socialize the citizenry to accept the values of their rulers and prepare young people for law-abiding adulthood, thereby preventing "tyranny of democratic anarchy."[12]

George Washington had both motivations. In his first state of the union message, he urged Congress to promote schools that taught citizens "to value their own rights" and protect themselves against those who would infringe upon them, "to distinguish between oppression and the necessary exercise of lawful authority," and "to discriminate the spirit of liberty from that of licentiousness...with an inviolable respect to the laws."[13]

In his farewell address upon leaving office, Washington urged establishment of public schools because "virtue or morality is a necessary spring of popular government"; to the extent public opinion makes policy in a democracy, "it is essential that public opinion should be enlightened."[14] Washington also wanted to bring youths of different backgrounds together at a national public university to develop a common identity: "In the general Juvenal period of life, when friendships are formed, & habits established that will stick by one, the Youth, or young men from different parts of the United States would be assembled together, & would by degrees discover that there was not just cause for those jealousies & prejudices which one part of the Union had imbibed against another part."[15] That youth should learn to accept diversity, as a goal of education, did not originate with contemporary affirmative action proponents.

Jefferson also wanted to empower citizens to choose good representatives and simultaneously to condition them to accept governmental authority. Public education, he wrote, should "raise the mass of the people to the high ground of moral respectability necessary to their own safety, and to orderly government." It will make citizens "see that it is their interest to preserve peace and order."[16]

But Jefferson also considered public education necessary to prepare citizens to vote wisely. This was not a concern for what we now call civics education, i.e., learning how a bill is passed, the length of a president's term, and so on. Rather, Jefferson thought, if schooling could enlighten students about "the experience of other ages and countries, they may be enabled to know ambition under all its shapes, and prompt to exert their natural powers to defeat its purposes."[17]

In the last decades of his life, retired from the presidency, Jefferson proposed a full system of public education goals (see **Figure A**), similar to the eight goals for which, this book argues, schools should be held accountable today. Jefferson's goals went beyond the preparation for citizenship he had emphasized earlier; they included basic academic skills and stressed the character traits he deemed essential for a well-functioning civil society.

This desire for public education with an expansive set of goals, articulated by Franklin, Washington, and Jefferson, was widely shared by their contemporaries. The 1780 Massachusetts Constitution, drafted by John Adams, included the first legal requirement for public education; it asserted that the duty of the legislative and executive branches "in all future periods" would be to maintain public schools because "wisdom and knowledge, as well as virtue, diffused generally among the body of the people, [is] necessary for the preservation of their rights and liberties." Adams' constitution specified that public schools, in addition to teaching academic subjects, should also be required to inculcate "the principles of humanity and general benevolence, public and private charity, industry and frugality, honesty and punctuality…sincerity, good humor, and all social affections, and generous sentiments."[18]

In 1787, the Northwest Ordinance provided funds for new states to establish public education systems. It stated: "Religion, morality, and knowledge, being necessary to good government and the happiness of mankind, schools and the

FIGURE A What public education should accomplish, as defined by Thomas Jefferson,1818

- to give every citizen the information he needs for the transaction of his own business

- to enable him to calculate for himself, and to express and preserve his ideas, his contracts and accounts, in writing

- to improve, by reading, his morals and faculties

- to understand his duties to his neighbors and country, and to discharge with competence the functions confided to him by either

- to know his rights; to exercise with order and justice those he retains; and to choose with discretion the fiduciary of those he delegates; and to notice their conduct with diligence, with candor, and judgment

- in general, to observe with intelligence and faithfulness all the social relations under which he shall be placed

---

Source: Jefferson et al. 1818, pp. 249-50.

means of education shall forever be encouraged."[19] New states were prohibited from altering this commitment without congressional consent. Thereafter, and throughout the 19th century, states adopted constitutions that set forth similar goals for public education. In all cases, the purposes of public schools were civic and moral, as well as academic.

The Jacksonian Era, and Horace Mann

As suffrage expanded in the 19th century, divisions between Jeffersonians and Federalists continued: Jacksonian Democrats wanted to empower the white working class, while conservatives worried that uneducated voters would misuse their power. Schools were the solution for both.

No different from today, there was controversy about whether poor children were being restricted to instruction in basic skills or whether they were receiving the same broad education as the middle class. In 1830, a Pennsylvania workingmen's committee investigated and denounced urban public schools that served mostly the poor and stressed basic skills, while children of the rich attended private schools with broader ambitions. Public schools, the committee complained, employed a curriculum that "extends, in no case, further than a tolerable proficiency in reading, writing, and arithmetic, and sometimes to a slight acquaintance with geography." But the report asserted, "there can be no real liberty without a wide diffusion of real intelligence;...members of a republic should all be alike instructed in the nature and character of their equal rights and duties, as human beings, and as citizens; and...education, instead of being limited as in our public poor schools, to a simple acquaintance with words and cyphers, should tend, as far as possible, to the production of a just disposition, virtuous habits, and a rational self governing character."[20]

In 1837, Horace Mann was elected secretary of the newly created Massachusetts Board of Education, and for a dozen years he wrote annual reports to mobilize support for public schools. Like the founders, Mann emphasized the training of youth for democratic citizenship, but he argued for other goals as well. His reports systematically covered the eight broad goal areas identified at the beginning of this chapter.

One report stressed the importance of vocal music in the curriculum, partly because it supported academic goals (musical tones, Mann noted, have mathematical relations), but also because the "Creator has made the human soul susceptible of emotions [patriotic feelings, for example] which can find no adequate expression but in song." Vocal music, Mann wrote, tends to unite those of diverse backgrounds who sing together, and to reduce conflict.[21]

Another report, written after Mann returned from a European trip, concluded that universal public schooling would not itself ensure democratic values. Although he admired the quality of academic instruction in Prussia, Mann noted that student literacy in that nation was used in support of autocracy. He insisted, therefore, that this nation's public schools must explicitly inculcate democratic moral and political values: "[I]f Prussia can pervert the benign influences of education to the support of arbitrary power, we surely can employ them for the support and perpetuation of republican institutions...and if it may be made one of the great prerogatives of education to perform the unnatural and unholy work of making slaves, then surely it must be one of the noblest instrumentalities for rearing a nation of freemen."[22]

The costs of poor health and lack of physical fitness, Mann observed, are borne by the entire community, both in lost worker productivity and in the burdens we assume to care for the infirm, so it is in the community's interest to ensure that all children receive instruction in health habits. Mann wanted schools to teach not only physical fitness and moderation in eating and drinking, but also sophistication about issues of public sanitation and hygiene. For example, he thought students should be trained to demand that government provide cities with pure drinking water and sewage systems.[23] In modern terms, Mann wanted to make students' environmental awareness and activism an outcome for which public schools should be accountable.

With reasoning that education reformers continue to employ today, Mann demonstrated that expansion of workers' academic skills would enhance economic competitiveness. To persuade the state legislature to appropriate public school funds, he conducted a survey of manufacturers to demonstrate that workers with education were more productive than those without.[24]

In defining political and civic sophistication as a necessary outcome of public education, Mann adopted the founders' insistence that democracy requires it. "[A] wise and enlightened constituency will refuse to invest a reckless and profligate man with office," Mann wrote.[25] And if "we do not prepare children to become good citizens…then our republic must go down to destruction."[26]

Another of Mann's public school priorities was moral, what we now call character education. Crime and vice would disappear, he said, if schools would teach ethical principles. Mann insisted that without teaching religious practice as such, schools should teach those biblical principles on which he thought all adult citizens were agreed: "piety, justice, and a sacred regard to truth, love to their country, humanity and universal benevolence, sobriety, industry, and frugality, chastity, moderation, and temperance, and those other virtues which are the ornament of human society."[27]

The Committee of Ten and the *Cardinal Principles*

As schooling expanded at the dawn of the 20th century, special attention was paid to secondary schools, where enrollment was rising most rapidly. Historians typically characterize this era as one in which two competing philosophies were at war; one focused on classical academic skills and the other on a broader range of practical life skills that diluted academic learning.

Two reports have come to symbolize this polarity. The first, calling for a heavily academic curriculum, was issued in 1893 by a "Committee of Ten," convened by the National Education Association (NEA). At that time, the NEA was a quasi-governmental organization that brought together elementary and secondary school administrators as well as college administrators, college professors, and education policy makers. Teachers played only a minor role in the organization. Its reports and recommendations, often commissioned by the federal government, effectively stated national education policy.[28]

The Committee of Ten was headed by Harvard President Charles W. Eliot. It arose from a concern of college leaders like Eliot that high school students were not being adequately prepared for college, and that their preparation was not sufficiently standardized in high schools and preparatory schools.[29] Its report, based on conferences for each subject area that were attended primarily by college professors and preparatory school instructors who taught those areas, urged that all high school students should follow an academic college-preparatory curriculum, not only of basic skills but of broader scope including Latin, Greek, English, modern languages (such as German or French), mathematics, physics, chemistry, astronomy, biology (including human hygiene), and social studies (ancient mythology; American, Greek, Roman, French, and English history; government; and geography). The committee recommended that instruction in each of these subjects begin in elementary schools, because otherwise there would not be sufficient time to prepare for college.[30] As to the arts and music, the committee supported teaching them, but not at the expense of essential academic subjects.[31] The Committee of Ten emphasized academic as opposed to citizenship or character outcomes to a greater extent than previous authorities, although earlier 18th and 19th century goal statements rarely applied to secondary education. With few students in schools at all, the founders and Jacksonians were primarily concerned with elementary schools.

Simultaneously with the release of the Committee of Ten's report, the NEA formed a "Committee of Fifteen" to issue a companion volume covering elementary education. It has received less attention than the secondary school report, but it reveals that it is probably mistaken to interpret the Committee of Ten as seeking an exclusively academic educational system for all students. The Committee of Fifteen report urged that academic topics like language, arithmetic, geography, history, and science should be "correlated" with (not taught in isolation from) the arts (vocal music and drawing), physical exercise, and hygiene. For seventh- and eighth-grade boys it recommended manual training (e.g., woodworking), and for girls it recommended sewing and cooking.[32] So although the Committee of Ten's report may not seem, at first glance, to be consistent with the eight goal areas around which there was a developing national consensus, educators in the 1890s were apparently somewhat more committed to a broad curriculum than their secondary school report appears to suggest.

Each of the Committee of Ten's subject-area conferences was asked to answer the question, "should the subject be treated differently for pupils who are going to college, for those who are going to a scientific school, and for those who, presumably, are going to neither?" The conferees unanimously reported that their subjects should be treated the same for all.[33] But this conclusion, really an afterthought, can hardly be taken seriously. The conferences were devoted to consideration of college preparatory curricula, and the conference reports made frequent references to college admission requirements, with only occasional asides that pupils not going to college might spend a semester of high school deviating from the basic curriculum to study bookkeeping or some other practical subject.[34] The conferences concluded that "college requirements for admission should coincide with the high school requirements for graduation."[35]

In 1892 when the Committee of Ten was formed, only about 4% of high-school-age adolescents actually attended secondary school. Almost all of those went on to graduate and then enroll in college. The Committee of Ten never conceived that secondary school would become universal, much less that adolescents preparing for the workforce would require a curriculum so heavily weighted toward college preparation. A quarter century later, however, secondary school enrollment had more than quintupled, to about 22% of high-school-age adolescents, nearly half of whom dropped out before graduating and fewer than a third of whom went on to college.[36] Whatever the merits of the Committee of Ten's recommended curriculum for college-bound students, it was no longer relevant to the rapidly expanding secondary school system. So in 1918, the federal government commissioned a new NEA report, *The Cardinal Principles of Secondary Education*, to summarize the goals of more universal schooling.

If the Committee of Ten's recommendations were too heavily weighted toward a classical academic curriculum, giving too little attention to the citizenship and character outcomes sought by education philosophers earlier in the nation's history, the *Cardinal Principles* were weighted in the opposite direction, diluting the academic focus of secondary schooling. The *Cardinal Principles'* bow to academic preparation consisted of a recommendation that "much of the energy of the elementary school is properly devoted to teaching certain fundamental processes, such as reading, writing, arithmetical computations, and the elements of oral and written expression." These should be continued in high school, the report added, but with an emphasis on their practical applications.[37]

Following the lead of the founders and Jacksonians like Horace Mann,[38] the *Cardinal Principles* also stressed health as a goal of schools and promoted physical activity for students, instruction in personal hygiene, and instruction in public health. The report said schools should teach the importance of "wholesome relations between boys and girls and men and women" and preparation for the traditional male-female division of labor in the home. It endorsed vocational education, including the selection of vocations appropriate to each student's "capacities and aptitudes," as well as maintenance of good relationships with fellow workers.

Also consistent with earlier statements, the *Cardinal Principles* gave greater emphasis to civic education than to any other goal, and the report stressed that students can learn democratic habits only if their classrooms and schools are run with more democratic methods. Even the study of English literature, it said, should aim to "kindle social ideals." Schools should prepare youth to participate in the neighborhood, town or city, state, and nation, and provide "a basis for understanding international problems." Schools should teach not only "practical knowledge of social agencies and institutions," but "good judgment" in political matters. Yet it failed to repeat the urgings of the founders, of Horace Mann, and of other education philosophers that good judgment must also flow from understanding the wisdom and follies of the past.

The *Cardinal Principles* also charged schools with preparing youth for the "worthy use of leisure," to be accomplished mainly by providing opportunities to appreciate great literature, art, and music so students will choose to continue these interests as adults, and by providing social activities in which students of different backgrounds and social classes can establish "bonds of friendship and common understanding."

And finally, the *Cardinal Principles* declared the development of ethical character to be "paramount among the objectives of the secondary school" in a democratic society. The goal included developing a sense of personal responsibility, initiative, and the "spirit of service."[39]

In retrospect, both the Committee of Ten and *Cardinal Principles* reports seem unbalanced. In recent years, some policy makers claiming to be admirers of the Committee of Ten have supported narrow, test-based accountability of the kind represented by NCLB – although schools that concentrate on preparing students for tests of basic skills could never develop the broad academic knowledge sought by the Committee of Ten. And throughout the 20th century, policy makers who claimed to be admirers of the *Cardinal Principles* sometimes seemed to wish that schools would focus only on social skills and the habits of intellectual inquiry, an agenda that ignores the foundation of knowledge upon which sophisticated inquiry must build. The authors of both reports probably had a more balanced view than did or do many of their followers. The members of the Committee of Ten and authors of the *Cardinal Principles* would probably have embraced the eight broad goal areas that have been common to Americans' expectations for public education, although the weights they gave to each of the goal areas might have varied considerably.

20th century commissions

As the 20th century progressed, commissions, government agencies, and scholars continued to examine public education's goals, and the consensus remained strong that these goals must include a balanced collection of academic, behavioral, health, artistic, and civic skills.

During the Great Depression of the 1930s, the NEA (still a quasi-governmental collection of all educators and education policy makers) established a committee to propose how public schools should respond to the nation's economic crisis. Chaired by Fred Kelly, an official of the U.S. Office of Education, the six-member committee (which included the philosopher of education John Dewey) worked for more than five years to set forth what it called the "social-economic goals" of American education. Its conclusions, encompassing both academic and behavioral goals, reflected the historic consensus around the eight outcome areas that had been developed in the 19th century.

The committee urged schools to improve Americans' health by teaching hygiene, nutrition, first aid, and healthful sexual practices.[40] Schools should also provide direct pediatric, dental, and psychiatric services: if private practitioners and public health agencies "persistently ignore their responsibility [to provide such care to all children], there may be no other way than for the school to take the initiative and provide such services."

The report emphasized the importance of schools teaching basic math and literacy skills, but it defined such skills somewhat more broadly than contemporary test-based accountability policies do. It is not only the techniques of reading that schools should be responsible for developing, but the habit of reading and, even more important, good judgment in selecting what to read. "A nation of illiterates is no less harmful than a nation where all can read but where no one reads anything which healthfully ministers to the need for beauty or the search for truth."[41] The report also considered essential an ability to distinguish between the "demagog and the statesman." This "demands the ability to read accurately, to organize facts, to weigh evidence, and to separate truth from falsehood."[42]

The Kelly committee expected schools to develop students' oral as well as written communication abilities – including social skills such as introductions, apologies, compliments, or criticisms.[43] Science, art, music, drama, and history should also be part of the curriculum. Schools should also develop students' morality – justice and fair dealing, honesty, truthfulness, maintenance of group understandings, proper respect for authority, tolerance and respect for others, habits of cooperation, and work habits such as industry and self-control – and encourage personal characteristics such as endurance and physical strength.[44]

It recommended increased attention to social studies, including a broad background in social and economic history, as well as ongoing discussion of current affairs. Schools should develop democratic habits, a commitment to promote social welfare, and ideals of racial equality.[45] School-sponsored extracurricular and community activities might be the most effective way of reaching these goals, the report concluded. "Good citizenship demands not only understanding but a habit of action as well. A habit of action with respect to life situations cannot be built up in school unless school life is part of real life."[46]

Also during the Depression and then during the Second World War, several other commissions, comprising distinguished scholars and government officials, issued similar reports on the goals of education.

The Educational Policies Commission (EPC), which included several state and district school superintendents, prominent scholars, and university presidents (among them James B. Conant of Harvard), produced a 1938 report that echoed Horace Mann's concerns about Prussian education. It stated that "the safety of democracy will not be assured merely by making education universal....The task is not so easy as that. The dictatorships [Germany, Italy, Japan, and the Soviet Union] have universal schooling and use this very means to prevent the spread of democratic doctrines and institutions."[47] We can preserve democracy only by making schools' highest priority the teaching of democratic principles and the development of habits and characteristics that enable citizens to utilize them. The most important purpose of our schools, the report said, is to teach the "ideals of democratic conduct" (see **Figure B**).

The commission's report also asserted that democratic ideals could only be taught by encouraging learners' active participation. "Democracy is a highly cooperative undertaking," the report said, and "can become more effective if children learn to cooperate in school."[48] Democratic habits cannot be taught solely in social studies classes. "The entire curriculum, the entire life of the school...should be a youthful experience in democratic living...agitating the social conscience."[49]

The EPC took note of the infatuation, even in 1938, with using basic academic skills tests as a way of measuring the outcomes of schools, and it called for an accountability system that covered the broader goals of education:

Most of the standardized testing instruments and written examinations used in schools today deal largely with information....There should be a much greater concern with the development of attitudes, interests, ideals, and habits. To focus tests exclusively on the acquisition and retention of information may recognize objectives of education which

FIGURE B Five ideals of democratic conduct that schools should teach, as defined by the Educational Policies Commission, 1938

- broad humanitarianism, "a feeling of kinship to other people more or less fortunate than oneself"

- respect for the moral rights and feelings of others

- the participation of all concerned in arriving at important decisions

- peaceful methods of settling national, international, and private disputes

- the pursuit of happiness, or judging the effectiveness of other policies by whether they contribute to human happiness

Source: EPC 1938, pp. 7-9.

are relatively unimportant. Measuring the results of education must be increasingly concerned with such questions as these: Are the children growing in their ability to work together for a common end? Do they show greater skill in collecting and weighing evidence? Are they learning to be fair and tolerant in situations where conflicts arise? Are they sympathetic in the presence of suffering and indignant in the presence of injustice? Do they show greater concern about questions of civic, social, and economic importance? Are they using their spending money wisely? Are they becoming more skillful in doing some useful type of work? Are they more honest, more reliable, more temperate, more humane? Are they finding happiness in their present family life? Are they living in accordance with the rules of health? Are they acquiring skills in using all of the fundamental tools of learning? Are they curious about the natural world around them? Do they appreciate, each to the fullest degree possible, their rich inheritance in art, literature, and music? Do they balk at being led around by their prejudices?[50]

In the early 1950s, the first baby boomers entered school (and overwhelmed school capacity). During his first year in office, President Dwight Eisenhower asked Congress to appropriate funds for conferences in every state on the goals of education. The conferences culminated in a 1955 national meeting of 2,000 civic and business leaders, two-thirds of whom were required to be non-educators. Led by Neil McElroy, a corporate executive later to become secretary of defense, the national meeting recommended a list of 15 goals of public education. They are somewhat more detailed than the eight areas defined in this book as making up the national consensus, but they cover the same territory (see **Figure C**). "Nothing was more evident at the White House Conference on Education," McElroy reported to the president, "than the fact that these goals, representing as they do an enormously wide range of purposes, are the answer to a genuine public demand."[51] And for schools to do all these things, McElroy added, they should be funded at higher levels. School spending, he advised, should be roughly doubled, and accountability should be enforced by denying funds to school districts that do not use money wisely.[52]

As memories of the Second World War receded, Americans' attention in the 1950s turned to anticipation of "automation" and the need for greater technical skills. Balancing the requirement for schools to train a technical elite with a commitment to equality of opportunity was a challenge. In this climate, the Rockefeller Brothers Fund convened panels of political, intellectual, technological, and economic leaders to make recommendations. Nelson Rockefeller, a future governor of New York and vice president of the United States, chaired the project, and Henry Kissinger, future secretary of state, was its staff director.

One Rockefeller Fund report, *The Pursuit of Excellence: Education and the Future of America*, asked how "may we best prepare our young people to keep their individuality, initiative, creativity in a highly organized, intricately meshed society?...Our conception of excellence must embrace many kinds of achievement at many levels....There is excellence in abstract intellectual activity, in art, in music, in managerial activities, in craftsmanship, in human relations, in technical work."[53]

The report predicted that testing would become an increasingly important technique for sorting future scientists and leaders for advanced training. But, the report warned, schools should not rely on test scores alone, nor, it implied, should test scores be the sole mechanism of school accountability: "Decisions based on test scores must be made with the awareness of the imponderables in human behavior. We cannot measure the rare qualities of character that are a necessary ingredient of great performance. We cannot measure aspiration or purpose. We cannot measure courage, vitality or determination."[54]

FIGURE C What should our schools accomplish? As defined by the Committee for the White House Conference on Education, Neil McElroy, Chairman, 1956

- a general education, with increased emphasis on the physical and social sciences

- patriotism and good citizenship

- moral, ethical, and spiritual values

- vocational education, tailored to the abilities of each pupil and to the needs of the community and the nation

- domestic skills

- training in leisure time activities such as music, dancing, avocational reading, and hobbies

- health services for all children, including physical and dental inspections, and instruction aimed at bettering health knowledge and habits

- special services for handicapped children, including those with speech and reading difficulties

- physical education, including systematic exercises and sports

- special programs for unusually talented students

- acquainting of students with other countries to help them understand international relations

- programs to foster students' mental health

- fostering of wholesome family life

- organized recreational and social activities

- promotion of safety, including drivers' education, swimming instruction, and civil defense

Source: McElroy 1956, pp. 8-9.

Accountability demands and reactions in the late 20th century: *A Nation at Risk*

In the late 1960s, policy makers began to demand accountability for test score improvement from public schools. Many reforms, popular today, were proposed 40 years ago, tried for a while, and then abandoned. In the early 1970s, for example, schools experimented with "performance contracting," in which private firms promised to raise test scores by specified amounts in return for payment.[55] This interest in test-based accountability lasted about 15 years, until policy makers and educators alike concluded that obsession with test scores, stimulating excessive test preparation and "teaching to the test," had produced illusory progress and narrowing of curriculums to the most easily tested basic skills.

In 1970, some of the nation's best-known testing experts addressed the growing interest in accountability in a special issue of the education magazine, *Phi Delta Kappan*. Henry Dyer, vice president of the Educational Testing Service (best known for producing the SAT exam for the College Board), noted that an accountability system must first define the goals for which schools should be held accountable. Dyer warned of a "mistake that could be made" in the design of such a system: "to concentrate all the effort on a single area of pupil development, namely, the 'basic skills.'"

Dyer added:

> The danger here – and it is one by which schools have all too often been trapped – is threefold. First, it encourages the notion that, as far as school is concerned, training in the basic skills is all that matters in a society where so many other human characteristics also matter. Secondly, it tends toward neglect of the fact that if a school gives exclusive attention to this one area of pupil development, it may purchase success in this area at the expense of failure in other areas – social behavior, for instance. Thirdly, it tends to blind people to the interrelatedness of educational objectives, that is, to the fact that pupil development in one area may be heavily dependent on development in other areas. Learning to read, for example, may be dependent on the pupil's maintaining good health. And the pupil's sense of his worth as a human being may be dependent on his ability to read.[56]

As a consequence, Dyer recommended that, if policy makers wanted to establish an immediate accountability system for schools, a temporary program must include at least two "widely different areas of pupil development," such as reading and health, until a full range of sophisticated measurement tools could be developed. In the longer run, an accountability system should "be capable of answering questions like the following:…has the school been more or less effective in developing children's number skills than in developing their sense of self-esteem, or their social behavior, or their health habits?"[57]

Dyer's ideas were consistent with mainstream thought at the time. Indeed, they may have been influenced by President Richard Nixon's message to Congress on education reform the previous March, in which he called for a National Institute of Education (NIE). In language probably provided by his aide, Daniel Patrick Moynihan, the president called for holding schools accountable for their outcomes, but he noted:

> To achieve this fundamental reform it will be necessary to develop broader and more sensitive measurements of learning than we now have. The National Institute of Education would take the lead in developing these new measurements of educational output. In doing so it should pay as much heed to what are called the "immeasurables" of schooling (largely because no one has yet learned to measure them) such as responsibility, wit, and humanity as it does to verbal and mathematical achievement....From these considerations we derive another new concept: accountability[58]

To refine the president's proposal, a government planning group specified goals for disadvantaged students, and the new NIE was to collect data to measure these students' progress. The planning group said that the institute should spend less effort on traditional academic outcomes (which we already know how to assess) and more on figuring out how to measure the development of motivation, the effects of character education, and the development of "useful and satisfied citizens."[59]

Congress established the National Institute of Education in 1972. But neither the NIE, the Office of Educational Research and Improvement (OERI) that succeeded it, nor the Institute of Education Sciences that has now replaced OERI, has pursued the kind of research into measurement of "immeasurables" called for by President Nixon and his contemporaries.

The late 1970s were a period of economic crisis – stubborn inflation, high unemployment, the beginning of a long period of income stagnation, low productivity growth, and a rising trade deficit. In 1983, President Ronald Reagan's National Commission on Excellence in Education issued *A Nation at Risk*, a report that claimed America's failing schools were not producing sufficient technological skills for the nation's industry to compete with imports of Japanese automobiles, Korean steel, or German machine tools. (Appendix 1 analyzes this and similar claims.)

The *Risk* report had a mixed message about the goals of education. It called for a revamped high school curriculum that included English, math, science, social studies, computer science, and (for the college bound) foreign languages, supplemented by the fine and performing arts that, all together, "constitute the mind and spirit of our culture."[60] It bemoaned the growth of tests that assessed only basic skills at the expense of critical thinking and reasoning, and denounced the minimum competency exams that were being given, and to which instruction was excessively directed, in 37 of the 50 states.[61] *Risk* worried that schools were emphasizing "such rudiments as reading and computation at the expense of other essential skills such as comprehension, analysis, solving problems, and drawing conclusions." It concluded: "Our concern goes well beyond matters such as industry and commerce. It also includes the intellectual, moral, and spiritual strengths of our people...."[62] By calling in these ways for a broad liberal education, *Risk* seemed to be associating itself with the previous two centuries of demands by government and private experts that public education fulfill a broadly defined academic, social, personal, and civic mission.

The countervailing message of the report, though, had enduring influence. It accused the nation of having "lost sight of the basic purposes of schooling" (proficiency in academic fields). Instead, the report worried, schools "are routinely called on to provide solutions to personal, social, and political problems that the home and other institutions either will not or cannot resolve." This diffusion of attention, it charged, "exact[s] an educational cost."[63] And although it denounced minimum competency testing, it called for even more standardized testing as a way to refocus schools on their academic mission and to raise student achievement. Predictably, this call spurred even more emphasis on the assessment of basic literacy and math skills and a tendency to evaluate schools and students solely by their test scores.

As the *Nation at Risk* report was being developed, but before its influence took hold, John Goodlad, dean of UCLA's Graduate School of Education, was considering the growing emphasis on basic academic skills. He examined the published policies of state and local boards of education, as well as 20th century commission reports described above, to see if their goals were consistent with the current mood. He reduced the varied goals in these policies to a complex set of 100, divided into 12 categories and 65 sub-categories. Not surprisingly, they included not only academics but citizenship, vocational preparation, problem solving, the arts, interpersonal relations, creativity, physical and emotional health, self-confidence, and moral and ethical character.[64]

Despite the fact that the balanced approach to educational goals was backed by a broadly based, long-time commitment, Goodlad predicted that it would not be immune to pressure in the future: "I think we are now [in 1983] entering an open, creative, exciting period of trying to reconstruct American schooling. And then, in the early 1990s, the cry will again be, 'Let's get back to simplicity. Let's get back to basics. Let's get back to more discipline.' We need to see what we can accomplish in about a decade before the negative forces begin again."[65]

Recognizing how the new testing fad might threaten the national consensus around the eight goal areas Americans had previously embraced, others also tried to resist the drive for more academic testing in the wake of *A Nation at Risk*. Four years after publication of the report, the National Academy of Education (NAE) established a committee to evaluate the National Assessment of Educational Progress (NAEP), a testing program that had been sampling students' academic skills for the previous 15 years.[66] The NAE committee worried that the literacy and mathematics assessed by NAEP, while important and fundamental, "represent only a portion of the goals" of schools. NAEP, it charged, did not test the humanities. "And then there are the aesthetic and moral aims of education that remain beyond the purview of current assessment techniques." The NAE committee expressed concern "lest the narrowness of NAEP may have a distorted impact on our schools." When academic tests are emphasized, "a subtle shift occurs in which fallible and partial indicators of academic achievement are transformed into major goals of schooling." The NAE committee concluded:

At root here is a fundamental dilemma. Those personal qualities that we hold dear – resilience and courage in the face of stress, a sense of craft in our work, a commitment to justice and caring in our social relationships, a dedication to advancing the public good in our communal life – are exceedingly difficult to assess. And so, unfortunately, we are apt to measure what we can, and eventually come to value what is measured over what is left unmeasured. The shift is subtle, and occurs gradually. It first invades our language and then slowly begins to dominate our thinking. It is all around us, and we too are a part of it. In neither academic nor popular discourse about schools does one find nowadays much reference to the important human qualities noted above. The language of academic achievement tests has become the primary rhetoric of schooling.[67]

Four years later, the U.S. Department of Education cited this warning, acknowledging that newly popular accountability systems in education would be misleading unless the nation had ways of measuring whether students were developing these more-difficult-to-measure qualities. Its National Center for Education Statistics (NCES) established the Special Study Panel on Education

Indicators to propose a national indicator system to reflect a broader balance of academic and non-cognitive education goals. The NCES report urged that, in addition to academic competence in the core subjects, measured "learner outcomes" should include tolerance, comprehending pluralism, self-direction, responsibility, commitment to craft, and other measures.[68] "We should assess what we think is important, not settle for what we can measure," the study panel urged.[69]

Subsequently, NCES commissioned the American Institutes for Research (AIR) to develop a proposal for collecting a variety of "input, output, outcome, and efficiency" indicators. AIR produced an inventory of such indicators, but NCES never published its report or followed up to develop such a system.[70] As the testing frenzy grew, culminating in *No Child Left Behind*, the warnings of the National Academy and the NCES study panel were forgotten.

Legislatures and courts: defining 'adequacy'

For nearly 30 years now, school districts and organizations representing minority children have litigated state constitutional provisions requiring state finance of an "adequate" education. Implicit in these suits were requirements that state courts define what such adequacy includes.

In 1979, the West Virginia Supreme Court issued a decision (*Pauley v. Kelly*) that became a model for courts in many other states. It defined a "thorough and efficient" education as one that develops "the minds, bodies and social morality of its charges to prepare them for useful and happy occupations, recreation and citizenship...." In language sometimes similar to that of Thomas Jefferson 200 years earlier, the court required the West Virginia legislature to fund a school system that would develop "in every child" the capacity to succeed in each of the eight broad outcome areas of the national consensus (see **Figure D**).

Ten years later, the Kentucky Supreme Court adopted the West Virginia reasoning and much of its language. Since then, state courts nationwide have cited these decisions as precedents for their own constitutional interpretations.

Contemporary policy, with its emphasis on testing basic academic skills, evolved not only from *A Nation at Risk* but from a 1989 conference of governors convened by the first President Bush, with Governor Bill Clinton of Arkansas the leading participant. The conference adopted national education goals that were heavily though not exclusively academic. Incorporated in a 1994 federal law, the goals aimed for American students to be "first in the world" in math and science. The national goals process was guided by Marshall Smith, a Stanford professor who was Governor Clinton's education

FIGURE D Outcomes that every child must be provided the opportunity to develop, as defined by the West Virginia Supreme Court, 1979

- literacy

- ability to add, subtract, multiply, and divide numbers

- knowledge of government to the extent that the child will be equipped as a citizen to make informed choices among persons and issues that affect his or her own governance

- self-knowledge and knowledge of his or her total environment to allow the child to intelligently choose life work – to know his or her options

- work-training and advanced academic training as the child may intelligently choose

- recreational pursuits

- interests in all creative arts, such as music, theater, literature, and the visual arts

- social ethics, both behavioral and abstract, to facilitate compatibility with others in this society.

Source: *Pauley v. Kelly* 1979, 705-706, 877.

advisor during the summit and who later served as undersecretary of education during Clinton's presidency. Looking back recently on what the last 15 years have accomplished, Smith now urges a change in course. He argues that we should "broaden our goals for schooling," and adds:

> Let's listen to what the early Greeks, the business world, developmental psychologists, good teachers, and parents tell us. Our basic goals for content and skills should embrace the language arts, mathematics, science, and history. We should strive to support all students to learn to more challenging standards in these areas, but this is not enough, for our children or our country. Broader goals should include service to our communities, exposure to and participation in the arts, and physical and health education....If schools expose children only to goals that emphasize self-interest [i.e., goals relating to more remunerative employment], we will lose our vision of a democracy that supports the common good.[71]

Today, two decades of excessive attention to basic skills has stimulated, as has so often happened before, second thoughts. But to translate these second thoughts into a reformed accountability policy, we need more than the insistence – albeit by political leaders, scholars, state constitutions, and courts – that schools produce both cognitive and non-cognitive knowledge and skills and both public and private behavioral outcomes. More specific definitions of adequacy are required if we are to design a system to hold schools accountable for them.

If a more balanced accountability system is to avoid the loss of credibility suffered so thoroughly by *No Child Left Behind*, it must have broad popular support. This chapter has reviewed what national leaders, education experts, and policy makers have thought about education goals. It concludes that there has been a historic consensus that schools should be held accountable for youth to achieve in eight broadly defined areas: basic academic knowledge and skills, critical thinking, appreciation of the arts and literature, preparation for skilled work, social skills and work ethic, citizenship and community responsibility, physical health, and emotional health.

Does the public today share this historic consensus? Or does the public believe that schools should concentrate on academics and leave other aspects of youth development to the family, church, and community? And if the public does continue to embrace the consensus that schools should be accountable for a broad set of academic and non-academic outcomes, how should each of the eight goal areas be balanced? How important is academic skill and knowledge, for example, relative to physical and emotional health?

It is not enough to define eight broad goal areas of education. To hold schools accountable for these goals, we need a judgment about the relative weight each goal should have. It is to this judgment that we now turn.

CHAPTER 2

Weighting the goals of public education
The public's opinion, and our own

To hold educators accountable in our representative democracy, we elect school board members and state legislators to define the goals of public schools. In a few cities, the power of elected school boards to establish goals has been assumed by elected mayors. Sometimes, as in the case of *No Child Left Behind*, Congress also has a say. We expect these elected officials to have the background, information, and judgment to make wise decisions, on behalf of their constituents, regarding issues as complicated as education goals.

The British parliamentarian Edmund Burke, in a now-classic speech, summarized the duties of elected legislators this way: "Your Representative owes you, not his industry only, but his judgment; and he betrays, instead of serving you, if he sacrifices it to your opinion."[72]

Certainly, to define the goals for which schools should be held accountable, elected officials should consider thoughtful public opinion. But surveys to elicit such opinion should require respondents to make choices – the same choices that elected leaders must ultimately make. Schools' time and resources are limited; greater effort to produce some outcomes necessarily requires lesser effort to produce others.

As Burke observed, public opinion is often relied upon unwisely by policy makers. In education nowadays, is has become commonplace for advocates of one policy or another to "prove" by polling that the public supports their positions. But by themselves, polls are an unreliable way of establishing education goals. Certainly, public opinion should inform the deliberations of elected officials. As is the case with most public issues, education policy alternatives are complex; choosing between specific policies requires more deliberation than most citizens take the time to conduct. This lack of detailed policy knowledge is why poll results typically reflect how questions are phrased, the order of their presentation, and the context of each question. Because many citizens, understandably having little time or background to deliberate complex issues, can simultaneously hold contradictory views, it is relatively easy for advocacy groups to prove the public's agreement with almost any position by constructing poorly worded questions.

One prominent polling group, Public Agenda, frequently uses one-sided alternatives to show public support for particular education policies. In 1994, for example, it demonstrated support for a basic-skills-only accountability policy by asking Americans if it was a serious problem that "there is not enough emphasis on the basics such as reading, writing and math" in schools. When 60% of respondents agreed, Public Agenda reported the "finding" that "teaching the basics" is one of the public's three top goals for public schools. The other top goals were elimination of school violence and maintenance of tougher discipline, also determined by asking for agreement with loaded statements, such as whether "there's too much drugs and violence in schools."[73] (One wonders how many respondents would think there's not enough drugs and violence in schools.) Although Public Agenda determined that Americans thought that there was "not enough emphasis" on basic skills, it failed to ask whether there was "not enough emphasis" on a range of other knowledge and skills that Americans have also historically valued. It is easy to elicit a view that there is not enough emphasis on basic skills if respondents are not asked to choose what should be sacrificed to make time for increasing that emphasis.

An earlier and more careful survey was published by Lawrence Downey in 1959. In response to critics who complained then, as they do today, that schools had abandoned academics to concentrate on "frills," and relying on many of the documents described in the last chapter, Downey and his University of Chicago doctoral students developed a synthesis of education goals previously embraced by Americans. The researchers then polled 12 representative communities around the nation, with an additional three in Canada. They did not use a random sample of adults in these communities, but instead surveyed educators and members of service, social, labor, management, church, ethnic, and racial organizations. Respondents received 16 cards, each of which described a distinct education goal. Nearly 1,300 educators and 2,500 non-educators were asked to sort these cards by relative importance.[74]

Figure E displays the average rankings by educators and community leaders of the 16 goals that had previously appeared in education policy making documents. Rankings by educators and community leaders differed only slightly. It is curious that a desire for knowledge and knowing how to acquire it were ranked at the top, while actually having a fund of knowledge ranked low. It is

FIGURE E The task of public education – the perceptions of people, ranks as surveyed by Lawrence Downey, 1959

1.   Intellectual skills (to acquire and transmit information)

2.   Desire for knowledge (love of learning)

3.   Creativity*

4.   Ability to cooperate with others in daily life*

5.   Ethics (moral integrity)

6.   Good citizenship (knowledge of rights and duties)

7.   Emotional health

8.   Patriotism

9.   World citizenship (understanding relationship of peoples)

10. Selecting vocations**

11. Physical health

12. Preparing for vocations (vocational skills)

13. Knowledge (having a fund of knowledge)

14. Aesthetic (cultural and leisure) pursuits

15. Home and family (including housekeeping and "do-it-yourself" skills)

16. Consumer sophistication

* Tied for third rank
** When only secondary, not elementary, school goals were considered, selecting vocations ranked 7th, tied with emotional health.

Source: Calculated from Downey 1960, Table 2, p. 36.

hard to imagine how schools could design an instructional program that could accomplish one without the other. Nonetheless, the Downey survey demonstrated that, in the late 1950s, both educators and community leaders embraced a consensus around the eight broad outcome goals that previous generations of Americans had described.

Nearly two decades later, a Stanford University research team responded to reports like *A Nation at Risk*, which seemed to place an exclusive focus on schools' important, but not exclusive, academic mission. The Stanford group undertook a survey similar to Downey's in which respondents were asked to make choices. The team collected the goals (usually called "mission statements") of 30 high school districts nationwide. From these, the researchers defined 10 primary goals that districts had set for themselves – five of which were academic (verbal, mathematics, science, social studies, and fine arts), and five of which the researchers termed "personal responsibility domains" (attitudes, interpersonal competence, moral development, health, and career development). They then asked teachers, students, and their parents to rank these goals, and the curricular emphases designed to achieve them, in importance.[75]

All three groups ranked the "personal responsibility domains" to be of greater importance, overall, than the academic subject areas. Of the former, parents and teachers considered moral development most important, followed by interpersonal competence, career, and health outcomes. These were followed by academic knowledge and skills – first verbal, then math, social studies, fine arts, and science, in that order. Respondents felt that other institutions – families, religious organizations, the media – should have a greater role in developing the "personal responsibility" outcomes, with schools playing a secondary role.[76] "Nevertheless," the 1987 Stanford report concluded:

> it seems clear that one of the top priorities of the schools is to promote moral development in the sense of helping young people become socially responsible adults….These data reveal a very disturbing discrepancy. In recent years schools have been directed by prominent goal-formulating groups to focus on a relatively narrow range of achievements within the category of cognitive goals. However, the goals that students, parents, and teachers seem to regard as being the most important for young people to achieve are largely within the domains of personal responsibility and practical intelligence.[77]

Some recent public opinion polls, more sophisticated than the Public Agenda effort described above, have surveyed attitudes regarding education goals. An annual Gallup poll, conducted for the education group Phi Delta Kappa (PDK), attempted in 2005 to determine how people balance academic proficiency and the social and other skills that students might gain in extracurricular activities. The pollsters asked respondents if they would rather have children get course grades of A's or get only average grades combined with participation in extracurricular activities. Nearly two-thirds (64%) preferred the combination of average grades and extracurricular activities, while only 29% preferred high grades.[78] The 2008 PDK poll found 52% agreeing that it would be a good thing if more math and reading resulted in less emphasis on other subjects, down from 56% in 2002.[79] But still, such questions are of only limited help to policy makers. While the responses indicate that the public considers "average" grades satisfactory, they do not reveal how much time devoted to extracurricular activities might be too much if it depressed grades below average. They fail to disclose which "other subjects" are now given too much priority or how much emphasis on these subjects should diminish.

Another ranking exercise, conducted in 1993 by the government's National Center for Education Statistics (NCES), surveyed only school professionals. The results suggest that educators place less importance on non-academic outcomes than does the public at large. NCES proposed a list of eight possible school goals to teachers and principals; 76% of teachers listed basic literacy skills either first, second, or third in importance; 62% listed personal growth as first, second, or third; 17% listed human relations skills; and 10% listed specific moral values. Principals' responses were similar.[80]

In 1998, the Shell Oil Company commissioned a poll of adults on a variety of public issues.[81] Respondents were given a choice of five education goals and asked which they thought were schools' *current* priorities. More respondents chose "preparing students for college" as the top current priority for schools, followed by providing vocational skills, teaching how to reason and think well, teaching basic values, and teaching about government and civic responsibility. But when asked to choose what school goals *should* be, more respondents chose "teaching basic values" as most important, with college preparation dropping to fourth place.

Also during the late 1990s, a U.S. Department of Education agency (the Mid-Continent Regional Laboratory, or McREL), examined state curricular requirements as well as high-quality programs like the International Baccalaureate, and developed a list of some 300 "standards" in 15 different subject areas. McREL then commissioned Gallup to present these standards to a random sample of adults. Because no respondent could handle, in time or cognitive challenge, all 300 in a single interview, each respondent was given from 80 to 90 overlapping standards; results were then coordinated statistically.[82]

McREL reported that more adults thought health education standards should "definitely be taught" than any other area, with work skills second in importance. These were followed by a series of academic competencies. **Figure F** ranks the various goals by the percentage of adults who thought they "definitely should be

FIGURE F Ranking of subject areas by average percentage of 'definitely should be taught' responses, as surveyed by McREL, 1999

1.	Health	9.	Behavioral studies
2.	Work skills	10.	Physical education
3.	Language arts	11.	Economics
4.	Technology	12.	History
5.	Mathematics	13.	Geography
6.	Thinking and reasoning	14.	Foreign languages
7.	Science	15.	The arts
8.	Civics		

Source: Marzano, Kendall, and Cicchinelli 1999.

taught." It is questionable whether meaningful conclusions can be drawn from this public reaction to such complex alternatives. Although relative priorities can be inferred statistically from these judgments, unless respondents are forced to make choices, we can't confidently establish what the public thinks are goals for which schools should be held accountable.

Yet along with other opinion polls just described, the McREL poll confirms that public opinion is roughly aligned with the consensus of scholars and policy makers described in the previous chapter. Although the relative importance of each goal of education may differ from poll to poll, from group to group, or from period to period, both professionals and the public are agreed that schools should in some measure be responsible for the eight broad outcomes identified in this book. And, we can infer, any accountability system that is faithful to this democratic consensus must require schools and other youth institutions to deliver this broad range. Accountability for test scores alone is disconnected from the outcomes we actually expect.

Eight broad goal areas for public education

The previous chapter reviewed historical documents about the goals of education and summarized what American policy makers have thought schools should accomplish. Any categorization scheme is necessarily arbitrary; a guiding principle for us was that eight broad goal areas was an optimal scheme because, if policy makers or the public were to weight the relative importance of different goals for purposes of an accountability system, eight was about as many as any of us can think about at one time.[83] Some polling experts with whom we consulted thought that even eight was too many, but we felt that collapsing the categories even more would sacrifice too much coherence within each category.

In 2005, we asked the Scripps-Howard News Service to include in its regular random-digit-dialing telephone poll of adult Americans a request that respondents rank these goals in priority order. Scripps-Howard did so, but the task proved too cognitively complex for a telephone poll. While many respondents were able to pick a top priority, few were able to rank-order the others. More respondents picked "providing students with good basic academic skills" as the top priority, but only one-third made it their top choice. Another third were unable to choose, either because they had no opinion or because they thought all (or several) goals were equally important. For the remaining third, the top priorities were, in order, problem-solving skills, citizenship, emotional health, vocational skills (for students not bound for college), social skills and work ethic, appreciation of the arts and music, and physical health.[84]

From the Scripps-Howard experience, we concluded that poll respondents could make the necessary choices between goals, and set realistic priorities for an accountability system, only with a more sophisticated survey method. So we contracted with Knowledge Networks,[85] a firm that conducts surveys online (it provides hardware for randomly selected American adults to attach to television sets), to poll the general public, as well as representative samples of state legislators and school board members, to determine these groups' views about the relative importance of the eight goal areas of public education.

Respondents in each of these populations were given a list of the eight goals and asked to assign percentage weights to each, with the requirement that all eight percentages must add to 100. The software permitted respondents continually to revise their weights until the 100% total was achieved. (Respondents who had computer access completed the survey at an online, password-protected website, not with television hardware.) For all respondents, whether in the general public or in the school board or legislator samples, the goals were listed randomly, so that average responses would not be influenced by the order in which the goals appeared. (Appendix 3 gives further technical detail on the survey methodology.)[86] **Table 1** shows the results.

The general public and their elected representatives are in fairly close accord regarding the relative importance of the goals of public education. Basic academic knowledge and skills are, in the considered judgment of Americans and their representatives, today more important than *any* of the other goals. But basic skills are not more important than *all* of the other goals. And *all* the categories that might broadly be termed "academic" (basic knowledge and skills, critical thinking, appreciation of the arts and literature, and preparation for skilled work) are of only slightly greater importance than the citizenship, character, and health goals. In consequence, an accountability system that created incentives to give too much stress to basic academic knowledge and skills, and too little stress to the other goals for youth, would not be faithful to the deliberative conclusions about which American adults and elected leaders concur today.[87]

Later chapters of this book begin to describe an appropriate accountability system, one that would be faithful to our goals for public education. Ultimately, it is up to our elected representatives, taking public opinion into account to the extent they deem appropriate, to determine the relative goal weights of an actual accountability system. This book's discussion, however, provisionally contemplates the weights listed in **Table 2**. They are influenced by our surveys and by recommendations of policy makers throughout American history.

These weights are necessarily arbitrary, and readers are invited to substitute their own weights until the political system actually adopts a well-considered accountability system.[88]

Federal and state accountability systems have proposed to judge schools solely by their accomplishments in the first two goal areas, basic knowledge and skills, and critical thinking. In practice, because basic skills are so much easier and less expensive to test, accountability has relied primarily on achievement in basic skills. As an unintended consequence, these accountability systems have interfered with, even destroyed, schools' efforts to achieve the other goals. The next chapter examines how contemporary accountability policies have affected the other goals of public education.

TABLE 1 Relative importance of eight goal areas of public education, as ranked by the general public, school board members, and state legislators

Goal	General public	School board members	State legislators
Basic academic skills	19%	22%	24%
Critical thinking	15	18	18
The arts and literature	8	9	9
Preparation for skilled work	11	11	11
Social skills and work ethic	14	12	11
Citizenship	10	11	12
Physical health	12	9	9
Emotional health	11	8	7
Total	100%	100%	101%*

* Sum = 101 because of rounding.

Source: Knowledge Networks survey commissioned by the authors.

TABLE 2 Relative importance of eight goal areas of public education, reflecting authors' analysis of survey findings and recommendations of policy makers

Goal	Relative importance
Basic academic skills	21%
Critical thinking	16
The arts and literature	10
Preparation for skilled work	10
Social skills and work ethic	13
Citizenship	13
Physical health	9
Emotional health	8
Total	100%

Source: Authors' analysis.

CHAPTER 3

Goal distortion

Teachers have only limited instructional time. With children present for only six hours, too many minutes devoted to math might mean too few left for physical education. Too much time for reading might mean not enough for civics. Too much attention to the arts might mean not enough for science. So with eight important goal areas, educators must allocate their efforts wisely, within each goal and between the eight goals.

Test-based accountability systems in many states, like the federal *No Child Left Behind*, hold schools accountable only for reading and math scores. Standardized tests concentrate mostly on basic skills in these subjects, not critical thinking or reasoning. If basic skills performance is inadequate, schools are subject to sanctions, ultimately a school staff's replacement. Nationwide, principals' tenure increasingly depends on whether basic skills scores are improving, so principals hold teachers accountable in similar fashion. In some districts, principals' and/or teachers' pay now varies, in part, by their students' scores.

With such pressure, it would be natural to expect schools to diminish their efforts in the other seven goal areas to spend more time improving basic skills. Even teaching of basic knowledge and skills in non-accountability subjects (like science or history) may decline. Critical thinking about literature, or mathematical reasoning, is likely to get less attention than the mechanics that are more easily tested.

And even the mechanics may be distorted. Because new test development is expensive, states use test questions that are similar, if not identical, from year to year. Teachers can soon "teach to the test" once they have seen which mechanical skills are emphasized more than others.[89] So, for example, students may learn more about triangles than rectangles only because teachers have learned to expect a triangle question on their state test.

This accountability-driven shift in priorities might not be a bad thing. It could be that schools were previously spending too little time on reading and math, so the incentives provided by the accountability system are a welcome correction. Or it could be that schools were previously using time inefficiently, and basic skill instruction could increase without taking time away from efforts to achieve the other goals.

But it is also easy to see how accountability-driven priorities could be harmful. In the context of one education goal, promoting students' physical health, consider our growing national diabetes epidemic. On average, blacks are 60% more likely to have diabetes than whites of similar age.[90] One cause, though not the only one, is a decline in physical activity of youth, particularly minority youth – exacerbated by the substitution of math and reading test preparation for physical education, particularly in schools where test scores are low and more academic drill might help meet accountability standards.

The Centers for Disease Control and Prevention (CDC) finds that 22% of black elementary school children are overweight, compared to 18% of whites. Perhaps not coincidentally, 47% of white elementary school children participate in organized daily physical activity, compared to only 24% of blacks.[91]

Yet black students are more dependent on physical education classes to protect their health because they have fewer opportunities for exercise outside school. They are more likely to live in unsafe neighborhoods and are less likely to participate in out-of-school sports. Overall, considering both in- and out-of-school exercise, 39% of white high school students now participate in a sufficient amount of strenuous physical activity necessary for good health, while only 30% of black high school students do so.[92]

Substituting test preparation for exercise may be short-sighted, even as a way to improve academic performance. Performance in all eight of the goal areas may improve when instruction has more balance. As Benjamin Franklin observed, and contemporary science confirms,[93] physical exercise is needed to keep mentally sharp.

Some prominent Americans have expressed concern that, as accountability demands for better math and reading scores have increased, attention devoted to other goals of education has decreased, particularly the role of schools in developing good citizenship habits.

The historian David McCullough concluded in testimony before a Senate committee: "Because of *No Child Left Behind*, sadly, history is being put on the back burner or taken off the stove altogether in many or most schools, in favor of math or reading."[94]

Retired Justice Sandra Day O'Connor now co-chairs a "Campaign for the Civic Mission of Schools" which laments that, under NCLB, "as civic learning has been pushed aside, society has neglected a fundamental purpose of American education, putting the health of our democracy at risk."[95] Justice O'Connor notes that NCLB "has effectively squeezed out civics education because there is no testing for that anymore and no funding for that....We can't forget that the primary purpose of public schools in America has always been to help produce citizens who have the knowledge and the skills and the values to sustain our republic as a nation, our democratic form of government."[96]

And deans of the five leading journalism schools have issued a report noting that schools should be the place where the nation's values are transmitted, but discussions of current events are being compromised by mandatory testing in math, reading, and science – especially among disadvantaged children whose curricula have been most affected by test-driven demands for more time on drill in basic skills.[97]

In his presidential campaign education policy statement, Barack Obama asserted that NCLB "has become so reliant on a standardized test model that... subjects like history and social studies have gotten pushed aside. Arts and music time is no longer there. So the child is not having the well-rounded educational experience I benefited from and most in my generation benefited from."[98]

Several surveys of school district officials, principals, and teachers confirm that the public school curriculum has been dangerously narrowed because of accountability pressures to post higher math and reading scores. Even testing in other basic knowledge and skills has declined. From 2001 to 2005, the number of states that tested history or other social studies dropped from 27 to 19.[99]

The narrowing did not begin with *No Child Left Behind*; there was evidence of it throughout the last several decades as math and reading tests have steadily gained in importance. In a 1994-95 survey of Maryland teachers, two-thirds said that they had reduced the amount of time they spent on instruction in non-tested subjects, especially art, music, and physical education.[100] In the 1990s, similar curricular shifts were also common in Texas, upon whose accountability system the national NCLB law was modeled. In that state, and especially in schools serving disadvantaged minority students, teachers of art, history, and science were required to put their curricula aside to utilize class time to drill students in the basic math and reading skills that were tested by the state exam.[101]

In a 2001 study of teachers in Kansas, Massachusetts, and Michigan, many reported that standardized testing had improved how they taught reading and math. But they also described having to drop "enrichment" activities that did not directly support higher scores on basic skills tests. Urban and rural teachers were more likely than suburban teachers to report such a shift. Thus, the achievement gap between disadvantaged and middle-class children probably grew in the goal areas not subject to standardized testing for purposes of accountability.

For example, in Kansas 75% of all elementary school teachers reported that they had removed areas previously taught to make room for more test preparation. An urban elementary school teacher noted being unable to teach a seasonal poem "because that's not really driving towards the standards they're going to be assessed on." A Kansas teacher complained about not getting to do as many "cooperative learning activities or projects....I've done a lot more direct teaching than being able to do student-led learning....That's what really suffers."[102]

An urban middle school teacher in Michigan said, "I remove a lot of the project-type activities such as writing plays, writing poetry, performance activities [to concentrate on] preparing for the tests." An urban high school teacher complained of being unable any longer to "prepare the kids to take their place in society....They don't understand taxation or financing an automobile. We used to teach business math...consumer math, and we used to teach some things that had real-world relevance. We eliminated all of that." Another urban middle school teacher said "I would like to be doing other things, like working more with public speaking....We...put that aside last year because we had to spend so much time on testing."[103]

Massachusetts teachers had the most praise for how standardized tests in math and reading had forced them to do a better job teaching these subjects. But these teachers were also twice as likely as those in Kansas or Michigan to say that removal from the curriculum of non-tested content was harmful to children's overall development.[104]

A survey of school principals in North Carolina, after the state implemented a test-based accountability system in 1999, found that over 70% had redirected instruction from other subjects and from character development to reading, math, and writing, and that this response was greatest in the lowest-scoring schools.[105] A 2003 survey of school principals in Illinois, Maryland, New Mexico, and New York found that those in high-minority schools were more likely to have reduced time for history, civics, geography, the arts, and foreign languages, to devote more time to math and reading.[106]

In New York's high-minority schools, for example, 38% of elementary school principals reported decreasing the time devoted to social studies (usually meaning history), but in low-minority schools only 17% reported doing so.[107]

The most comprehensive investigations of test-driven curricular shifts have been conducted by the Center on Education Policy (CEP), which surveyed 349 representative school districts during the 2006-07 school year. It found that accountability does work: 62% of these districts had increased time devoted to reading and math. The increases were greatest in urban districts sanctioned under NCLB because their test scores were too low; in such districts, the

TABLE 3 Changes in instructional time, districts with at least one NCLB-sanctioned school

Subject area	Average weekly change in instructional time (minutes), 2001-07
English	+ 183
Math	+ 86
Social studies	- 90
Science	- 94
Art and music	- 61
Physical education	- 57
Recess	- 60

Source: McMurrer 2007, Table 4.

increase in reading and math instruction totaled an average of over four hours a week.[108]

This is just what test-based accountability systems intend to accomplish. Students whose reading and math performance was lowest were getting a lot more instruction in these subjects. But in an accountability system, what doesn't get measured doesn't get done; increased time for test preparation in reading and math comes at the expense of time for something else. As **Table 3** shows, these districts cut an average of an hour or more from instruction in social studies, science, art and music, physical education, and recess. Most districts facing sanctions cut time from several of these subject areas to make room for more reading and math test preparation.

Anecdotal accounts from teachers confirm these trends. An elementary school teacher in California reports:

> We go by the standards [in language arts and mathematics]. We are being told that your students have to meet these standards; they have to, have to. So we started getting rid of things that had nothing to do with the standards. That's when we got rid of social studies and science.... The standards are it; and if it doesn't fit the standards, then toss it, because we have to stick to the standards.[109]

A Colorado teacher reports:

> Our district has told us to focus on reading, writing, and mathematics. Therefore, science and social studies, unless I can teach them in a reading, writing, or mathematics format, then they don't get taught. I don't teach science and social studies nearly as often and not purely as science or social studies. In the past I had hatched out baby chicks in the classroom as part of a science unit. I don't have time to do that. I have dissected body parts and I don't have time to do that. I have waited until now to start my economics unit for mini-society because it takes so much time. I can do it now because [it is the end of the year and the state accountability testing] is over. We don't take as many field trips. We don't do community outreach like we used to like visiting the nursing home or cleaning up the park because we had adopted a park and that was our job...to keep it clean. Well, we don't have time for that anymore.[110]

And another California teacher, from a Los Angeles low-income and low-performing school, serving mostly Hispanic immigrant children, adds:

> [T]he pressure became so intense that we had to show how every single lesson we taught connected to a standard that was going to be tested. This meant that art, music, and even science and social studies were not a priority and were hardly ever taught. We were forced to spend ninety percent of the instructional time on reading and math. This made teaching boring for me and was a huge part of why I decided to leave the profession.[111]

Appendix 4 includes excerpts from additional interviews with teachers from several states on the extent to which such goal distortion has occurred. Their anecdotal accounts describe a reallocation of instruction from non-tested subjects to reading and math, and a reallocation within language arts instruction itself from literary activities to basic skills.

The role of excessive basic skills testing in curriculum distortion has not gone unnoticed by some prominent policy makers who had earlier advocated more testing as a suitable way to hold schools accountable for better performance. Robert Schwartz, for example, was the founding president of Achieve, the joint business-governors group that was largely responsible for the testing and accountability demands in the 1990s that spurred greater state-level testing and culminated in NCLB. He now writes:

> [T]he goal of equipping all students with a solid foundation of academic knowledge and skills is leading to an undue narrowing of curricular choices and a reduction in the kinds of learning opportunities for academically at-risk students that are most likely to engage and motivate them to take school seriously. This is a painful acknowledgment from someone who considers himself a charter member of the standards movement...."[112]

Chester Finn and Diane Ravitch, early advocates of NCLB who had been assistant secretaries of education in previous Republican administrations, now say: "NCLB puts a premium on reading and math skills....Worthy though these skills are, they ignore at least half of what has long been regarded as a 'well rounded' education in Western civilization...."

Noting that these shifts disproportionately affect minority and disadvantaged students, and expressing a sentiment not much different from that of the Pennsylvania workingmen's committee in 1830, Ravitch and Finn add that, if the testing craze continues:

> Top private schools and a few suburban systems will stick with education broadly defined, as will elite colleges. Rich kids will study philosophy and art, music, and history, while their poor peers fill in bubbles on test sheets. The lucky few will spawn the next generation of tycoons, political leaders, inventors, authors, artists, and entrepreneurs. The less lucky masses will see narrower opportunities.[113]

Regretting their earlier support of state and federal accountability-by-testing, they conclude:

> We should have seen this coming...should have anticipated the "zero sum" problem... more emphasis on some things would inevitably mean less attention to others....We were wrong. We didn't see how completely standards-based reform would turn into a basic-skills frenzy....[114]

Policy makers, however, should have seen this coming because it had come before – in the 1970s and '80s, most states required standardized "minimum competency testing" and utilized these test scores as a way to identify, shame, or intervene in failing schools. Yet higher scores on math and reading tests of basic skills were accompanied by worse performance in areas for which teachers were not held accountable: science, writing, mathematical problem solving, and analytical reading.[115]

Disappointing results from minimum competency tests were one influence on the *Nation At Risk* report (discussed in Chapter 1) that denounced the quality of American education. The report noted that "schools may emphasize such rudiments as reading and computation at the expense of other essential skills such as comprehension, analysis, solving problems, and drawing conclusions."[116] It complained that "'[m]inimum competency' examinations (now required in 37 States) fall short of what is needed, as the 'minimum' tends to become the 'maximum,' thus lowering educational standards for all."[117] It is ironic that these cautions were lost in the academic skills panic that was stimulated by the report. Although intended to reject the excesses of minimum competency testing, the effect of *A Nation at Risk* was to promote the new wave of such testing that we experience today.

Accountability policies based on math and reading test scores not only distort the curriculum by creating incentives to ignore important education goals. Such policies corrupt the educational process in other ways as well. The next chapter reviews some of these corruptions.

CHAPTER 4

Perverse accountability

At least when it comes to basic academic knowledge and skills, it seems reasonable to most people that we should be able to measure schools' and teachers' effectiveness by their students' test scores. But, alas, test scores turn out not to be an adequate accountability device, even for basic skills. The goal distortion described in the last chapter is only one of the serious flaws of a test-based accountability system.

Test reliability

Test-based accountability plans (like those of *No Child Left Behind* and similar state systems) rely on a single test in math and reading, administered annually. But single tests can be misleading. Every parent knows children have good or bad days. Even students having consistently normal days don't get precisely the same scores when they re-take a test. Sometimes on testing days, entire classes can be attentive or distracted. Accurate measurement requires multiple re-tests. Only then can we estimate students' true performance by averaging the results.

Yet multiple re-tests are expensive to design because each test must be different from previous versions. Otherwise precise questions would be predictable, teachers would prepare students for these questions, and test results would not reflect students' abilities. And if we want to measure multiple subjects (math, reading, writing, science, history, and perhaps others), requiring multiple re-tests for each subject, each year, would drastically cut into instructional time.

If we hope to use tests for school or teacher accountability, we might be tempted to ignore the unreliability of any single student's score and assume that some students' good days would offset other students' bad ones; then, the average results for an entire grade or class would be accurate, a fair indication of schools' and teachers' effectiveness even if individual student scores could not provide such an indication. In any assessment or survey, the larger the number of students tested, the more likely it is that erratic scores will cancel each other out in an average. But as it turns out, most schools are too small to support statistical confidence that children's good and bad days will average out on a single test. On any day in one grade in one school, it would not be unusual for more students to be having bad days than good ones (or vice-versa). As a result, the grades' scores have to be reported as an approximation – usually by reporting the average score together with its margin of error.[118] But this margin of error could be greater than the true differences in average scores that would distinguish effective schools from ineffective ones.

If we could ensure that every student's score on a particular test day reflected that student's own average performance, the small number of students in a school cohort would still render accountability measures inaccurate. This is because students vary in the native ability they bring to schools. Every teacher knows classes can be unusually talented or unusually difficult in any year. The variation in human ability is substantial.[119] A single school cohort is not likely to be large enough to allow confidence that the average native ability of students, and the distribution of their ability, is similar to that of the population as a whole. In any class or grade or school, there may well be an unusually large number of bright students one year and slower students the next. So a school may seem to be raising its test scores from one year to the next, but it may only be teaching a brighter group of students. This human variability necessitates a further margin of error in reporting test scores.

Making matters worse, test-based accountability systems, such as those adopted by states leading up to and following passage of *No Child Left Behind*, aim to hold schools accountable not only for their average scores in each grade but for the average scores of subgroups, like black students, Hispanic students, or low-income students. Subgroups, of course, are smaller in size than an entire grade – a fourth grade might have 60 students, but only 15 black students, for example. The smaller the subgroup, the bigger the margin of error in reporting that subgroup's average score. So ironically, while NCLB purported to focus on disadvantaged minority children, the more integrated a school, with more distinct subgroups, the more inaccurate federal test-based accountability became.[120]

In sum, the test scores of students in a school, or changes in those scores from year to year, may not accurately reflect that school's performance in comparison to the performance of other schools: the students in that school may not be typical of students generally of the same age and grade, or even typical of students in the same school the previous year; and the students' scores on a particular testing day may not be typical of the same students' scores on other days that testing might have taken place.

When the Bush administration and Congress were designing NCLB in 2001, two economists (Thomas Kane and Douglas Staiger) demonstrated that, without permitting very large margins of error, many schools would be rewarded or punished solely because of these statistical challenges.[121] Their paper derailed NCLB's adoption for six months while administration and congressional experts tried to finesse these problems. They couldn't, but they enacted NCLB anyway, resulting in remarkable anomalies: schools rewarded one year and punished the next with no changes in effectiveness; schools rewarded under a state's system and simultaneously punished under the federal one, or vice-versa. When states try to avoid these absurdities by reporting large margins of error in schools' test scores, state education officials must necessarily fail to identify many schools that are truly low-performing (as well as castigate schools that might be doing quite well). As a result, some supporters of test-based accountability denounce state departments of education for claiming such large error margins and making a mockery of accountability policy.[122] The accusations of mockery are fair – smaller error margins would be more conventional, but would also misidentify more schools as either failing or succeeding.

Holding all to a single standard

As noted above, children's native ability varies widely. Indeed, human variation characterizes any trait we want to measure, whether it is academic achievement, height, weight, athletic ability, artistic inspiration, resistance to disease, or courage. Yet today's test-based accountability policies expect all students to reach the same standard of proficiency. The *No Child Left Behind Act*, for example, demanded that all students in each state pass a single "challenging" standard by 2014. But even if test-based accountability policies were to succeed in giving schools and teachers incentives to devote inordinate attention to math and reading, it is practically and conceptually ludicrous to expect all students to reach identical levels of challenging proficiency. NCLB hoped to eliminate disparities based on children's race and socioeconomic status, but it overlooked the reality that disparities *within* any race or social group are greater than the disparities between these groups.

In any subgroup, or in the population as a whole, even in the best of environments, "challenging" achievement in a particular subject for higher-ability children would be impossibly hard for those who were slower, and "challenging" achievement for slower students would be too easy for the brighter ones.

The challenging standards that federal law now requires nearly all students to meet are the standards of proficiency defined by the National Assessment of

Educational Progress (NAEP), periodic federal tests of national student samples. NCLB's use of the term "challenging" to define proficiency was taken from NAEP's definition of proficiency as "demonstrated competency over challenging subject matter." Under NCLB, states have had to permit administration of the NAEP as the benchmark for state testing.[123] But while NAEP tests are excellent, their cut-off scores that define proficiency have no credibility. Passing points are arbitrary, fancifully defined by panels of teachers, politicians, and laypeople. Most children in the highest-scoring countries don't achieve them. On international tests, places like Taiwan and Singapore come out on top in math, but more than half of students in these high-scoring countries seem to be less than proficient by NAEP's standard. Swedes are the best readers in the world, but two-thirds of Swedish students do not read well enough to be considered proficient by NAEP's criteria.[124]

Expecting *all* American students to perform at this level by 2014 (or any date) can only set them, their teachers, and their schools up for failure.[125]

NCLB's expectation of proficiency for all confused a minimum standard, one that all (even the least able) students should meet, with a challenging standard, one that requires typical students to reach well beyond their present level of performance. The consequences for accountability of this breathtaking illogic are evident. In a rare bow to local control, the NCLB Act permitted each state to define proficiency separately, with only the vague expectation that these definitions would be similar to NAEP's. Not surprisingly, many states defined proficiency quite low, yet the law prohibited the Department of Education from enforcing the provision that standards must be "challenging." If the department had been permitted to forbid low state passing scores, the already unacceptably large number of failing schools would have been astronomical. Nonetheless, low state proficiency cut points have become a sore point with advocates of test-based accountability, who propose to correct this flaw in NCLB by establishing national standards.[126] This proposal, if adopted, would result in an accountability system that made wholesale failure inevitable.

In response to this argument – that no standard can serve as both a minimum standard and as a goal – some advocates of test-based accountability note that commonplace tests do exist in which all test takers are expected to be proficient. They say, for example, that if we can expect all drivers to pass a licensing exam and be proficient at understanding the rules of the road, then we can also expect all fourth graders to be proficient in math.[127]

This analogy fails for three reasons. First, not *all* test takers pass the written exam to get a drivers' license – although almost all do, eventually, having taken the test multiple times, something not permitted in contemporary school accountability systems.[128] Second, every state recognizes that passing a paper-and-pencil test cannot alone demonstrate proficiency; applicants for driver's licenses must also pass a performance assessment by getting behind the wheel and demonstrating skills like making turns, parking, etc. And third, anyone who has taken a written driver's license test knows that the level of difficulty is extraordinarily low. Passing can be assured by devoting only a few minutes to review of the state manual published for this purpose. Nobody would call written state driver's tests "challenging." If they were indeed challenging, the goal of having everyone pass would be no more in reach than the goal of having all fourth graders proficient in math.

If we define proficiency low enough, as driver's tests do, it is certainly possible to achieve the goal of having almost all students proficient in math and reading by some future date. But such a standard would not be challenging to most students, and would do little to spur typical students to perform at higher levels than they do today.

Besides driver's exams, other tests also require proficiency – for example, physicians, accountants, hairdressers, and others obtain licenses to practice only after satisfying boards of examiners that they possess proficiency in their fields; passing examinations is part of these processes. But the professional boards that establish passing cut scores – i.e., proficiency levels – on such examinations are attempting to maintain existing professional standards in the licensing of new practitioners. Experience determines what competent physicians, accountants, or hairdressers should actually be able to do; licensing boards do not use cut scores to require newly licensed practitioners to perform at radically higher levels than most existing practitioners. In practice, cut scores on such licensing examinations are often changed based on supply and demand factors: if there is a shortage of job seekers in a profession, licensing boards lower the cut scores for passing the test, confirming that even for licensing exams, the concept of proficiency has no objective meaning.[129] Further, there is considerable selectivity in the pool of candidates taking the exam. Because not all young people are qualified to enter training to become candidates in medicine, accounting, or hairdressing, the variability in performance among candidates is much narrower than among the full national universe of students in a particular grade level. And then, professional schools are expected to weed out students whom they admitted but who are not likely to pass the licensing exam at the end of their training.

In contrast, test-based school accountability policies establish achievement levels intended to apply to 99% of all students.

The importance of how assessment results are reported

The origins of this confusion between a minimum and an aspirational standard can be traced to a shift in how we describe student achievement. In the past, certainly until 30 years ago, it was usual to describe achievement in what educators refer to as "norm-referenced" terms. After administering a standardized test to a nationally representative sample of students in a given grade, psychometricians calculated a median score and then reported each student's score, and each subgroup of students' average score, in reference to this national average.[130]

Such norm-referenced reports took a variety of forms. In cases where the public was familiar and comfortable with a test, scale scores were reported with no further explanation. An example of a norm-referenced test with which we are fully comfortable is the college admission test, the SAT, where instead of reporting that a given student is at about the 84th percentile (scoring better than 84% of all test takers in the year the test norms were established), we say that the student has a score of 600. By definition, 600 is the score of an 84th percentile test taker in the original national sample (and 500, the average score of the sample).[131] The scale score of 600 has no absolute significance; it is only a norm-referenced score, a convention with which the public is familiar. When we are told that a student scored 600 on the SAT math test, most of us, comfortable with this norm-referenced scale, have an intuitive understanding of what that student can do.

For 25 years now, NAEP has also reported scale scores that allow norm-referenced interpretation. But because the public was never familiar with the NAEP scale, and because NAEP added unnecessary complexity by employing different scales for different grade levels, NAEP scale score reports have no intuitive meaning for the public.[132] Unlike the SAT, which uses the easily remembered 500 for average performance and the easily remembered 400 or 600 for performance that was about 34 percentile points below or above average in the base year (1991) when SAT scoring rules were last calculated, NAEP scale scores for public schools are much more difficult to contextualize. In 2006, for example, 237 was the score for average fourth-grade math performance (and 266 for one standard deviation above), but for average eighth-grade math performance the score was 278 (and 314 for one standard deviation above).[133] Because neither the public nor even relatively sophisticated policy makers could ever become familiar with these needlessly obscure conventions, Congress sought an alternative.

Many policy makers advocated the desirability of defining performance cut scores (i.e., proficiency levels) as an alternative to scale scores, but gave little consideration to the complexities involved. In the 1988 congressional reauthorization of NAEP, the Senate bill instructed the National Assessment Governing Board (NAGB), which oversees NAEP, to "identify feasible achievement goals for each age and grade in each subject area under the National Assessment." The final bill that emerged from the conference committee somehow substituted the word "appropriate" for "feasible."[134] "Feasible" cut points would have to be somehow anchored to what students actually can accomplish, but "appropriate" cut points had no anchor at all, and were left entirely to the discretion of NAGB board members.

Arbitrariness of proficiency definitions

When NAGB attempted to carry out Congress' instruction to identify achievement goals, NAGB asked the Senate education staff member who drafted the bill to explain what "appropriate" meant. He stated that Congress' choice of language was "deliberately ambiguous" because neither congressional staff nor education experts were able to formulate it more precisely. "There was not an enormous amount of introspection" on the language, he reported.[135]

A few experts protested at the time. One was Harold Howe II, former U.S. commissioner of education, who had played an important role in developing the NAEP some 20 years before. In May 1988, Howe wrote to the Commissioner of Education Statistics:

> …[M]ost educators are aware that any group of children of a particular age or grade will vary widely in their learning for a whole host of reasons. To suggest that there are particular learnings or skill levels that should be developed to certain defined points by a particular age or grade…defies reality.[136]

Nor was Howe the first to sound such a warning. Six years earlier, when momentum was first building for NAEP reports that went beyond scale scores, the federal governing body for NAEP asked former U.S. Labor Secretary Willard Wirtz and his colleague Archie Lapointe to make recommendations about how NAEP should be improved.[137] The Wirtz-Lapointe report warned that NAEP should not attempt to define passing points, a task that, the report said, "would be easy, attractive, and fatal….Setting levels of failure, mediocrity, or excellence in terms of NAEP percentages would be a serious mistake….[T]he making of judgments about what is 'good' or 'bad' is reasonable and responsible only in terms of particular educational environments."[138]

Ignoring this advice of its own commissioned experts, NAGB in 1990 adopted the policy of reporting whether NAEP scores had reached an appropriate, or proficient, level, acknowledging, with no apparent embarrassment, that "appropriateness is a matter of taste."[139]

For 12th graders, proficiency was defined as the level of performance that *all* students should achieve; as NAGB put it: "At grade 12 the proficient level will encompass a body of subject-matter knowledge and analytical skills, of cultural literacy and insight, that all high school graduates should have...; the knowledge and skills all students need to participate in our competitive economy... and the levels of proficiency needed to handle college-level work."[140] At the time NAGB made this pronouncement, approximately 29% of all 17-year-olds eventually went on to graduate from college.[141] NAGB's unexamined assumption that the NAEP proficiency standard could be defined at a level that would more than triple this rate illustrates the fanciful thinking underlying the achievement level process.

Today, many state standardized tests, employed for accountability purposes, use similar terminology about the competitive economy and college readiness to describe their passing scores.

There is nothing scientific about defining a standardized test's passing score, and there are several methods for doing so. But all require subjective decisions by panels of judges who decide what constitutes proficiency for a particular subject and grade – although the federal and state governments are normally not so candid as NAGB when it stated that appropriate achievement levels are simply a matter of taste. One common method is to ask each judge to imagine what a barely proficient student can generally do, and then estimate, for each question on a test, the probability that such a student will answer the question correctly. The minimum test score (in percent correct) that a student must achieve to be deemed proficient is determined by averaging the judges' probability estimates for all the questions.[142] This is the method NAGB used to set NAEP's proficiency definitions. About half of NAGB's panelists were teachers, and about one-third were members of the general public. Other professional educators (e.g., administrators, specialists) made up the balance. NAGB gave its panelists no standards by which to make judgments of proficiency; they were to rely simply on their own opinions, which varied widely.[143]

NAGB panelists' subjective judgments, while well intentioned, almost inevitably lead to overestimates of proficient performance. When teachers and educators, as well as members of the general public, imagine proficiency, they tend to think of a performance level that is higher than students actually achieve, but one that they hope students will achieve or think students should achieve. It is a rare teacher who considers that her students' average performance should not have been higher than it was, if only the students had been a little better prepared and tried a little harder, if only parents could have been persuaded to be a little more supportive, if only the teacher had organized the curriculum a little differently, or if only some distracting event had not occurred during the school year. So it is not surprising that the NAGB judges established definitions of NAEP achievement levels that were unreasonably high, despite the judges having gone through several days of training designed to avoid that very result.

Indeed, commonplace mis-estimation of how students perform characterized the earliest development of NAEP in the late 1960s. The designers of early NAEP attempted to include some "easy" exercises that they expected 90% of all students to answer correctly. But to the surprise of NAEP officials, each time their sophisticated contractors developed such exercises, and then tried them out on a sample student population, far fewer than 90% were able to answer these questions correctly. NAEP officials concluded that "even experienced exercise writers cannot 'armchair' the difficulty level of 'easy' exercises. Writers, and perhaps adults in general, do not have a feel for the kinds of information which are common to almost all youngsters of a given age level."[144] This institutional wisdom had been forgotten when, a quarter century later, NAGB set out to establish proficiency cut scores.

In 1978, still more than a decade before NAGB began to define cut scores for NAEP, a measurement expert warned that judges in such an exercise almost invariably set unrealistically high criteria. He described the mental process that judges typically apply as one of "counting backwards from 100%":

> An objective is stated and a test item is written to correspond to it. Since the objective is felt to be important – or else it wouldn't have been stated – its author readily endorses the proposition that everyone should be able to answer the test question based on it….But reason and experience prevail and it is quickly recognized that perfection is impossible and concessions must be made for mental infirmity, clerical errors, misinformation, inattention, and the like. Just how great a concession should be made becomes distressingly arbitrary….[145]

If this is an accurate description of how NAGB judges approached their task, it is not surprising that NAEP proficiency is defined unreasonably stringently. The mental burden of proof fell on deviations from perfection.

After it established the first achievement levels for math, NAGB conducted a forum to hear public comments about the new standards. One judge who had established the cut scores was the mathematics education director for the National Academy of Sciences. She testified: "We were uncomfortable that we did not do the best job we could do. It was a rushed process."[146] The president of the Educational Testing Service, which administered NAEP, urged NAGB to delay employing achievement levels until it could be certain that they had been established properly.

In response, Chester E. Finn Jr., a former NAGB chairman and still a board member, explained why he was unwilling to defer to this expert advice. The realism of proficiency cut scores was unimportant, he suggested, compared to the desirable impact on public psychology of demonstrating that large numbers of students were failing. If we delay, he said, "we may be sacrificing something else – the sense of urgency for national improvement."[147]

More recently, Finn asserted that if statistical experts have contempt for such proficiency definitions, then there must be something wrong with the experts:

> I lost a lot of respect for the technical types in the course of these conflicts. They…turn out to be very effective at criticizing somebody else's decision and totally unable to suggest a viable alternative….A large number of technical experts have bitched and moaned about the way [setting proficiency levels] is done, but I have yet to see any of them propose another way to do it. So, I get fed up with technical experts… [who] have marginalized themselves by appearing to take an adversarial stance toward some of the things that are most important in the views of those operating NAEP, such as setting standards.[148]

The ill-considered drive for substituting proficiency cut points for NAEP scale scores was bipartisan. Finn had been an assistant secretary of education under President Reagan and was appointed to NAGB by the first President Bush. The Congress that demanded such cut points was controlled by Democrats; the Senate staff member who had substituted "appropriate" for "feasible" in the legislation was an aide to Senator Ted Kennedy, Democrat of Massachusetts.

For nearly two decades now, the National Assessment Governing Board itself has issued contradictory statements regarding how seriously its achievement levels should be taken. In 1990, it stated that the proficiency level represented merely "acceptable" achievement.[149] More recent NAGB publications acknowledge that the definitions are indefensible, although government reports continue to use them. NAGB now puts it this way:

Nor is performance at the Proficient level synonymous with "proficiency" in the subject. That is, students who may be considered proficient in a subject, given the common usage of the term, might not satisfy the requirements for performance at the [Proficient] NAEP achievement level.[150]

In the early 1990s, NAGB, Congress, and the Department of Education all commissioned studies to evaluate the achievement-level-setting process and the validity of the results. Each study concluded that the achievement levels were misleading and even harmful, and urged NAGB to discontinue their use or to use them only with the most explicit warnings about their arbitrariness. The government's response to each of these studies was to commission yet another study, hoping that a different group of scholars would emerge with a more favorable conclusion.

The first of these, by three nationally prominent statisticians, was conducted in 1991, following the initial efforts of judges to establish math proficiency cut scores.[151] According to the statisticians' preliminary report, "the technical difficulties [with NAGB's achievement level definitions in math] are extremely serious," and to repeat the process in standards setting for other subjects would be "ridiculous." The statisticians charged that the governing board was technically incompetent and urged Congress to reconstitute it with members who had more sophistication. NAGB's response was to cancel the statisticians' contract before the final report could be submitted.[152]

But the preliminary report had been publicized, so the House Education and Labor Committee asked the General Accounting Office (GAO) to decide whether the statisticians were right. In 1993 the GAO published its report, entitled *Educational Achievement Standards: NAGB's Approach Yields Misleading Interpretations.* The report concluded that defining proficiency cut-off scores is not a task that laypeople can reasonably perform. For example, the GAO found that NAGB judges could not properly distinguish between easier and more difficult test items. Judges had a tendency to classify multiple choice items as easy, when they were not necessarily so, and classify open-ended items as difficult, even when they were not. The GAO concluded that the cut score for proficiency should have been set considerably lower than it was, based on the NAGB panel's own standards. This would have resulted in much larger numbers of students being deemed proficient.[153] The GAO reached these conclusions:

> We conclude that NAGB's...approach was inherently flawed, both conceptually and procedurally, and that...the approach not be used further until a thorough review could be completed....
>
> These weaknesses are not trivial; reliance on NAGB's results could have serious consequences. For example, policymakers might conclude that since [performance seemed poor], resources should be allocated so as to emphasize fundamental skills for most classes....[T]his strategy could retard their progress toward mastering more challenging material....
>
> In light of the many problems we found with NAGB's approach, we recommend that NAGB withdraw its direction to NCES that the... NAEP results be published primarily in terms of levels. The conventional approach to score interpretation [i.e., reports of scale scores] should be retained until an alternative has been shown to be sound.[154]

The GAO concluded that NAGB had ignored the advice of statistical experts because "the benefits of sending an important message about U.S. students' school achievement appeared considerable, and NAGB saw little risk in publishing scores and interpretations that had yet to be fully examined."[155]

Still not satisfied, the Department of Education commissioned yet another study of the NAEP proficiency definitions, this one performed by a National Academy of Education (NAE) panel.[156] Confirming the GAO's findings, the NAE panel concluded that the procedure by which the achievement levels had been established were "fundamentally flawed," that they were "subject to large biases," and that the achievement levels by which American students had been judged deficient were set "unreasonably high."[157] The NAE recommended that the method used for establishing NAEP achievement levels should be abandoned and that the achievement levels themselves should not be used. In fact, the NAE panel stated, continued use of these standards could set back the cause of education reform because it would harm the credibility of NAEP itself.[158]

And again, the Department of Education responded by contracting for yet another evaluation of NAEP, this time with the National Academy of Sciences. The academy's panel held a conference in 1996 on the achievement-level-setting process and published its conclusions three years later. The "process for setting NAEP achievement levels is fundamentally flawed," the academy report repeated. "[P]rocesses are too cognitively complex for the raters, and there are notable inconsistencies in the judgment data....Furthermore, NAEP achievement-level results do not appear to be reasonable compared with other external information about students' achievement."[159]

None of this advice has been followed. In the 1994 reauthorization of the Elementary and Secondary Education Act, of which NCLB was the subsequent reauthorization, Congress acknowledged the judgments of the scientific community and instructed that proficiency level definitions should be used only on a "developmental basis" until the Commissioner of Education Statistics re-evaluates them and determines that the levels are "reasonable, valid, and informative to the public."[160] Similar language remained in NCLB. The result has been that all NAEP reports now include disclaimers about the validity of the proficiency levels being used. Yet the same NAEP reports continue to highlight data on these proficiency levels, while government officials continue to issue pronouncements about the percentages of students who are not proficient, never mentioning the disclaimers.[161]

In 2000, NAGB commissioned one more review of the controversy by James Popham, a nationally respected testing expert. Acknowledging that the cut scores are widely regarded as being too high, Popham noted that resistance to lowering them was based on a belief that doing so "would present a clear admission to the world that the Nation's much touted pursuit of *demanding* levels of student performance was little more than public-relations rhetoric." Nonetheless, Popham concluded, "if not modified, [the achievement levels policy] may make NAEP an educational anachronism within a decade or two."[162]

The subjectivity of state proficiency standards

Federal law now requires each state to use a similarly flawed methodology to establish proficiency cut scores that all students must surpass. State officials' manipulation of these definitions has sometimes been even more flagrant than the National Assessment Governing Board's.

As noted, NAGB has established definitions of proficiency that are unreasonably high. It has also established a lower cut point, which it describes as not proficient but "basic." Several states have established their own proficiency definitions that are even lower than NAEP's definition of basic.[163] These cut points attempt to ensure that more schools can escape the sanctions required by NCLB. Colorado established two cut scores for proficiency: one was termed "proficient" for purposes of compliance with NCLB, but the same cut score was termed only "partially proficient" for purposes of compliance with state accountability rules. Eighth-grade mathematics students in Montana, who achieve far above their state's proficiency standard, can walk across the border to Wyoming and, with the same math ability, fall far below proficiency in that state.[164] In Missouri, 10% fewer students are deemed proficient on the state eighth-grade math test than on NAEP, while in Tennessee, 66% more students are deemed proficient on the state test than on NAEP.[165]

In the mid-1990s, South Carolina students were four times as likely to be deemed proficient by South Carolina's own accountability system as were proficient on the NAEP.[166] Today, however, South Carolina has raised its cut point to NAEP's level,[167] presumably because, like federal officials, South Carolina's leaders hoped reports of large numbers of failures would communicate an urgency for improvement.

Capricious state standards in other state test-based accountability systems produce anomalies of their own. In the 1990s Massachusetts established cut scores on its state test that resulted in only 28% of its eighth graders being deemed proficient in science. But at about the same time, Massachusetts' eighth graders scored higher, on average, than students in every country in the world (except Singapore) on an international exam.[168]

One state, Louisiana, found that its proficiency definition was too high to permit many of its schools to avoid sanctions under NCLB, so the state simply decreed that for NCLB purposes its "basic" cut score would be considered a challenging standard of proficiency.[169]

To sum up, the goal of all students, in all subgroups, achieving proficiency by 2014, or by any subsequent date, is not achievable for two reasons. First, inevitable variation in student performance makes it logically necessary that all students cannot be at or above a level that typical students find "challenging." Second, the concept of proficiency in multiple academic subjects and grade levels is so subjective that basing an accountability system upon it, involving sanctions and rewards, will almost inevitably impose these sanctions and rewards either on too many or too few schools, depending on the policy goals of the standards setters.

The bubble kids

Any single proficiency standard for accountability, no matter how reasonable it might seem, invites another perverse consequence – sabotaging the goal of teaching all children, because the only ones who matter are those just below the cut-off point. In schools nationwide, such children are now labeled "bubble kids," a term taken from poker and college basketball, where bubble players or teams are those just on the cusp of elimination. Explicit school policies now demand that teachers focus attention only on those bubble students, because inching them past the standard is the only accomplishment for which schools can claim "adequate yearly progress." So teachers have incentives to ignore already-proficient children in order to devote more attention to the only students for whom they get credit, those just below the passing point.

Less obvious is the incentive also to ignore children sufficiently below proficiency that even constant drill won't pull them across the finish line. Under NCLB rules, because all children were eventually (by 2014) expected to pass, ignoring poorer performers should, in the long run, have been counterproductive. But the NCLB Act placed no premium on the long run. Teachers and principals didn't worry about punishment a decade hence when they may not still be around. And since most educators always considered the 2014 goal absurd, they had good reason to expect its abandonment, further reducing incentives to worry about the lowest-performing children.[170]

As noted above, some proponents of test-based accountability complain that many states' low definitions of proficiency make it too easy for students in these states to seem to make progress at the rates required by law, and these proponents urge that national, higher definitions be established. Yet the higher the proficiency standard, the greater will be the number of children who are too far below it for teachers to worry about. Thus, if national standards were established, the result would be even greater numbers of low-achieving students being "left behind" than were left behind by NCLB in its initial years.[171]

For the bubble students in particular, schools have substituted drill and repetitive test practice for good instruction. Because test development is expensive, states re-use similar tests from year to year, effectively guiding teachers to stress content they suspect will re-appear. As noted above, this re-use makes results even more unreliable than they would be from a test that varied enough from year to year to make direct instruction on anticipated items more difficult. Teachers devote a lot of time to test-taking skills (for example, how to guess multiple choice answers) that have little to do with learning math and reading. Schools drill expected question types in the weeks before testing; this does little to help children retain what they learned and may persuade students that academic work is uninteresting and a chore. Some of these practices are illustrated in the teacher interviews reported in Appendix 4.

Gaming

Directing instruction only to children just below a passing point, or concentrating instruction only on narrow topics likely to appear on a state test, while not unlawful, are the kinds of gamesmanship for which test-based accountability creates incentives. While any accountability system is subject to some gaming, tricking the accountability system would be more difficult if schools and teachers were accountable for a broader collection of outcomes, and if the achievement of these outcomes were measured in more varied ways, using both qualitative and quantitative methods. For example, if experienced observers were to spend time in teachers' classrooms, evaluating the quality of instruction, it would be immediately obvious if teachers were disproportionately drilling the bubble students and ignoring children at the extremes of the distribution – those who need even more help, and those who are in no danger of failing. But once we base accountability primarily on the generation of a single number, a test score, the accountability system must overlook how that number was generated – except in cases of outright cheating.

Cheating is likely to increase when teachers and administrators are faced with strong sanctions (such as loss of job) for students' poor test performance. Unlawful cheating can include obtaining advance copies of an exam and coaching students on specific questions, providing assistance during an exam, or changing answers after exam booklets have been collected. There is no reason to believe that test-based accountability policies have led to widespread dishonesty in American schools, but it has apparently led to some – occurring in at least 5% of classrooms, according to one estimate based on Chicago data from the late 1990s.[172] The state of Texas recently commissioned a statistical analysis to identify schools where unusual patterns in test booklets made score gains seem improbable. The analysis found such improbable gains in nearly 9% of the state's schools, although in almost all these cases developing specific evidence for prosecutions is not feasible. The state is now implementing a new security system that includes statistical analyses of score patterns as well as other measures, such as identifying schools that achieved unusual gains or that had test booklets with an unusually high number of erasures.[173]

Other gamesmanship of more borderline legality has also apparently now become commonplace in American schools subject to high-stakes, test-based accountability policies. For example, it is a matter of discretion for school administrators to suspend students who commit disciplinary infractions. In some cases, such students could be given in-school suspensions rather than being sent home; in other cases, they might only be given warnings, denied athletic privileges, or required to remain after school to do homework. When school administrators are evaluated primarily by their schools' average test scores, the accountability system may influence disciplinary enforcement: specifically, students with disciplinary problems and whose academic performance is poor are more likely to be suspended just before testing days than they would be at other times of the year, and are more likely to be suspended during testing periods than are students with similar disciplinary problems whose academic performance is satisfactory. An analysis of Florida data in the late 1990s, just after the state adopted a test-based accountability system, found that, in over 40,000 cases where two students were involved in a disciplinary infraction (fighting, for example), the student whose prior-year test score was lower was more likely to be suspended, or suspended for longer periods, than the student whose prior-year test score was higher. This cannot be attributed to the possibility that lower-scoring students are more likely to be the primary instigators of incidents, because this relationship held more strongly for students in grades subject to accountability testing than for students in other grades, and held more strongly during testing periods than during other times of the year.[174] However, during the period immediately before testing, when cramming and test preparation for low-scoring students is most intense, such students were less likely to be suspended, or suspended for shorter periods, than at other times.[175]

Other gaming is also designed to manipulate the simple quantitative targets of a test-based accountability system. Some state accountability systems, for example, have excluded some students with disabilities from testing requirements; the federal NCLB system did not exclude them, but permitted these students to be given additional time and other support when taking accountability tests. This procedure gave school administrators incentives to designate more students as disabled than they would have designated in the absence of test-based accountability.[176] In some cases, low-scoring students have been inappropriately assigned to special education programs because they can get higher scores if given additional time; in other cases, high-scoring students have been inappropriately assigned to special education programs because their test scores can help the school demonstrate that its special education students are making adequate progress for accountability purposes. Analyses of data from Florida, Texas, and Chicago confirm that test-based accountability plans have caused the rate at which students were designated as disabled to increase.[177] In some cases, gaming was even more blatant – scheduling low-scoring or special education students to watch movies in the library, or even to take field trips to a zoo on testing days.[178] Student scores on state tests, when used for accountability purposes, may artificially be inflated by all of these gaming practices.

One way to confirm whether gaming and inappropriate test preparation is taking place is to look for cases where students take different exams covering the same subject matter: one used for purposes of accountability, where teachers or schools are faced with punishment (for example, closing of a school and loss of jobs); and the other used to assess student achievement but without serious consequences for teachers or schools if scores do not rise. If students' scores go up on the high-stakes accountability exam, but the same students' scores do not rise on the low-stakes exam, there is a likelihood that the accountability exam score increases were unduly inflated. This was the case in Chicago in the late 1990s, when students began to take an accountability exam but continued to take an earlier test as well. Apparently, teachers began to focus on the narrower set of skills likely to appear on the accountability exam, perhaps ignoring the broader skills required by the curriculum.[179]

A comparison of state test scores with NAEP scores suggests a similar phenomenon. NAEP is less subject to test-prep corruption because it is administered only to representative samples of schools and students, because it has more emphasis on critical thinking, and because different students taking the NAEP get test booklets covering different aspects of a subject area, enabling NAEP to report on the achievement of a broader curriculum. Not surprisingly, once NCLB was adopted, the share of students reaching proficiency on NAEP math and reading assessments did not shoot up to the degree that the share of students reaching proficiency on state tests had done. Math (but not reading) scores in NAEP increased a little, but at about the same (or slower) rate of improvement as before NCLB was adopted. Besides suggesting gaming and inappropriate test preparation, this experience offers damning evidence that, for all its other problems, NCLB was apparently a waste of time.[180]

Schools and social policy

Inadequate schools are only one reason disadvantaged children perform poorly. They come to school under stress from high-crime neighborhoods and economically insecure households. Their low-cost day care tends to park them before televisions, rather than provide opportunities for developmentally appropriate play. They switch schools more often because of inadequate housing and rents rising faster than parents' wages. They have greater health problems, some (like lead poisoning or iron-deficiency anemia) directly depressing cognitive ability, and some (like asthma and vision difficulties) causing more absenteeism or inattentiveness. Their households include fewer college-educated adults to provide more sophisticated intellectual environments, and their parents are less likely to expect academic success.[181] Nearly 15% of the black-white test-score gap can be traced to differences in housing mobility, and 25% to differences in child and maternal health.[182]

Yet contemporary test-based accountability policies that establish the goal of all students being proficient require that school improvement alone – higher expectations, better teachers, improved curriculum, and more testing – should raise all children to high levels of achievement, poised for college and professional success. Natural human variability would still distinguish children, but these distinctions would have nothing to do with family disadvantage. If true, there really would be no reason for progressive housing or health and economic policies. The nation's social and economic problems would take care of themselves, by the next generation.

Teachers of children who come to school hungry, scared, abused, or ill consider this absurd. But increasingly, in our test-based accountability environment, pronouncements of politicians and some educational leaders intimidate teachers from acknowledging the obvious. Instead, teachers are expected to repeat the mantra "all children can learn," a truth carrying the false implication that the level to which children learn has nothing to do with their starting points. Policy makers and school administrators warn teachers that any mention of children's socioeconomic disadvantages only "makes excuses" for teachers' own poor performance.

Of course, there are better and worse schools and better and worse teachers. And of course, some disadvantaged children excel more than others. But our federal and state test-based accountability policies, anchored to the demand for a single standard of proficiency for all students, regardless of background, have turned these obvious truths into the fantasy that teachers can wipe out socioeconomic differences among children simply by trying harder.

Denouncing schools as the chief cause of American inequality – in academic achievement, thus in the labor market, and thus in life generally – stimulates cynicism among teachers who are expected to act on a theory they know to be false. Many dedicated and talented teachers are abandoning education; they may have achieved exceptional results with disadvantaged children but, with state and federal proficiency bars set so impossibly high, even these teachers are labeled failures.

Continuation of the rhetoric of test-based accountability will also erode support for public education. Under pressure, educators now publicly vow they can eliminate achievement gaps, but they will inevitably fall short. When these educators then fail to fulfill the impossible expectations they themselves have endorsed, the reasonable conclusion can only be that they and their colleagues in public education are hopelessly incompetent.

'Fixing' NCLB

At this writing, few policy makers have yet publicly acknowledged NCLB's demise. Instead, they talk of fixing it. But fixes are impossible. Some so-called fixes would credit schools for student test score growth from year to year, rather than for passing arbitrary proficiency points.[183] Clearly, adequate progress from different starting points will likely lead to different ending points, but proponents of growth models still insist that all children should be proficient at challenging standards. The implication of growth models should be to have lower goals for students who started out farther behind, even if they gained as rapidly as students who started out farther ahead. But acknowledging lower goals, on average, for disadvantaged children is too much to swallow in today's unsophisticated political climate. Consequently, this fix to NCLB lacks coherence – we can either expect all children to achieve the same growth rate, or we can expect them all to achieve the same final level, but as long as students start at different places, we can't expect them to simultaneously achieve both.

Growth models have even bigger error margins than single-year test results because they rely on two unreliable scores (last year's and this year's), not one. In each of these two years, the "good days-bad days" problem, and the unrepresentative collection of student ability present in a school's grade cohort in any particular year, can result in a false score; but the error is greater because each year's error could be in the opposite direction – students having a good day when the test is given in the first year and a bad day when the test is given in the second, or vice-versa.[184] The unrepresentativeness of natural student ability in any grade or school leads to another problem: higher-ability students may gain more from one year to the next than lower-ability students, so a cohort's growth may not reflect much about school effectiveness. Or the opposite may be the case: lower-ability students may gain more from one year to the next than higher-ability students, perhaps because the material to be made up is at a relatively low level and easy to master.

And such an NCLB "fix" would not reduce goal distortion: accountability for growth in math and reading retains all the incentives to abandon non-tested knowledge and skills that are present when schools are accountable for fixed score levels in math and reading. Even if other subjects were added to the testing regime, presently quantifiable knowledge and skills are too few to minimize goal distortion – the federal government is unprepared to monitor, for instance, whether students express good citizenship or whether they are physically fit.

Some advocates proposed to counter the distorting effects of holding schools accountable only for math and reading scores by including "multiple measures" in any reauthorization of NCLB. For example, they proposed that high school graduation rates be included along with test scores in evaluating schools. This proposal was adopted by Representative George Miller, chairman of the House of Representatives committee with responsibility for education policy. But any mention of diluting the math and reading focus as the essential core of NCLB accountability elicited the wrath of the remaining "basics" fundamentalists – politicians and advocacy groups who continued to support NCLB. These loyalists, including the Bush Administration, would have countenanced multiple measures only if they come into play after schools were qualified exclusively by their math and reading test scores; the measures could not be used in an overall, balanced evaluation.[185]

It is surprising that so many education policy makers have been seduced into thinking that simple quantitative measures like test scores can be used to hold schools accountable for achieving complex educational outcomes. After all, similar accountability systems have been attempted, and have been found lacking, in other sectors, both private and public, many times before. The corruptions and distortions resulting from test-based accountability are no different from those that have been widely reported in the business world, as well as in fields like health care, welfare, job training, law enforcement, and other government services. These experiences are the subject of Chapter 5.

CHAPTER 5

Accountability by the numbers

In 1935, a 19-year-old political science major at the University of Chicago interviewed Milwaukee city administrators for a term paper. He was puzzled that, when money became available to invest in parks, school board and public works officials could not agree on whether to hire more playground supervisors or improve physical maintenance of the parks themselves. He concluded that rational decision making was impossible because "improving parks" included multiple goals: school board members thought mostly of recreational opportunities for children, while public works administrators thought mostly of green space to reduce urban density.

The next year, the director of the International City Managers' Association hired the young graduate as a research assistant. Together they reviewed techniques for evaluating municipal services, including police, fire, public health, education, libraries, parks, and public works. Their 1938 book, *Measuring Municipal Activities*, concluded that quantitative measures of performance were mostly inappropriate because public services have goals that can't easily be defined in simple numerical terms.

The senior author, Clarence E. Ridley, directed the city managers' association until retiring in 1956. His assistant, Herbert A. Simon, went on to win the Nobel Prize in economics for a lifetime of work demonstrating that organizational behavior is characterized by "bounded rationality": weighing measurable costs and benefits in simple numerical terms does "not even remotely describe the processes that human beings use for making decisions in complex situations."[186]

In *Measuring Municipal Activities*, Ridley and Simon observed that public services have multiple purposes and, even if precise definitions for some purposes were possible, evaluating the services overall would require difficult judgments about which purposes were relatively more important. Also, it was never possible to quantify whether outcome differences between cities were attributable to differences in effort and competence of public employees, or to differences in the conditions – difficult to measure in any event – under which agencies worked.

The authors concluded that "[t]he most serious single problem which still stands in the way of the development of satisfactory measurement techniques is the difficulty of defining the objectives of municipal services in measurable terms."[187] Objectives, for example, like "improve health... or develop good citizens must be stated in much more tangible and objective terms before they adapt themselves to measurement."[188]

Ridley and Simon noted that, before attempting quantitative measurement, questions should be addressed such as: For evaluating library services, should judgments be made about the quality of books being circulated?[189] For a mortality index for public health, should all lives be considered equally valuable – those of the elderly, of very young children, and of productive workers?[190]

Ridley and Simon had something to say about measuring school effectiveness as well:

> The chief fault of the testing movement has consisted in its emphasis upon content in highly academic material....The fact that a particular pupil shows a marked improvement in reading or spelling may give some indication that a teacher is improving her performance...but the use to which the pupil puts that knowledge is the only significant point in determining the significance of subject tests in measuring the educational system.[191]

And

> The final appraisal of the school system must be in terms of its impact upon the community through the individuals that it trains. How effective is the school system in raising the cultural level of the community?...What is the delinquency rate in the community?... Is the economic situation improving as a result of intelligent effort on the part of the people?...What is the proportion of registered voters to the eligible voting population?...
>
> From a practical standpoint, no one is so optimistic as to believe that all these results can be directly measured, but...serious attempts will be made in the future to devise measures which will approximate these end-products as closely as possible.[192]

There is today growing enthusiasm by politicians and policy makers for quantitative accountability systems that might maximize public service efficiency. But they have rushed to develop measurement systems without giving great thought to whether these systems were truly measuring ultimate outcomes of the kind that Ridley and Simon described 70 years ago.

In Great Britain a quarter century ago, Margaret Thatcher attempted to rationalize public enterprises: where they could not be privatized, her government hoped to regulate them, using rewards and sanctions for numerically specified outcomes. Tony Blair later accelerated these efforts, while in the United States, the Clinton Administration's Government Performance Results Act of 1993 proposed to "reinvent government" by requiring measurable outcomes for all government agencies.

Enthusiasm for holding schools accountable for student test scores is but part of this broader trend that has proceeded oblivious to the warnings of Herbert Simon and other notable social scientists. Scholars have often concluded that, when agents in other sectors are held accountable for improving production of a simple numerical output, performance on that easily measured output does improve. But overall performance frequently deteriorates. So economists, sociologists, and management theorists generally caution against accountability systems that rely exclusively, or even primarily, on numerical outcome measures.

In 1975, Donald T. Campbell formulated what he called his "law" of performance measurement:

> The more any quantitative social indicator is used for social decision-making, the more subject it will be to corruption pressures and the more apt it will be to distort and corrupt the social processes it is intended to monitor.[193]

Such corruption occurs primarily because of the problem Herbert Simon identified – an indicator that can be quantified often reflects only an aspect of the outcome of interest, so undue attention to this aspect will distort the balance of services being provided.

In his 1989 study, *Bureaucracy*, James Q. Wilson wondered why public agencies did not employ "carefully designed compensation plans" that would permit public employees to benefit, financially, from good performance. "Part of the answer," he said, "is obvious. Often we do not know whether a manager or an agency has achieved the goals we want because either the goals are vague or inconsistent, or their attainment cannot be observed, or both. Bureau chiefs in the Department of State would have to go on welfare if their pay depended on their ability to demonstrate convincingly that they had attained their bureaus' objectives."[194] We could, of course, pay diplomats based on the number of dinners they attended because informal contacts with representatives of other nations should have a positive relationship to the goal of advancing the national interest. But if we did implement such a performance-based pay system, we might find that diplomats got fatter while the national interest was ignored.

Soviet central planning

Before the Soviet Union collapsed, Western scholarly and popular publications often reported about the goal distortion and corruption resulting from Soviet attempts to manage an economy by mandating the achievement of numerical output goals. State industrial planners established targets for enterprise production and punished managers who failed to meet them. For example, there were targets for the number of shoes to be produced. Certainly, increasing output was an important goal of the Soviet shoe industry, but it was not the only goal. Factories responded to the accountability requirements by using a limited leather supply to produce a glut of small sizes that consumers couldn't use. Planners specified the number of kilometers that freight transport enterprises should cover each month. Certainly, transporters who cover more distance can deliver more goods. But when distance itself was incentivized, haulers fulfilled quotas by driving circuitous routes.[195] Planners specified the number of meters to be drilled each quarter by geological prospectors. Certainly, geologists who drill more holes should discover more oil. But when drilling became an end in itself, geologists fulfilled quotas by digging rather than by finding oil.[196] (Geologists could not be held accountable for finding oil, because digging is completely within their control, success somewhat less so.) A cartoon in a Soviet satirical magazine showed managers of a nail factory admiring their goal fulfillment: suspended from a crane was a gigantic nail that extended across the entire length of the factory; this was the most efficient way for the plant to fulfill its monthly quota, expressed in weight, for nails produced.[197]

Some Soviet incentives retarded technological progress. Electrifying the vast country was an important economic objective, but creating incentives to increase output gave electricity managers no reason to reduce inefficiency from the loss of current in transmission.[198] Quotas for other industries set in tons created incentives to avoid developing lighter materials.[199]

Education parallels

Soviet experience with simple quantitative accountability has been duplicated in modern times, in education and in other sectors. Previous chapters showed how attempts to hold schools accountable for math and reading test scores have

corrupted education by reducing the attention paid to other important curricular goals; by creating incentives to ignore students who are either above or
far below the passing point on tests; by misidentifying failing and successful
schools because of test unreliability; by converting instruction into test preparation that has little lasting value; and by gaming, which borders (or may include)
illegality.

Each of these corruptions has parallels in other fields, often studied and
reported by social scientists and management theorists. But education policy
makers have paid little attention to this expertise.[200] Instead, state and federal
governments adopted test-based accountability as the tool for improving student achievement, duplicating the worst features of flawed accountability systems in other public and private services.

Some advocates of test-based accountability in education, confronted with
evidence of goal distortion or excessive test preparation, have concluded that
these problems stem only from the inadequacy of teachers. As one critic argues,
good teachers "can and should" integrate subject matter so that raising math
and reading scores need not result in diminished attention to other curricular
areas.[201] But this expectation denies the intent and power of incentives that,
if successful, *should* redirect attention and resources to those outputs that are
rewarded. The consistency with which professionals and their institutions respond in this fashion in all fields should persuade us that this is not a problem
with the ethos of teachers, but an inevitable consequence of any narrowly quantitative incentive system.

Familiar examples: body counts, ticket quotas, television sweeps, best-seller lists, college rankings, crime clearance rates, and Nixon's war on crime

Donald Campbell observed that a tragic example of goal distortion from
quantifiable accountability stemmed from the work of a former Harvard Business School professor, financial analyst, and business-executive-turned-pub-
lic-official. During the Vietnam War, Secretary of Defense Robert McNamara
believed strongly in quantitative measures of success and demanded reports
from his generals of American and North Vietnamese "body counts." It is
true that, just as high reading test scores are usually a reliable indicator of
reading proficiency, relative casualties are usually a reliable indicator of the
fortunes of a nation at war; a strong inverse correlation between a nation's
casualties and its success in the broader political and economic objectives
of warfare should normally be expected. But an army can be corrupted if

imposing or avoiding casualties become ends in themselves, and if local commanders' performances are judged by this relatively easily measured indicator. Generals or civilian leaders may then lose sight of political and economic objectives. In the Vietnam War, American generals attempted to please their superiors by recording more enemy deaths than their own. As it was impossible to hide American deaths from political leaders, generals found ways to inflate the numbers of enemy deaths. In some cases, death became an end in itself, in other cases the categorization of deaths was corrupted (for example, by counting civilian as enemy deaths) or the numbers simply exaggerated. High enemy body count numbers led American leaders to believe the war was being won. These leaders confused superiority in body counts with achievement of political and economic objectives. The war was then lost.[202]

Other unfortunate consequences of quantitative accountability are familiar. Motorists stopped by police for trivial traffic violations may have experienced an accountability system in which police sergeants evaluate officers by whether they meet ticket quotas. Certainly, issuing citations for traffic violations is one measure of good policing, but when officers are disproportionately judged by this easily quantifiable outcome, they have incentives to focus on trivial offenses that meet a quota, rather than investigating more serious crimes where the payoff may be less certain. The numerical accountability system generates false arrests, and creates incentives for police officers to boost their measured productivity by disregarding suspects' rights. In New York City a few years ago, the use of quantifiable indicators to measure police productivity resulted in the publicized (and embarrassing, to the police) arrest of an 80-year-old man for feeding pigeons and of a pregnant woman for sitting down to rest on a subway stairway.[203]

Management theorists and criminologists have long decried the quota practice, but police departments continue to be seduced by an apparently easy way to ensure that officers do not waste excessive time on coffee breaks.[204] In 1966, the criminologist Jerome Skolnick wrote, "The goals of police and the standards by which the policeman's work is to be evaluated are ambiguous.... Even within the ranks of police specialists there is no clear understanding of goals," making judgment based on simple quantitative indicators bound to distort police priorities.[205]

Television programming offers another example of Campbell's law. Stations sell advertising at rates throughout the year determined by viewership during three designated "sweeps" months, November, February, and May. A survey company (Nielsen) sends surveys to a sample of viewers during these months to determine what programs typical viewers watch. The system assumes that sweeps-month programming is representative of programming throughout the year for which advertising is sold. Yet the stations respond to these high-stakes surveys by scheduling programs during sweeps months that are more popular, or attention-grabbing, than those of a typical month. Some stations even award cash prizes to viewers who watch programs at times the survey is being conducted.[206] Certainly, viewership numbers at sampled times should reflect whether station programming is likely to draw viewers. But when viewership numbers become ends in themselves, they distort and corrupt the processes they are intended to monitor.

Several newspapers, most notably the *New York Times*, publish weekly best-seller lists. Books on the list get special displays and promotions in book stores, resulting in substantial increases in sales (and authors' royalties). The best-seller list is compiled from computerized reports sent to the *Times* from a national sample of bookstores. But publishers attempt to "teach to the test," identifying which book stores are going to be sampled and organizing bulk purchases, thereby bumping the book up to the best-seller list. The *Times*, not always successfully, monitors book store sales to identify such artificial purchases that corrupt the representativeness of the index. "People do try to game the list," the editor in charge has acknowledged.[207]

U.S. News and World Report publishes an annual ranking of colleges. The rankings are truly an accountability system; many college boards of trustees consider the rankings when determining presidential compensation. In at least one case, a university president (at Arizona State) was offered a large bonus if the university's ranking moved up on his watch.[208]

U.S. News rankings are based on several factors, including the judgments of college presidents and other administrators about the quality of their peer institutions, and the selectiveness of a college, determined partly by the percentage of applicants who are admitted (a more selective college admits a smaller percentage of applicants). Thus, the rankings are a candidate for illustration of Campbell's law, because these factors would be quite reasonable if there were no stakes attached to measuring them. College presidents and other administrators are in the best position to know the strengths and weaknesses of institutions similar to their own, and asking them for their opinions about this should be a good way to find out about college quality. But once an accountability rating is based on these answers, presidents have incentives to dissemble by giving competing institutions poorer ratings and making their own institutions appear relatively superior.

Likewise, higher-quality colleges are likely to accept relatively fewer applicants because demand for admission is strong. But once this indicator became an accountability measure, colleges had incentives to recruit applicants who were bound ultimately to be rejected. Colleges, for example, have sent promotional mailings to unqualified applicants and waived application fees in order to attract unsuccessful (and unsuspecting) applicants. The indicator nonetheless persists in *U.S. News* ratings, although it now has questionable value.[209]

The Federal Bureau of Investigation (FBI) tracks crime clearance rates to evaluate police departments' effectiveness. The clearance rate is the percentage of reported crimes that result in perpetrators' convictions. Just as high math scores characterize effective schools, high clearance rates characterize effective police departments. But as with math scores, once clearance rates become ends in themselves, Campbell's law sets in, and the indicator distorts and corrupts the social processes it is intended to monitor. Police can increase the clearance rate by offering reduced charges to suspects who confess to other crimes, even those they may not actually have committed. Such plea bargains give detectives big boosts in their clearance rates. Meanwhile, those who plead guilty only to the crime for which they were arrested typically get harsher penalties than those who make false confessions to multiple crimes.

Incentives to raise clearance rates are commonplace, although this use of a numerical measure undermines justice – the true, and difficult to quantify, objective of law enforcement.[210]

As a 1968 presidential candidate, Richard M. Nixon promised a "war" on crime. After his election, the FBI publicly reported crime statistics by city. It judged whether police departments were effective by the sum of crimes in seven categories: murder, forcible rape, robbery, aggravated assault, burglary, auto theft, and serious larceny (defined as theft resulting in a loss of at least $50). Many cities subsequently posted significant reductions in crime.[211] But the crime reductions were apparently realized by playing with crime classifications. The biggest reductions were in larcenies of $50 and over in value. Valuing larceny is a matter of judgment, so police departments placed lower values on reported losses after the implementation of the accountability system than before.[212] Although the number of alleged $50 larcenies (which counted for accountability purposes) declined, the number of alleged $49 larcenies (which did not count) increased.

Policemen nationwide were under orders to downgrade the classification of crimes to show progress in their cities' crime index numbers.[213] Donald Campbell concluded: "It seems to be well-documented that a well-publicized, deliberate effort at social change – Nixon's crackdown on crime – had as its main effect the corruption of crime-rate indicators, achieved through underrecording and by downgrading the crimes to less serious classifications."[214]

A not-so-familiar example: Santiago bus drivers

A curious example of goal distortion that arises from setting a purely quantitative standard for public services comes from the bus system of Santiago, Chile.
Most bus drivers worldwide are paid a flat wage. And almost everywhere, passengers complain of waiting too long for a bus to come, only to have several
arrive together. To prevent this, Santiago pays most (but not all) bus drivers per
passenger carried. In establishing this system, the authorities reasoned that if
bus drivers were accountable for the number of passengers carried, and drivers
found themselves too close to the previous bus, they would slow down to give
additional passengers time to congregate at bus stops. The result would be better service from more evenly spaced buses.

The system works: typical Santiago passengers wait 13% longer for buses
whose drivers are paid a flat rate than for those whose drivers are paid per passenger. But instead of slowing down to allow passengers to congregate at stops,
incentive-drivers speed up, to pass buses in front and thus collect passengers
before other drivers do so. Drivers accountable for the number of passengers
have 67% more accidents per mile than fixed-wage drivers. Passengers complain that buses on incentive contracts lurch forward as soon as passengers
board, without their having a chance to sit.[215]

Bus drivers have to balance several goals – delivering passengers rapidly
to their destinations, safety, and comfort. By creating an accountability and
compensation system based only a more easily measured output, Santiago bus
companies undermined other goals.

Goal distortion in health care report cards

Quantitative accountability has corrupted aspects of health care, both in Great
Britain and the United States. Heart surgery is an example in both countries.
Beginning in the late 1980s, both national governments (and several American
states) hoped to persuade patients to choose more effective care, especially
because public funds (Medicare and Medicaid in the U.S.) might otherwise
be wasted. So the governments created "report cards" to compare the extent
to which patients of different doctors and hospitals survived open-heart surgery. Goal distortion resulted.

Health care, like education, has multiple goals that providers must balance.
For heart patients, one goal is certainly to prolong life. But a second is to respect
wishes of terminally ill patients who choose to avoid artificial life-prolonging
technology and hope for a more dignified experience when death is inevitable.

To this end, federal legislation requires hospitals to provide patients with information about living wills. The two goals are difficult to balance and can be reconciled only by the judgments in specific cases of the physicians and families involved. Heart surgery report cards undermined this balancing process. By rewarding hospitals only for reducing easily measured mortality rates, accountability systems created incentives to ignore the other goal of encouraging appropriate use of living wills.[216]

Britain's National Health Service (NHS) also ran up against Campbell's law when it attempted to compare the performance of maternity services so that it could encourage mothers to use those of higher quality. To this end, NHS published comparative data on providers' perinatal mortality rates – the rate of infant deaths immediately before and after birth. This is certainly the most easily quantifiable outcome of obstetrics. But there are other objectives as well, including reducing the severity of handicaps with which high-risk infants survive, and providing a more comfortable and competent experience for pregnant mothers.

These more difficult-to-quantify objectives require maternity services to devote more resources to prenatal care. The incentive system, publishing only the quantifiable perinatal mortality rate, led maternity services to re-balance their efforts between community-based prenatal care and hospital deliveries. With limited resources, maternity services invested less in prenatal care so they could invest more in hospital services. The perinatal mortality rate declined, just as the incentive system intended. But there were worse developmental outcomes for live births – more low birthweight babies and more children born who later had learning difficulties and behavioral problems – because less attention had been paid to prenatal care.[217]

NHS also established a standard that no patient should wait more than two years for elective surgery. This created incentives for surgeons to perform more operations and spend less time on post-operative care, which was unmeasured in the accountability system.[218] Such a shift may have reduced overall patient welfare. Because surgical urgency is on a continuum, not neatly divided between elective and urgent procedures, the target for elective surgery caused practitioners to make relatively minor procedures (some cataract surgeries, for example) a greater priority and more serious but not quite urgent procedures a lesser priority; in that way all surgeries could be performed within the target time frame.[219] A consequence was that *average* waiting times for surgery increased, even though more surgeries were performed within two years.[220]

In 2002, following highly publicized cases of mistreatment of the elderly in nursing homes, the Health Care Financing Administration (HCFA, now renamed the Centers for Medicaid and Medicare Services, or CMS) established a report card, the Nursing Home Quality Initiative (NHQI), which required nursing homes to report publicly whether they adhered to 15 recognized quality standards – for example, the percent of residents who have pressure sores (from being turned in bed too infrequently). These public reports were intended to provide information about relative quality to consumers who were selecting nursing homes for themselves or elderly relatives. However, administrators of nursing homes, and nurses caring for the elderly, must balance many more than these 15 aspects of quality. For example, because nurses' time is limited, if they spend more time turning patients in bed (an NHQI standard), they may have less time to maintain hygienic standards by washing their hands regularly (not an NHQI standard). Although the NHQI was intended to be easily understood by consumers and is limited to 15 standards, CMS monitors some 190 measures (such as handwashing) on a checklist when it inspects nursing homes for purposes of certifying eligibility for Medicaid or Medicare reimbursement. Following the introduction of NHQI, performance on the 15 selected indicators improved, but adherence to the 190 standards overall declined, resulting in more citations for violations issued by CMS.[221] Infections from less handwashing by nurses increased.

In 1994, the U.S. General Accounting Office (GAO) published an analysis of health care report cards. It concluded: "[A]dministrators will place all their organizations' resources in areas that are being measured. Areas that are not highlighted in report cards will be ignored."[222]

Risk adjustment

Test-based accountability systems in education should (though often do not) adjust results for differences in student characteristics. A school with large numbers of low-income children, high residential mobility, great family stress, little literacy support at home, and serious health problems may be a better school even if its test scores are lower than another whose pupils don't have such challenges. Education policy makers sometimes try to adjust for these differences by comparing only "similar" schools – those, for example, with similar proportions of minority students, or similar proportions of students who are low income (eligible for the federal free and reduced-price lunch program).

But this solution doesn't really solve the problem. Stable working class families, with incomes nearly double the poverty line, are eligible for the federal lunch program; schools with such students can easily get higher scores than schools with very poor students, yet the latter schools may be more effective. Charter schools can enroll minority students whose parents are more highly motivated than those in neighborhood schools, tempting charter school promoters to make false claims of superiority when their test scores are higher.[223]

The difficulty of adjusting for differences in unmeasured background characteristics was identified by Clarence Ridley and Herbert Simon in their 1938 study of municipal functions. To compare the effectiveness of fire departments in different cities or years, they found it impossible to use simple quantitative measures, such as the annual value of fire losses or the number of fires per capita. From one year or place to another, there might be a change in the amount of burnable property or in the proportion of industrial property, a more severe winter that might lead to greater use of flammable materials within buildings, or "a multitude of other factors beyond the control of the administrator [that] would have an important effect upon the loss rate."[224]

And Ridley and Simon considered fire the easiest of municipal activities to measure.[225] Comparisons of police effectiveness, they argued, had to account not only for racial and ethnic differences in populations but also the quality of housing, economic conditions, the availability of "wholesome recreational facilities," the administration of the courts, and "other intangible factors of civic morale."[226] Evaluation of public health workers' performance had to adjust for similar factors, as well as for climate, epidemics, and other chance fluctuations in population health. Construction of a mortality index for measuring the adequacy of public health departments must distinguish "only those diseases which are partly or wholly preventable through public health measures."[227]

Medicine faces similar problems; some patients are much sicker, and thus harder to cure, than others with the same disease. Patients' ages, other diseases, history of prior treatment, health habits (smoking, for example), diet, and home environment must all be taken into account. So before comparing outcome data, health care report cards must be "risk-adjusted" for the initial conditions of patients. Although risk adjustment in medicine is far more sophisticated than controls for minority status or lunch eligibility in education, health policy experts still consider that the greatest flaw in medical accountability systems is their inability to adjust performance comparisons adequately for patient characteristics.

The Health Care Financing Administration initiated its accountability system for cardiac surgery in 1986 with its reports on death rates of Medicare patients in 5,500 U.S. hospitals. HCFA used a complex statistical model to identify hospitals whose death rates after surgery were greater than expected, after accounting for patient characteristics. Yet the institution labeled as having the worst death rate, even after sophisticated risk-adjustment, turned out to be a hospice caring for terminally ill patients.[228]

The following year, HCFA added even more patient characteristics to its statistical model. Although the agency now insisted that its model adequately adjusted for all critical variables, the ratings invariably resulted in higher adjusted mortality rates for low-income patients in urban hospitals than for affluent patients in suburban hospitals.[229] Campbell's law swung into action – when surveyed, physicians and hospitals began to admit that they were refusing to treat sicker patients.[230] Surgeons' ratings were not adversely affected by deaths of patients who had been denied surgery. Surveys of cardiologists found that most were declining to operate on patients who might benefit from surgery but were of greater risk.[231] Some hospitals, more skilled at selection, got higher ratings, while others did worse because they received a larger share of patients with more severe disease. In 1989, St. Vincent's Hospital in New York City was put on probation by the state after it placed low in the ranking of state hospitals for cardiac surgery. The following year, it ranked first in the state. St. Vincent's accomplished this feat by refusing to operate on tougher cases.[232]

Just as some schools that are failing in comparison to all schools may be judged satisfactory when compared only to similar schools, whether hospitals have unsatisfactory mortality rates depends on the particular risk-adjustment formula employed in the ratings. An analysis of gastrointestinal hemorrhage cases in Great Britain found successive revisions of hospital rankings as additional adjustments for patient characteristics were applied.[233] A study of stroke victims in the U.S. applied 11 alternative (and commonly used) systems for measuring severity of risk and found that hospitals deemed better-than-average according to some systems were deemed worse-than-average according to others.[234]

HCFA's Medicare performance indicator system was abandoned in 1993. Bruce Vladeck, the HCFA administrator at that time, conceded that the methodology was flawed. "I think it's overly simplistic," he told an interviewer. "[I]t doesn't adequately adjust for some of the problems faced by inner-city hospitals."[235] Added Jerome Kassirer, then editor-in-chief of the *New England Journal of Medicine*, "The public has a right to know about the quality of its doctors, yet…it is irresponsible to release information that is of questionable validity, subject to alternative interpretations, or too technical for a layperson to understand…." He concluded that "no practice profile [i.e., physician report card] in use today is adequate to [the] task."[236]

In 1994, when the GAO published its health care report card study, several state incentive systems were still in place, as were some that had been devised by private insurers. The GAO found that no public or private report card had been able to develop a method to adjust for patient characteristics that was "valid and reliable."[237] Kaiser Permanente in Northern California, for example, published a report card that included over 100 measures of performance.[238] Yet the GAO observed that "each performance indicator may need its own separate adjustment because patient characteristics have a unique effect on every condition and disease."[239]

Similar problems arise when we attempt to adjust for risk factors in education – for example, family characteristics apparently have a more powerful impact on reading scores than on math scores, the latter being more sensitive to school quality and the former to family intellectual environment.

Gaming health care accountability

Quantitative accountability in health care has also inspired gamesmanship by providers not so different from the games educators have learned to play under test-based accountability plans. Obstetricians, for example, can never precisely define the date of conception, so in Britain, when they were held accountable for reducing mortality after a gestation cutoff of 28 weeks, obstetricians improved their performance indicators in borderline cases by reporting that mortality occurred before, not after, the 28-week cutoff.[240]

Britain's NHS also established a target that no patient should sit in an emergency room for more than four hours before seeing a physician. Hospitals soon dramatically improved their consistency in meeting this threshold. But average waiting times sometimes also increased and health care deteriorated. Previously, the highly publicized cases that gave rise to the target were mostly patients with relatively minor injuries or illnesses who were forced to wait on the infrequent (but not unheard of) occasions when emergency rooms were overwhelmed by more serious cases. To meet the new accountability requirement, hospitals ensured that patients with less serious problems were seen before the four hours expired but, as a result, patients with more serious problems had to wait somewhat longer than they had previously. A review committee of the Royal Statistical Society concluded that the accountability target had undermined medical ethics that require treatment priority based on need.[241]

Moreover, because the four-hour waiting standard did not begin until patients actually arrived at an emergency room, some ambulances parked and did not discharge patients to the emergency room until advised that the hospital could now see a patient within four hours. This gaming had detrimental effects on the delivery of health care, as patients with relatively minor problems were not treated any sooner, but fewer ambulances were available for dispatch to pick up seriously ill patients.[242]

Another NHS standard was that patients should be able to see their primary care physicians within 48 hours of making appointments. Some physicians met this accountability threshold simply by refusing to schedule appointments more than 48 hours in advance.[243] When asked about this at a press conference, Prime Minister Tony Blair said it was "absurd" to think that doctors would do such a thing, but his health secretary later confirmed that this was, indeed, a perverse consequence of the accountability target.[244]

Medical data corruption is another kind of gaming that results from quantitative accountability systems. Many background characteristics used for risk adjustment must be coded by and collected from the physicians themselves who are being held accountable for risk-adjusted outcomes. Physicians have always used great discretion in coding. As the General Accounting Office noted in its evaluation of health care report cards, many Americans have had the experience of friendly physicians who creatively code a routine office visit to qualify for insurance reimbursement. Physicians sometimes alter coding to protect patient privacy, masking diagnoses of alcoholism, HIV, or mental illness, for example.[245] Thus it is no surprise that after incentive systems were put in place, physicians used their discretion to classify symptoms that patients initially present as more severe than the same symptoms would have been classified prior to the incentive system.[246] For example, after New York State began to report death rates from cardiac surgery, the share of cardiac patients reported by physicians to have serious risk factors prior to surgery rose dramatically. Patients reported also to suffer from chronic obstructive pulmonary disease more than doubled, and those reported to be suffering from renal failure jumped sevenfold.[247] Since the definitions of many co-morbid conditions are not precise, it is unclear to what extent physicians consciously manipulated the data. Nonetheless, 41% of the reduction in New York's risk-adjusted mortality for cardiac bypass patients was attributable to the apparently artificial increase ("upcoding") in reported severity of patients' conditions.[248]

In 2003, a team of American health care economists published an analysis of health care report cards. Their academic paper concluded that report cards on health care providers "may give doctors and hospitals incentives to decline to treat more difficult, severely ill patients." The accountability system has "led to higher levels of resource use [because delaying surgery for sicker patients necessitated more expensive treatment later] and to worse outcomes, particularly for sicker patients....[A]t least in the short-run, these report cards decreased patient and social welfare."[249]

One of the paper's co-authors was Mark McClellan, who had been a member of President George W. Bush's Council of Economic Advisers while *No Child Left Behind* was designed and implemented. The paper concluded that, although report cards advertised that some hospitals got dramatically better outcomes, "On net, these changes were particularly harmful….Report cards on the performance of schools raise the same issues and therefore also need empirical evaluation."[250]

Dr. McClellan subsequently served as administrator of the Centers for Medicare and Medicaid Services from 2004 to 2006. Apparently ignoring his earlier conclusions, the federal government reinstituted Medicare accountability report cards in 2007, publishing the names of 41 hospitals with higher-than-expected death rates for heart attack patients. The government planned next to add a report card for pneumonia. The Bush Administration's secretary of health and human services, Michael Leavitt, acknowledged that the list of failing hospitals still imperfectly adjusted for patient characteristics, but promised that "[i]t will get nothing but better as time goes on."[251]

Ignoring McClellan's conclusions, six states continue to publish report cards on cardiac surgery mortality rates in their hospitals, and three publish performance reports for individual surgeons.[252]

Accountability in job training and welfare

In 1955, the organizational sociologist Peter M. Blau studied a state employment agency's tasks of registering jobless workers for benefits and providing assistance in finding new jobs. Initially, Blau found that the state attempted to hold case workers accountable by rating them according to the number of interviews they conducted. But this resulted in goal distortion; case workers had incentives to sacrifice quality for speed. So the state added seven new quantitative indicators, including the number of job referrals and actual placements, and the ratio of placements to interviews. Even these quantitative indicators were still deemed insufficient to balance all aspects of effective performance, so the agency prohibited supervisors from basing more than 40% of an employee's evaluation on quantitative indicators.[253]

The government has frequently attempted to impose accountability systems on job training and welfare agencies that use federal funds. As in health care, Campbell's law usually wins out: the reliance on quantitative indicators distorts and corrupts the agency functions that these indicators hope to monitor.

Under the Job Training Partnership Act (JTPA) of 1982, the government offered financial rewards to agencies that had better records of placing workers in jobs. The Department of Labor defined successful placements as those that lasted at least 90 days. This created incentives for agencies to place workers in low-skilled and short-term jobs that might last not much longer than 90 days.[254] Training for long-term stable employment required more resources, and success rates in that area were somewhat lower, although placement in long-term stable employment was an important though unmeasured JTPA goal. The federal program could have reduced goal distortion by extending the monitoring program beyond 90 days, but the Department of Labor could not afford the additional expense.[255]

When JTPA rewarded agencies for the share of clients placed in jobs, it provided perverse incentives to recruit and train only those unemployed workers who were most easy to place, that is, workers who had been unemployed for only a short period, had the best skills or educational credentials, or had favored race or ethnic backgrounds.[256] In these ways, the law's purpose to provide training to workers who "are most in need of training opportunities" was subverted.[257] James Heckman, a Nobel laureate in economics, concluded that JTPA "performance standards based on short-term outcome levels likely do little to encourage the provision of services to those who benefit most from them...."[258]

Gaming job training and welfare accountability

Accountability under the job training program created many opportunities for gaming. Placements (or lack of them) were counted only for job seekers formally enrolled in training programs. This counting method gave agencies incentives to train clients informally, then formally enroll them only after it was determined that the job seekers were certain to find employment. In other cases, because employment was verified 90 days after the end of formal training, agencies failed to graduate and continued "formally training" some clients who had little hope of finding employment, long after any hope for success had evaporated. Such gaming behavior continued under the Workforce Investment Act (WIA) of 1998, the JTPA successor program.[259] As the General Accounting Office observed, "[t]he lack of a uniform understanding of when registration occurs and thus who should be counted toward the measures raises questions about both the accuracy and comparability of states' performance data."[260]

In some cases, agencies provided special services to support employment, such as child care, transportation, or clothing allowances. Such services were often terminated after the 90th day of employment. Similarly, case managers followed up with employers and urged them to keep recent trainees on the payroll. Follow-up often ended on the 90th day. Such gaming did not take place prior to JTPA's establishment of a 90-day standard for measuring performance.[261]

The accountability plans of both JTPA and WIA required local agencies to demonstrate continuous performance improvement each year. As with education's NCLB, the law recognized that conditions differed from state to state, so states were permitted to establish their own target levels. As a result, many states established deliberately low initial targets for their training agencies, to ensure more room for subsequent improvement.[262] This too anticipated states' behavior in education, where many would attempt to meet NCLB proficiency standards by defining proficiency at a level far below "challenging." Public administration theory refers to this behavior as the "ratchet effect," a term taken from analyses of similar behavior in the Soviet economy.

As in health care, the inability to adjust performance expectations adequately for background characteristics has also frustrated accountability designs in job training and welfare programs.

Following adoption of the 1996 welfare reform law, Temporary Assistance to Needy Families (TANF), most states hired private contractors to administer at least some aspects of the program. Wisconsin Works (W-2) was the state program most frequently cited as a national model. The program rewarded private contractors on the basis of participants' employment rate, average wage rate, job retention and quality (whether employers provided health insurance), and educational activities.[263] However, because Wisconsin's contracts did not employ risk-adjustments for economic conditions or recipients' relevant qualifications (for example, whether they had high school diplomas), contractors discouraged enrollment of the harder-to-serve cases, and contractors' profits were excessive. Every two years, Wisconsin redefined the incentive criteria to account for changes in economic conditions and in contractors' opportunistic selection of clients; otherwise, meeting the state's accountability requirements would have become even easier. After six years of this, Wisconsin gave up, eliminating performance standards and even rescinding bonus money that had been awarded.[264] And the federal government has discontinued using quantitative incentive systems to manage TANF programs in all states.[265]

Unlike TANF, the JTPA and WIA job training programs employed statistical adjustments to account for some local agencies having an easier time placing the unemployed in jobs. If accurate adjustments were not made, agencies located in areas with booming economies, or where unemployed workers were more likely to have high school diplomas, could post better placement numbers than agencies in depressed areas with more high school dropouts. Nonetheless, despite the Department of Labor's relatively sophisticated attempts at risk-adjustment, the General Accounting Office found that subtle differences in local economic conditions – growth in new or existing businesses, for example – were not captured by the statistical models. Thus, the incentive system still encouraged agencies to select only those unemployed workers who were easiest to place.[266] The GAO concluded: "Unless the performance levels can be adjusted to truly reflect differences in economic conditions and the population served, local areas will continue to have a disincentive to serve some job seekers that could be helped."[267]

Federal job training regulations also attempted to make accountability requirements sensitive to the population served by requiring the reporting of enrollment separately by subgroups, much as in education, where results are reported separately for minority and low-income students. Unlike education, however, where contemporary accountability programs require all students to achieve the same level of performance, each subgroup of job seekers had a unique target, considered appropriate for its unique challenges; the handicapped, racial minorities, and welfare recipients each had specific training targets. However, these categories were too broad to defeat the ability of counselors to distinguish potentially more successful trainees from within these targeted groups (e.g., blacks and welfare recipients who were relatively more able than others). Those with more education were disproportionately recruited for training.[268] As the GAO reported to Congress, "the need to meet performance levels may be the driving factor in deciding who receives WIA-funded services....Local staff are reluctant to provide WIA-funded services to job seekers who may be less likely to get and keep a job....As a result, individuals who are eligible for and may benefit from WIA-funded services may not be receiving services...."[269]

In any accountability system, no matter how carefully policy makers define subgroups, professionals who have direct contact with clients will always know more detail than policy makers about client characteristics and be able to game the system. In health care, Mark McClellan and his colleagues observed, "Doctors and hospitals likely have more detailed information about patients' health than the developer of a report card can, allowing them to choose to treat unobservably (to the analyst) healthier patients."[270] This is certainly true in schools, where teachers know more about their students' potential than administrators or policy makers can infer from prior test scores and a few demographic markers.

The private sector

When New York City Mayor Michael Bloomberg announced a 2007 teachers' union agreement to pay cash bonuses to teachers at schools where test scores increase, he said, "In the private sector, cash incentives are proven motivators for producing results. The most successful employees work harder, and everyone else tries to figure out how they can improve as well."[271] Eli Broad, whose foundation promotes incentive pay plans for teachers, added, "Virtually every other industry compensates employees based on how well they perform....We know from experience across other industries and sectors that linking performance and pay is a powerful incentive."[272]

These claims misrepresent how private sector firms motivate employees. Although incentive pay systems are commonplace, they are almost never based exclusively or even primarily on quantitative output measurement for professionals. Indeed, while the share of private sector workers who get performance pay has been increasing, the share who get such pay based on numerical output measures has been decreasing.[273] The business management literature nowadays is filled with warnings about incentives that rely heavily on quantitative rather than qualitative measures.[274]

For business organizations generally, quantitative performance measures are used warily, and never exclusively. Even stock prices or profit are not simple guides to public companies' performance and potential. The Securities and Exchange Commission has complex regulations designed to prevent publicly traded firms from using numerical indicators to mislead investors. Yet financial data are still too complex for laypersons to interpret – that's why investors rely on sophisticated analysts, employed to discern the underlying and often non-quantifiable potential that stock prices or other easily measured characteristics might obscure.[275] Analysts sometimes disagree – equities markets exist only because quantitative indicators are not sufficiently transparent, and buyers and sellers have different interpretations of what firms' financial data mean.

SEC and private accounting standards are often defeated by an inability to control "creative accounting" to maximize bonuses. Among the most easily manipulated financial rules and business practices are depreciation schedules for long-term assets; accelerated or delayed shipments to or from inventories at the end of accounting periods; transfer of revenues or expenses between accounting periods; the allocation of overhead to inventories; and the expensing or capitalizing of major repair activities, research and development, or even advertising expenses.[276] As with gaming in schools' test-based accountability systems, some but not all such manipulation is criminal. But before crossing that line, managers have considerable discretion.[277]

Most private sector jobs, as do teaching and other jobs in the public sector, include a composite of easily measured and less-easily measured responsibilities. Holding agents accountable only for the easily measured ones leads to goal distortion. Adding multiple measures of accountability is, by itself, insufficient to minimize such distortion.

Because of the ease with which most employees game purely quantitative incentives, most private sector accountability systems blend quantitative and qualitative measures, with most emphasis on the latter. This method characterizes accountability of relatively low- as well as high-level employees. McDonald's, for example, does not evaluate its store managers by sales volume or profitability alone. Instead, a manager and his or her supervisor establish targets for easily quantifiable measures such as sales volume and costs, but also for less easily quantifiable product quality, service, cleanliness, and personnel training, because these factors may affect long-term profitability as well as the reputation (and thus, profitability) of other outlets. Store managers are judged by the negotiated balance of these various factors.[278] Wal-Mart uses a similar system. A like practice of negotiating qualitative as well as quantitative performance goals is also common for professionals in the private sector.[279]

Certainly, supervisory evaluation of employees is less reliable than numerical output measurements such as storewide sales or student test scores. Supervisory evaluation may be tainted by favoritism, bias, inflation and compression (narrowing the range of evaluations to avoid penalizing or rewarding too many employees), and even kickbacks or other forms of corruption.[280] Yet the widespread management use of subjective evaluations, despite these flaws, suggests that, as one personnel management review concludes, "it is better to imperfectly measure relevant dimensions than to perfectly measure irrelevant ones."[281] Or, "the prevalence of subjectivity in the performance measurement systems of virtually all [business] organizations suggests that exclusive reliance on distorted and risky objective measures is not an efficient alternative."[283]

Management of accountability systems in the private sector is labor intensive. Bain and Company, the management consulting firm, advises clients that judgment of results should always focus on long- and not short-term (and more easily quantifiable) goals. A company director estimated that, at Bain itself, each manager devotes about 100 hours a year to evaluating five employees for purposes of its incentive pay system. "When I try to imagine a school principal doing 30 reviews, I have trouble," he observed.[283]

A widespread business reform in recent decades has been "total quality management," promoted by W. Edwards Deming. He warned that businesses seeking to improve quality and thus long-term performance should eliminate work standards (quotas), eliminate management by numbers and numerical goals, and abolish merit ratings and "management by objective," because all of these encourage employees to focus on short-term results. "Management by numerical goal is an attempt to manage without knowledge of what to do, and in fact is usually management by fear," Deming insisted.[284]

A corporate accountability tool that has grown in popularity is the balanced scorecard, first proposed in the early 1990s because business management theorists concluded that quantifiable short-term financial results were not accurate guides to future profitability. Firms' goals were too complex to be reduced to a few quantifiable measures, and future performance relies not only on a track record of financial success but on "intangible and intellectual assets, such as high quality products and services, motivated and skilled employees, responsive and predictable internal processes, and satisfied and loyal customers."[285] Management experts who promote the balanced scorecard approach to corporate accountability recommend that executives should supplement numerical output measures with judgments about the quality of organizational process, staff quality and morale, and customer satisfaction. Evaluation of a firm's performance, they say, should be "balanced between objective, easily quantifiable outcome measures and subjective, somewhat judgmental, performance drivers of the outcome measures." [286]

For "best-practice firms"[287] employing the balanced scorecard approach, the use "of subjective judgments reflects a belief that results-based compensation may not always be the ideal scheme for rewarding managers [because] many factors not under the control or influence of managers also affect reported performance [and] many managerial actions create (or destroy) economic value but may not be measured."[288]

Curiously, the federal government adopted a balanced scorecard approach simultaneously with its quantitative outcome-focused Government Performance Results Act and its test-based *No Child Left Behind Act*. Each year since 1988, the U.S. Department of Commerce has handed out Malcolm Baldrige National Quality Awards for exemplary institutions in manufacturing and other business sectors.[289] Numerical output indicators play only a small role in the department's award decisions: for the private sector, 450 out of 1,000 points are for "results" although, even here, results such as "ethical behavior," "social responsibility," "trust in senior leadership," "workforce capability and capacity," and "customer satisfaction and loyalty" are based on points awarded from qualitative judgments. Other criteria, also relying on qualitative evaluation, such as "how do senior leaders set organizational vision and values," and "protection of stakeholder and stockholder interests, as appropriate" make up the other 550 points.[290]

The Department of Commerce concluded that Baldrige principles of private sector quality could be applied as well to health and education institutions, so these were added to the reward system in 1999. For school districts, only 100 of 1,000 points are for "student learning outcomes," with other points awarded for subjectively evaluated measures such as "how senior leaders' personal actions reflect a commitment to the organization's values."[291]

The most recent Baldrige award in elementary and secondary education was presented in 2005 to the Jenks (Oklahoma) school district. In making this award, the Department of Commerce cited the district's generally good test scores as well as its low teacher turnover and innovative programs such as an exchange relationship with schools in China and the enlistment of residents of a long-term care facility to mentor kindergartners and pre-kindergartners.[292] Yet the following year, the federal Department of Education deemed the Jenks district to be sub-standard according to NCLB rules, because Jenks' economically disadvantaged and special education students failed for two consecutive years to make "adequate yearly progress" in reading scores.[293]

That exclusively quantitative accountability systems result in goal distortion, gaming, and corruption in a wide variety of fields is not inconsistent with a conclusion that such systems nonetheless improve average performance in the narrow goals they measure. At the very least, they may direct attention to outliers that warrant further investigation. Several analyses by economists, management experts, and sociologists have concluded that narrowly quantitative incentive schemes have, at times, somewhat improved the average performance of medical care, job training, welfare, and private sector agents. The documentation of perverse consequences does not indicate that, in any particular case, the harm outweighed the benefits of such narrow quantitative accountability. The Soviet Union did, after all, industrialize from a feudal society in record time.

The General Accounting Office, while condemning the perverse incentives resulting from report cards in health care, nonetheless concluded, "We support the report card concept and encourage continued development in the field."[294] Performance incentive plans in medicine, both in the United States and Great Britain, did improve average outcomes in many respects, including cardiac surgery survival rates, the most frequently analyzed procedure.[295] Accountability for waiting times for elective surgery in Great Britain did reduce average waiting times, notwithstanding some other perverse consequences.[296] One careful analysis of emergency room waiting times in Great Britain was unable to find evidence of perverse consequences expected from a narrow quantitative incentive. It could be, the authors concluded, that "it is better to manage an organization using imperfect measures than using none at all."[297]

In education, how much gain in reading and math scores is necessary to offset the goal distortion – less art, music, physical education, science, history, character building – that inevitably results from rewarding teachers or schools for score gains only in math and reading? How much misidentification of high- or low-performing teachers or schools is tolerable in order to improve their average performance? How much curricular corruption and teaching to the test are we willing to endure when we engage in, as one frequently cited work in the business management literature puts it, "the folly of rewarding A while hoping for B"?[298]

But no accountability at all is not the only alternative to the flawed approach of exclusive reliance on quantitative output measures. It is possible, indeed practical, to design an accountability system in education to ensure that schools and educators meet their responsibilities to deliver the broad range of outcomes that the American people demand, without relying exclusively on measures as imperfect as test scores. Such a system would be more expensive than our current regime of low-quality standardized tests, and would not give policy makers the comfortable, though false, precision that they want quantitative measures like test scores to provide.

We know that such a system is practical, because many of its components have already been employed. When NAEP was developed in the 1960s, its early design assessed a much broader range of outcomes than it does today. And throughout the nation, school accreditation teams provide the framework within which important elements of a balanced accountability system could be developed. Other nations have developed school inspection systems that illustrate such development. The following chapters describe these precedents in turn.

CHAPTER 6

Early NAEP

In 1867 Congress established a Department of Education to collect "such statistics and facts as shall show the condition and progress of education in the several States and Territories."[299] But for its first hundred years, the department reported only on how much money was being spent and how many students were enrolled.

Francis Keppel, appointed U.S. commissioner of education in 1962, thought the law required him also to report on student achievement.[300] So he asked John Gardner, then president of the Carnegie Foundation, to form a committee to design a system for measuring what American students had learned. Gardner recruited a distinguished group of statisticians, survey researchers, and educational measurement experts; they began meeting in 1963 to create the National Assessment of Educational Progress.[301]

Ralph W. Tyler, one of the nation's most respected education scholars, chaired the committee, called ECAPE (the Exploratory Committee on Assessing the Progress of Education). Thirty years earlier, Tyler had directed an evaluation of the "Eight Year Study," an experiment in which 30 high schools implemented new curricula, with elite colleges agreeing to admit graduates of these high schools based on their ability to apply what they learned, not on standardized test scores or completion of courses with traditional disciplinary titles. Tyler's evaluation considered whether these students could analyze problems from various disciplines, find data from multiple sources (books and libraries, interviews, letter writing), and develop plans for solutions. To assess students' attitudes, values, and breadth of interests, the evaluation relied on examination of student diaries, as well as interviews and paper-and-pencil tests.[302]

In a 1949 book, Tyler had recommended that educational evaluation should not rely exclusively on standardized test scores but "must appraise the behavior of students since it is changes in these behaviors which is sought...." He urged that tests be administered after students leave school, because material not well taught may be "rapidly dissipated or forgotten."[303] While agreeing that some knowledge and skills can be assessed with paper-and-pencil exams, he insisted that other objectives of education, such as social skills, are "more easily and validly appraised through observations of children under conditions in which social relations are involved," both when they are playing and working together.[304] Evaluation should include collection of actual products made by students, such as paintings or written themes. He suggested that, if a school's reading program aimed to develop mature interests, evaluators could assess this by seeing what books students checked out of libraries.[305] In a 1963 memo to Francis Keppel, Tyler explained how such approaches might be developed for a national assessment.[306]

ECAPE encountered resistance from politicians and educators who feared that Keppel planned to develop a national test that would destroy America's traditional local control of education. Because local conditions were so different, educators also worried that test results would be used to make unfair comparisons between states, school districts, and schools. For these reasons, both the National Education Association and the American Association of School Administrators initially refused to cooperate with Tyler's committee.[307]

The opposition was fortunate, because it forced ECAPE to design an assessment that would yield only national results, but none at the state, school district, school, or student level. ECAPE planned to have samples large enough to obtain average results by geographic region (Northeast, Southeast, Central, and West), type of community (e.g., large city, suburb, small city, or rural town), gender, parental education level, and poverty status. Race was subsequently added.[308] But the samples were too small to report state-by-state results. This necessity, forced on ECAPE by political opposition, was a blessing in disguise because ECAPE instead could plan to invest limited resources in a much broader range of outcomes than tests normally covered.

Further, the NAEP design – that no student took an entire test and no individual student scores could result – permitted NAEP to assess a much broader range of knowledge and skills than typical tests. Each student who took a NAEP exam took only part of it, and answers were combined to generate national results. Although no student typically took the test for more than 45 minutes or an hour, NAEP was still able to get results in each subject from several hours of material in the various test booklets given to different students.

When the first planning meetings were held at the Carnegie Corporation in late 1963 and early 1964, the participants devoted considerable attention to their fear that a national assessment would cause a narrowing of school curricula, because if the tests covered only basic academic skills then other subjects, like music, might be ignored or downgraded.[309] So ECAPE then surveyed documents covering all of what Americans in the 20th century had wanted education to accomplish, beginning with the *Cardinal Principles* of 1918 and including reports of the Educational Policies Commission during the 1930s and '40s.[310] ECAPE stated that NAEP should assess any goal area for which schools devote "15-20% of their time…" the "less tangible areas, as well as the customary areas, in a fashion the public can grasp and understand."[311] These should include all areas that "thoughtful laymen consider important for American youth to learn,"[312] that is, art, citizenship, career and occupational development (including vocational education), foreign language, health and physical fitness (including such aspects of emotional health as self-image and self-confidence), literature, mathematics, music, reading, science, social studies, and writing. Consumer protection was also a subject of assessment; the committee felt that the ability to resist false advertising claims, and budget appropriately, was an important life skill with which youth should emerge from schools.[313]

Following Ralph Tyler's insistence that educators should assess the behavioral outcomes of education, not only the abstract skills that led to such outcomes, ECAPE designed survey questions to assess behavior as well as skill. For example, ECAPE members agreed that schools should not teach the mechanics of reading as an end in itself. Rather, schools should want students to use the skill in behaviors like reading a newspaper, and effective teaching should lead to such use. An assessment of outcomes should determine not only whether students have basic reading skills, but whether, as they grow older, students actually read newspapers. This behavioral outcome does not stem from direct instruction in language arts classes, but also from classes in other curricular areas such as social studies.[314]

In civics education, ECAPE was also interested in assessing behavior as well as factual knowledge. The committee defined the goals of assessment as discovering whether students showed concern for the welfare and dignity of others, supported rights and freedoms of all, helped maintain law and order, knew the main structure and functions of government, sought community improvement through active democratic participation, understood problems of international relations, took responsibility for their own personal development, and helped and respected their own families.[315]

Conventional written exams alone could not assess all of these goals. Some outcomes of schools could only be assessed by observation of student behavior, or by survey techniques that verify the activities in which students engage.

Survey-type questions posed a problem, because ECAPE recognized that students or adults may exaggerate when asked about things they have done. Therefore, early NAEP assessors were trained to ask follow-up questions in a way to ensure they obtained accurate data. For example, in the citizenship assessment, if a respondent answered that he or she had written a letter to a congressman, the NAEP assessor then asked for details, such as what the letter was about, to ensure that the respondent was describing a real event.

ECAPE was troubled that test results might be misleading if NAEP were administered to children in the same grade level nationwide. Schools vary in the ages at which they enroll children. Different birthday cutoffs for starting kindergarten or first grade mean that in some states students at a particular grade are older than students in the same grade in other states. States and even districts have different social promotion policies; students in a particular grade in some districts may be older than students in districts where students are held back less often. Therefore, ECAPE decided that, to obtain consistent data, students should be assessed at particular ages, not grades. For example, if NAEP were to assess a sample of 9-year-olds in a school, a random sample of children of that age in that school should be assessed, regardless of what grade level they happen to have attained.

If the assessment covered high school students, some dropouts would be missed. Therefore, an assessment of youth in their late teens must include students who were no longer in school as well as those who were still enrolled.

One member of ECAPE was Peter Rossi, a prestigious sociologist who headed the National Opinion Research Center. Rossi observed that "[a]lthough the immediate goal of school systems is to produce graduates with appropriate skills, knowledge and values, the long range goal is to produce an adult population with levels of these attributes sufficient to meet the needs of our society." Reinforcing Tyler's views, Rossi observed that educators often face the problem of decay – students may learn something that enables them to pass a test in the short run, but it does not stay with them after the school year is over. Therefore, Rossi argued, to truly measure whether an educational system is effective, young adults must also be assessed to see what has stuck with them a few years after they left school. "In short, whether or not a school system is an effective institution depends as much on whether its products as *adults* retain enough of the knowledge, skills and values that were characteristics of graduates."[316]

ECAPE estimated that assessing each sampled out-of-school 17-year-old and young adult would be 10 times more costly than assessing a student in school – in current dollars, about $330 per out-of-school respondent vs. $33 per in-school student.[317] Nonetheless, ECAPE concluded that "it is of substantial practical importance to have facts about the achievement level of those who have left school."[318]

ECAPE members understood that families, communities, religious institutions, and schools all contributed to the outcomes of education. This was as true of reading proficiency as it was of developing a good work ethic. It is not possible to separate what was learned in school from what was learned outside; schools influence all the cognitive and non-cognitive outcomes of education. So ECAPE thought of NAEP as testing "what people have learned, not necessarily all within the school system."[319] Information on student outcomes can influence policy makers' decisions about how to improve academic and non-academic school programs, without implying that such programs alone can fully achieve the desired results.

ECAPE did not model NAEP on standardized tests then used, and still used, by American schools. Rather, its models were surveys conducted by the Bureau of the Census, the Bureau of Labor Statistics (BLS), and the Centers for Disease Control (CDC).[320] These provide data, but policy makers must interpret them. Nobody "passes" or "fails" the Census or the National Health Survey. Respondents get no scores on their answers. Rather, when official surveys report, for example, that unemployment was higher this year than last, or that the diabetes rate among women was rising from one survey to the next, policy makers take this information to design improvements in job training or public health programs.

ECAPE wanted NAEP to serve a similar function for education. If NAEP were to report that the percentage of 13-year-olds who could calculate the area of a triangle had declined, this should spur policy makers to examine mathematics instruction to see where it might be falling short. Or if NAEP were to report that the percentage of 17-year-olds who knew the correct technique for applying artificial respiration had increased, this should encourage policy makers that this aspect of health education was improving.

Thus, the only reporting for which ECAPE designed NAEP to engage was the kind of reporting done by the Census, BLS, or CDC. Early NAEP did not report scores, but only specific test questions or activities, along with the percentages of students who could successfully answer the question or conduct the activity, broken down by region, sex, poverty status, and race.[321] Such percentages, ECAPE believed, would be easily understood by the public, which could (with its representatives) then draw its own conclusions about implications for educational policy.

These principles all guided the NAEP that ECAPE designed. NAEP exams were first administered nationwide in 1969 and continued pretty much according to the ECAPE design through 1973. NAEP assessed 9-, 13-, and 17-year-olds, as well as young adults (ages 26 to 35), regardless of what grade students were in or even whether they were still enrolled in school.[322] For respondents who were not in school, trained NAEP staff assessed a random sample of youth and young adults of the appropriate ages in their homes and communities. NAEP covered all important outcomes to which schools aimed to contribute, some of which could be assessed by paper-and-pencil tests and others of which could only be assessed by trained observers who recorded student behavior.

In retrospect, some aspects of early NAEP seem flawed. With hundreds of test items covering many subject areas, it was unrealistic to expect policy makers or the public to derive meaning from the percentages of students who could complete each specific item. Had the original NAEP design been maintained, some way of summarizing the results, with some kind of "score," would have had to be developed to make the results useful for the public at large. In addition, it proved to be overly cautious for NAEP to report results only at the regional level. Larger samples could produce state-by-state results, and these would have been useful to policy makers without opening the door to flawed comparisons between schools or students. If students in some states do better on geometry questions, or on first-aid questions, policy makers in the lagging states might be inspired to take appropriate action.

However, NAEP never had the opportunity to consider these adjustments. Congressional leaders were not persuaded that such a census of educational outcomes could be used to improve policy. In 1974, Congress cut NAEP's $6 million annual budget in half; by 1980, it had climbed back only to $3.9 million.[323] Gradually, important design elements in the original NAEP were dropped. After 1974, NAEP eliminated the young adult sample, although it was briefly reinstated for one year, in 1977. After 1976, NAEP ceased assessing out-of-school 17-year-olds.[324] NAEP ceased observing behavioral outcomes and, with the exception of an arts and music assessment conducted in 1997, NAEP became exclusively a pencil-and-paper test. In 1998, attempts to sample students of similar age were dropped, and NAEP now assesses students in fourth, eighth, and 12th grades, regardless of their ages.[325] These changes were almost entirely motivated by cost savings, not because they would improve the quality of test data.

As NAEP began to look more like a typical standardized test, the government wanted results that looked more like typical test scores. The intention of NAEP's original designers was abandoned – to model the assessment on surveys like the Census and to let the public draw its own conclusions about whether such percentages were satisfactory. NAEP had initially been administered by the Education Commission of the States, a consortium of governors and other state policy makers. But in 1983, the government switched the NAEP contract to the Educational Testing Service (ETS, the organization that administers the College Board's SAT), and statistical sophistication became a higher priority than public understandability.[326] ETS began to report overall subject-area scale scores;[327] then, as we saw in Chapter 4, in the early 1990s NAEP began to report whether students had passed a fanciful "proficiency" point. In the 1980s, Congress again began to increase the NAEP budget, but by this time debates about education were obsessed with a belief that we were a "nation at risk" from having low test scores. Thus, new money was now mostly used to increase the frequency of math and reading tests and to increase the sample size for state-level score results in math, reading, science, and writing alone.[328] NAEP's budget is today over $100 million annually, 10 times its inflation-adjusted 1980 level.[329] An obsession with math and reading test scores was not the only reason why early NAEP items covering behavioral outcomes were not reinstated when funds again became available. In the decades after the budget was initially slashed, organized interest groups on the left and right pressed Congress to restrict NAEP, and some urged its abolition. Pressure groups from the left were so suspicious that discussions of real social problems might include stereotypes that it became impossible to craft test questions that avoided racial, ethnic, gender, or historical landmines. Further, these advocates felt it necessary to ensure that no test question placed any group of students at a disadvantage: the context of the question, these advocates argued, might be more foreign to the experience of some students than it might be to others.

Test developers for the National Assessment Governing Board responded to pressure from the left by having a "bias and sensitivity review" panel edit every question proposed for inclusion in the NAEP. Diane Ravitch, a member of NAGB from 1997 to 2004, recounts that these panels rejected a reading passage about a friendly dolphin because it might discriminate against students who did not live near the ocean; they excluded a passage about how owls hunt rodents, because owls are associated with death in Navajo culture; they excluded a passage about an old woman whose overladen bicycle tumbled over, because it might stereotype old women as having poor judgment; they excluded a story about the African American educator and civil rights leader Mary McLeod Bethune because she had been divorced; and so on.[330]

Meanwhile, pressure groups from the right worried that, if a NAEP test posed questions involving personal judgment or values, or views on controversial issues, NAEP would then be able to collect reports of children's thoughts into a national database of totalitarian proportions that the government could use to track every American's personal opinions and habits. In the 1980s, right-wing groups organized letter-writing campaigns, bombarding the Department of Education and Congress with demands that NAEP stop snooping on American children.[331]

By 1996, the NAGB felt compelled to issue a policy statement explicitly asserting that NAEP "tests academic subjects and does not collect information on individual students' personal values or attitudes."[332] Although information on individual students had never been part of NAEP's plan, the new statement made clear that NAEP would avoid any assessment of the values and attitudes that have always been central goals of American education.

But some fanatics were still not satisfied. During the debate over *No Child Left Behind* in 2001, conservative Republicans succeeded in attaching an amendment prohibiting NAEP from assessing students' "personal or family beliefs or attitudes."[333] In the same spirit, NCLB prohibited states from conducting their own tests that touch on these topics, whose definitions were never specified. NCLB also required that NAGB ensure that all NAEP items are "free from racial, cultural, gender, or regional bias and are secular, neutral, and non-ideological."[334] Such undefined language, while unexceptionable on its face, is intended to, and does, intimidate NAGB from including anything but the most uninteresting items and certainly not any that ask students to think creatively about controversial topics. The text of NCLB included more detail about how NAGB should respond promptly to parent complaints about NAEP questions (including a requirement that the secretary of education report to Congress summarizing responses to such complaints) than it does about the questions themselves.

No doubt, these are tough issues. But students cannot gain the ability to deal with controversial issues if their teachers never raise topics that some parents will find objectionable and if students are never assessed on their proficiency in weighing complex problems. Back in the 1840s, Horace Mann's attempt to design a public education system took place in the context of fierce national disputes about constitutional protections for slavery, the role of the federal government in public works, and the Mexican War. A great weakness of Mann's design for public schooling was his inability to reconcile his desire to train for citizenship and his need to avoid controversial issues in the classroom. He wrote:

> those articles in the creed of republicanism, which are accepted by all, believed in by all, and which form the common basis of our

political faith, shall be taught to all. But when the teacher, in the course of his lessons or lectures on the fundamental law, arrives at a controverted text, he is either to read it without comment or remark; or, at most, he is only to say that the passage is the subject of disputation, and that the schoolroom is neither the tribunal to adjudicate, nor the forum to discuss it."[335]

This was then, and is today, a formula for putting students to sleep. And if students are never permitted to practice the debate of controversial public issues, such pedagogy cannot fulfill Mann's goal for education of developing good citizens. Yet unsatisfactory though Mann's solution may have been, we have done no better since. In the 1980s, when NAEP's budget was finally restored at a time when sensitivities from both right- and left-wing censors were intimidating public officials, it is inconceivable that NAGB could have added back items that assessed whether students exhibited good citizenship behaviors, had satisfactory interpersonal skills and social responsibility, or followed good physical and mental health practices.

The abandonment of ECAPE's original design sparked protest. In 1982, the Wirtz-Lapointe report,[336] commissioned by NAEP, recommended reinstatement of out-of-school assessments of 17-year-olds and young adults, and reinstatement of the broad goal-area coverage that had been abandoned to focus more narrowly on less-expensive-to-test academic skills. Continuing NAEP with such a narrow focus, the report said, "would not make sense" and "will virtually assure the Assessment's not playing a major role in informing the general public about the educational achievement picture....Covering subject areas not covered by other assessment systems is critical." Not doing so "would contribute to the narrowing of American education.[337]

In 1986, the U.S. secretary of education appointed a study group, led by Tennessee Governor Lamar Alexander (Hillary Rodham Clinton was also a member), to evaluate NAEP. The group's 1987 report protested the narrowing of subject areas NAEP was assessing, and urged that coverage be re-expanded, especially to include "higher-order cognitive skills," often "involving value judgments of some subtlety," which had been minimized as NAEP moved toward easily quantifiable and tested basic skills. The study group also urged that the out-of-school 17-year-old and young adult populations be restored.[338] In a companion report to Alexander's, the National Academy of Education concluded that NAEP's narrow coverage "may have a distorted impact on our schools."[339]

Narrow though NAEP may have become with respect to the broad goals of American education, NAEP's academic items have remained significantly more sophisticated than those of typical standardized tests. NAEP assesses not only student competence in basic skills but their reasoning and critical thinking abilities as well. Missing from the modern NAEP, however, are the noncognitive behavioral traits and skills that we expect schools to develop, as well as non-academic factual knowledge (such as of appropriate health behaviors) that youth need to succeed and flourish.

Today, the early history of NAEP has become a quaint curiosity. Few officials in the U.S. Department of Education, even those responsible for NAEP, are even aware of it. But knowledge of the work of ECAPE, and of NAEP's experiences during its first decade, should be revived. They illustrate how assessment could be used to create the context for a balanced accountability system for education, a system upon which the public could rely to learn if schools perform satisfactorily.

Earlier, this book defined eight goal areas of American public education and asserted that schools should be held accountable for satisfactory outcomes in each of these goal areas, appropriately weighted by their relative importance. The balance of this chapter describes a few typical early NAEP exercises to illustrate that it truly is possible to know if such satisfactory outcomes are being produced. It is not necessary to provide illustrations for the first two goal areas, basic knowledge and skills and critical thinking, because these purely academic areas can mostly be assessed by familiar types of paper-and-pencil exams; early NAEP assessed them in this way, and modern NAEP continues to do so. Some of the illustrations that follow might appropriately assess more than one goal area. They include both questions of fact that might still appear on standardized tests, and questions of behavior, value, and judgment that are no longer tested. Some of these questions might seem dated nearly 40 years after they were administered. However, they clearly demonstrate the possibilities of what could be assessed if there were a will to do so.

Appreciation of the arts and literature (Goal 3)

Early NAEP planned regular assessments of art and music, and NAEP exams covered these in 1972 and 1978. The arts, however, were subsequently dropped as NAEP narrowed its subject area coverage.

The 1994 reauthorization of the Elementary and Secondary Education Act (eventually supplanted by *No Child Left Behind*) stated that "the arts are forms of understanding and ways of knowing that are fundamentally important to education."[340] As a result, NAGB briefly responded to public concern that NAEP's narrowed subject coverage was inconsistent with national goals and ordered an arts assessment in 1997. Because of limited funds, only eighth graders took the test,[341] but within this constraint the arts assessment was of high quality. It included paper-and-pencil test items as well as performances rated by NAEP observers. Results were reported for all eighth graders and separately for males and females and for blacks and whites. The 1997 NAEP report was accompanied by a CD-ROM that displayed nationally representative eighth graders engaged in creating art and music in response to NAEP prompts.[342]

For the visual arts, for example, NAEP displayed reproductions of mother/child portraits from several historic periods and assessed whether students could identify techniques and interpret themes. NAEP asked students to observe a full-size collage by Romare Bearden and to recount the "story" they believed Bearden was attempting to tell. On a postcard-size copy in test booklets, they were asked to draw arrows to aspects of the artwork they believed the artist wanted them to notice. They were asked to categorize the Bearden collage as "impressionism," "photographic realism," "surrealism," or "semiabstract representation" (the correct answer). They were then given a packet of materials and asked to create their own semiabstract representational collages, which NAEP evaluated based on effective use of the technique.[343]

In the early NAEP music assessments as well as in the 1997 eighth-grade assessment, paper-and-pencil items determined whether students could identify notes and time signatures in written music.[344] Students listened to recordings of passages from well-known classics such as the "Hallelujah Chorus" from Handel's "Messiah" or the "March" from Tchaikovsky's "Nutcracker Suite"; in some cases, students were asked to identify the composers, in others the periods in which the works were written.[345] NAEP assessors played a selection of jazz pieces; students responded to a multiple choice item asking whether each piece was in the ragtime, boogie-woogie, Chicago school, or modern style.[346] NAEP assessors played a recording of the French folk song, "Au Claire de la Lune." Students were then asked to identify the instrument on which the music was played and to determine which of the four phrases of the recording were similar. Portions of the recording were replayed, and students were asked to say whether the steps in that portion went up or down.[347] NAEP assessors played a recording of "Wade in the Water," and students were asked to identify the piece as a spiritual and to explain how such music was important in the daily lives of the people who originally sang it.[348]

Survey questions asked whether students participated in a variety of in-school and out-of-school musical activities, ranging from playing in a band or orchestra or singing in a choir, to attending concerts or listening to musical tapes, CDs, or records. They asked students what kinds of music they liked to listen to, whether they played a musical instrument, and whether they liked to sing.[349] As always, such questions produced no "scores" but were posed in the expectation that if curriculum designers knew, for example, what types of music children do and do not appreciate, it would help to improve the music curriculum.

The test also assessed students on their musical performances. Presented with two written measures of music, students were asked to write two additional measures that complemented those given. They were asked to sing a line of simple written music;[350] to sing the song, "America," first accompanied by recorded voices, and then alone; to sing a simple round, "Are You Sleeping?";[351] and to play back a simple tune ("Twinkle, Twinkle, Little Star") on a keyboard.[352]

Preparation for skilled employment (Goal 4)

Early NAEP attempted to determine whether students were developing the ability to take responsibility for their own development. It assessed whether they were insightful about their own strengths and weaknesses and whether they knew the characteristics of different jobs and occupations for which such strengths and weaknesses might be relevant.[353] The test asked young adults, for example, whether they had taken any adult education courses in the last two years. It asked 13- and 17-year-olds if they had talked about future employment plans with a teacher or school advisor or counselor, and with their parents.[354] Illustrating how NAEP data should be used to prod school improvement, an early NAEP report wondered "why, in an age that has seen the growth of the counseling profession, only 35% of the 17-year-olds said they had spoken with a counselor about their future plans."[355]

ECAPE understood that relatively few young people (only 20-25%) would go to college. Thus, it considered an important high school goal to be familiarizing students with a wide variety of occupations so the students could make informed choices about careers and make sure they were developing the skills needed for their chosen fields.[356] Early NAEP asked 17-year-olds what jobs they might like to have, and then to assess how seriously these youths had considered them, to describe what abilities were needed for the jobs, and to name aspects of the jobs they would like and those they would dislike.[357] To assess whether 9- and 13-year-olds were on a path to make informed choices, early NAEP asked them to identify things they did well and things they did poorly. [358]

Early NAEP gave 17-year-olds and young adults a job advertisement in a newspaper and asked them to write a letter of application. To assess whether schools were exposing younger students to a variety of settings, NAEP asked 9- and 13-year-olds whether they had visited such places as a museum, a farm, a factory, a college, a planetarium, and a newspaper printing plant.[359]

And early NAEP did not hesitate to assess the ability to make rational decisions about policies in the work world, even where rationality was not generally accepted. For example, in 1973 NAEP described for 17-year-olds and young adults a contemporary airline hiring policy: "all stewardesses must be unmarried women between the ages of 21 and 35." It then asked these test takers how they would change the policy, and to write their own substitute policy for the airline.[360] It should not be too difficult for NAEP to find comparable challenges that are relevant today.

Social skills and work ethic (Goal 5)

Employers frequently report that high school graduates are unprepared for work, not so much because of cognitive deficits but because they lack interpersonal skills to work in teams and solve problems collaboratively.[361] These skills are as essential to civic, community, and family life as they are to the workplace. Early NAEP was determined to assess them.

Early NAEP identified skills "that are generally useful in the world of work" and assessed students on them: numerical, communication, manual-perceptual, information-processing, decision-making, and interpersonal skills. It assessed work habits, such as accepting responsibility for one's own behavior, the ability to plan work, the use of initiative, adaptation to varied conditions, even good grooming.[362]

For example, early NAEP showed 13- and 17-year-olds a film of a supervisor interacting with his employees and asked the adolescents to list four things the supervisor did best and worst.[363]

To see whether students were learning to cooperate effectively in small groups, NAEP sent trained observers to present a game to 9-year-olds in sampled schools. In teams of four, the 9-year-olds were offered a prize (such as crayons or yo-yos) to guess what object was hidden in a box. The students were only permitted to ask yes-or-no questions, and two teams competed with each other to see who could identify the toy first. Cooperation was necessary, because all team members had to agree on each question asked, and then the role of posing questions publicly was rotated. Trained NAEP observers rated the students on whether they suggested a new question to ask, gave reasons for their own viewpoints, sought additional information that would be helpful to the team's work, helped organize the procedure, or otherwise demonstrated cooperative problem-solving skills. Students were also rated on whether they impeded teamwork, for example by making discouraging or irrelevant comments.[364]

A different cooperative exercise was given to 13- or 17-year-olds. NAEP assessors presented groups of eight students with a list of a dozen issues about which teenagers typically had strong opinions. They asked the students to reach a consensus on what they considered the five most important issues and then to write a recommendation, supported by a majority of the group, on how to resolve at least two of them. The list included, for 13-year-olds, issues such as whether they should have time limits for being at home or going to bed, whether they should be allowed to watch adult movies, and whether parents should have the right to approve their choices of friends. For 17-year-olds, the list included issues such as compulsory school attendance and military service requirements, and the age eligibility minima for voting, drinking, or smoking. As they did with 9-year-olds, the NAEP assessors observed these groups, rating whether students took clear positions, gave reasons for points of view, sought additional information helpful to completing the task, helped organize or change internal procedures, defended the right to hold contrary viewpoints, and never demeaned the group's work or did something totally unrelated to the task. NAEP then reported, for example, that only 4% of the 13-year-olds defended the right of another group member to be heard or to hold a different opinion, while 6% were willing to continue to defend their own viewpoint even in the face of opposition.[365]

NAEP asked young adults and 17-year-olds to imagine they were operating a machine without a proper safety shield and, as a result, another worker was injured by a flying piece of metal. NAEP then asked them, "are you responsible for the injury to the other person"? Credit was given for answers in which the test taker took complete responsibility, partial responsibility, or only moral responsibility (because legally, management was responsible for enforcing safety regulations).[366]

To assess whether students were developing the kind of responsibility the work world would require, early NAEP asked students at all three age levels whether they did regular chores around the home.[367] If students had younger siblings at home, NAEP interviewers asked whether the students helped answer tough questions that their younger siblings may have asked.[368] As always, interviewers asked follow-up questions to verify the accuracy of answers.

Citizenship and community responsibility (Goal 6)

When NAEP was first administered in 1969, the nation was in the midst of a civil rights revolution with segregation still commonplace; certain questions about race were more sensitive than they might be today. NAEP's willingness to probe such areas reflects its initial determination to assess the full range of outcomes schools aim to produce, since these topics were certainly lively ones in classrooms at that time – or should have been. Thus in 1969, NAEP interviewers asked 13-year-olds, 17-year-olds, and young adults what they felt they should do if they walked past a park and observed an attendant barring minority children from entering. NAEP reported that 82% of 13-year-olds, 90% of 17-year-olds, and 79% of young adults said they thought they should do something and gave acceptable illustrations, ranging from tell their parents, report it to a public authority, report it to a civil rights or civil liberties organization, write letters to the newspaper, or take social action (such as picketing or leafleting).[369] The three age groups were also asked, in a paper-and-pencil exercise, if they would be willing to have someone of a different race be their dentist or doctor, live next door, be elected to public office, sit next to them in a crowded restaurant, or stay in the same motel or hotel. Generally, the percentages of 13-year-olds who answered affirmatively was highest, with the percentages declining for 17-year-olds and then for adults.[370]

NAEP attempted to determine if students understood that individuals should be judged on their own merits and not held responsible for misdeeds of others. So in 1969, NAEP interviewers asked both 9- and 13-year olds whether, if the father of a friend was jailed for theft, they would still invite the friend to their houses to play.[371] To assess students' commitment to civil liberties, 13- and 17-year-olds and young adults were asked if they thought someone should be permitted to say on television that "Russia is better than the United States," that "Some races of people are better than others," or that "It is not necessary to believe in God." For 13-year-olds, the questions were posed by an interviewer while the questions appeared on a paper-and-pencil test for the older groups. Only a bare majority of young adults thought that the statements about Russia and God should be permitted, and only a minority in each of the age groups would permit statements of racial superiority. Only 3% of 13-year-olds, 17% of 17-year-olds, and 24% of young adults thought all three statements should be permitted.[372]

Although the early NAEP exams were not designed to reveal longitudinal data (for example, by asking 13-year-olds the same questions as 9-year-olds had been asked four years previously), the exams do suggest the possibility of growth as students mature. For example, only 24% of 9-year-olds thought it was all right to say publicly that you thought the president was doing a bad job, whereas 55% of 13-year-olds thought this would be all right.[373] And a steadily increasing percentage of 9-, 13-, and 17-year-olds and young adults stated that the president does not have the right to do anything affecting the nation that he wants to do (49%, 72%, 78%, 89%).[374]

In 1969, NAEP interviewers asked 17-year-olds and young adults to list five ways in which citizens can influence government actions. Acceptable answers included voting, writing letters, attending public meetings and expressing opinions at them, campaigning for a candidate, participating in a protest, signing a petition, and many others – even bribing a legislator or participating in a riot was rated as technically correct. Only 11% of 17-year-olds and 8% of young adults were able, even after prompting, to come up with five ways, although much higher percentages came up with fewer than five.[375]

In addition, NAEP interviewers also asked the young adults if, in the last five years, they themselves had ever talked with or written to a government official about a civic issue; if adults answered yes, the interviewer pressed for details to verify that the action had actually taken place.[376]

NAEP assessors assembled a dozen randomly selected 13- and 17-year-olds and presented controversial issues to them, such as whether the death penalty should be available in murder cases, whether schools should have dress codes, whether women should be drafted (during the Vietnam War, only men were drafted), and whether gun ownership should be registered. About two-thirds volunteered either to state an initial position or take a contrary position on one of these issues.[377]

NAEP also attempted in 1969 to assess whether 17-year-olds and young adults were able to consider alternative viewpoints on controversial public issues by asking them to state arguments both for and against one of the most heated public issues of the time – whether students enrolled in college should be granted deferments from the military draft.[378] It asked 9- and 13-year-olds if something must be true if it is reported in the newspaper.[379] And NAEP asked young adults if, in the previous year, they had performed any unpaid volunteer work to improve their communities; if the answer was yes, NAEP interviewers asked follow-up questions to verify its accuracy. NAEP asked 17-year-olds if they belonged to any non-school clubs or organizations, and similarly followed up to verify.[380]

Physical health (Goal 7)

In 1977, 17-year-olds and young adults were asked what they should do if they were ill and their doctors prescribed medication that was too expensive. NAEP reported that 35% of 17-year-olds and 65% of young adults got the correct answer (from multiple choices) – to ask the doctor to prescribe the drug by its "generic or chemical name."[381] The young adult survey included items measuring knowledge of sex, particularly hygiene and venereal disease, but these items were not included in the survey of 17-year-olds (although such knowledge may be a necessary outcome of the educational process for teenagers as well).

Seventeen-year-olds were asked questions about drug abuse, such as what to do if a friend at a party passed out from a drug overdose (correct answers were get the friend up and walk him or her around, get immediate medical help, and preserve the remaining drugs so the doctor can identify what the friend took); and whether "speed" or "uppers" led to jitteriness, shortness of temper, sleeping difficulties, dependence (the correct answer was yes), or increased appetite (the correct answer was no).[382] There were similar questions about the effects of alcohol and smoking.

Young adults and 17-year-olds were assessed on whether they knew the proper procedure for lifting heavy objects (e.g., using leg more than back muscles), whether they were familiar with key first-aid principles (what to do in the case of burns, animal bites, objects in the eye, poisoning, bleeding), whether it was safe to run an automobile in a closed garage in cold weather, and whether excessive speed was the most frequent cause of automobile accidents.[383]

To assess the healthy eating habits of young adults and 17-year-olds, NAEP presented food choices and asked respondents to recognize which had fewer calories.[384]

Emotional health (Goal 8)

Early NAEP included questions to assess the emotional health of 17-year-olds and young adults. For example, some questions probed whether youths were adequately prepared for responsible parenting. Seventeen-year-olds and young adults were presented with a list of baby behaviors – fear of strangers, speaking in short sentences, following objects with eyes, recognizing parents, crawling on hands and knees, controlling urine and bowel movements – and asked whether these were typically found in babies younger or older than 18 months of age.[385]

For young adults who had children of their own already in school, NAEP assessed parenting by asking if they had looked through their children's school books and could describe them to the interviewer.[386]

Seventeen-year-olds were also asked whether it was normal or abnormal at their age to have blurred vision (abnormal), feelings of doubt about the future (normal), desire for independence from family (normal), concern about appearance (normal), dental cavities (normal), frequent headaches (abnormal), a mole that increases in size (abnormal), and facial pimples (normal).[387]

Young adults and 17-year-olds were asked whether seeking psychiatric help necessarily was a sign of mental illness (false), or whether people may seek such help for objective advice about handling problems (true).[388]

Another set of questions attempted to determine whether youth had the self-assurance to make difficult decisions in situations that require courage or emotional maturity. In 1977, both young adults and 17-year-olds were asked, in a multiple choice exercise, what to do if visiting a friend whose six-month-old baby had visible bruises. The correct answer was "suggest that your friend call her baby's doctor about the bruises." Incorrect choices included "ignore the bruises because they are none of your business" and "accuse your friend of beating her child." A follow-up question asked what to do if, later, bruises remain and the friend says that the baby fell out of her crib. The prompt said "you are now suspicious that your friend may have hurt the baby intentionally, because she did not seek help," and asks what to do next. The correct answer was "call the local child health agency and report your suspicions." Incorrect choices included "do nothing more because you have done all you can…" "call the police…" and "stay with your friend to make sure she does not harm the baby again."[389]

NAEP then and now

For all items, early NAEP reported only the percentages of students who were able to correctly answer or acceptably perform them; no overall scores were given. NAEP reports did not imply what percentage should be deemed acceptable. ECAPE believed it was up to the public, not NAEP officials, to determine what percentage of the entire population should, for example, have written to a public official or be able to play a tune on a keyboard, following effective instruction.

The illustrative items described in this chapter may not have been ideal; NAEP was never fully developed to generate a balanced assessment of American student achievement on the eight goal areas of public education. As noted above, opposition from individuals and interest groups would today make it politically impractical for NAEP to ask questions that touch on controversial issues or that ask for knowledge and performance that some Americans consider "personal" – although NAEP's sampling design assures that no results can ever be attributed to individual students.

Issues of reliability also loom large – however accurate such sample results might be for the nation at large, it would be impractical, and in most cases statistically invalid, to engage in such time-consuming assessment of large enough numbers of students to generate reliable school-level results.

But if, for example, an assessment like early NAEP demonstrated that too few students in a particular state had awareness of vocational options that would be open to them, policy makers in that state might require schools to take eighth graders on field trips to museums, to hospitals, to laboratories, to corporate offices. If an assessment like early NAEP demonstrated that too few students were practiced in tolerating and responding to contrary opinions, that state might be inspired to develop and require a curriculum that gave students such practice.

After seeing some initial NAEP results, the first staff director of NAEP expressed the goals of the designers this way:

> One citizenship exercise demonstrated clearly that most young people and young adults do not believe that the government should allow certain very controversial statements to be aired on radio or TV. If I were a member of a board of education and saw that result, I would want to inquire of my superintendent whether our students were studying the issue of freedom of expression, freedom of the press, etc.[390]

Contemporary accountability policy in education assumes that assessments must generate reliable student- and school-level results, must rely heavily upon the multiple choice format to ensure accuracy, and must assess student knowledge, not student behavior. However, the original intention of NAEP and its early administration challenge these assumptions and demonstrate that what really stops us from pursuing a balanced educational index is cost and vision, not capability. Reflection on early NAEP should put to rest the notion that standardized test scores are the only outcomes that can practically be reported and that schools, therefore, can only be held accountable for these narrow results.

Schools would perform differently, and better, if they were held accountable for a wider range of student performance than math and reading test scores alone. Many of the items initially included in NAEP exams demonstrate that such accountability is not unrealistic. But NAEP itself cannot and should not be used for accountability purposes. As ECAPE originally intended, NAEP can only provide a context for accountability policies by guiding policy makers toward the outcome areas of education where schools in their states are most in need of improvement. Although ECAPE was not able to persuade public officials that NAEP could provide this guidance at a state level, there is today a consensus that state-by-state comparisons are one of the most valuable services NAEP performs.

However, before describing how state policy makers might use the information NAEP provides as a context for accountability, let's turn to the ingredients of a coherent school-level accountability system.

CHAPTER 7

School boards, accreditation, and Her Majesty's Inspectors

Other nations have ways to hold educators accountable, but American schools' unique governance system should, if it works, make further accountability unnecessary. Almost every school district in the country is governed in part by an elected school board. School boards could and should hold their superintendents and staffs accountable for student performance across the eight broad goal areas of public education.

But because school boards usually fail to fulfill this accountability role, some other institution is needed to ensure that schools are achieving the eight goals.

For insights about how school board accountability should be supplemented, the current voluntary accreditation system in the United States, as well as the system of school inspections in England, can help. Elements of both can be borrowed to design a workable accountability system for public education.

School boards

Accountability for outcomes was the original inspiration for school boards. In 1642, the Massachusetts colonial legislature required parents to teach their children to read and to understand both religious and secular law. To ensure compliance, the legislature required town selectmen (councilmen) to check up on parents and fine those whose children did not display the expected learning.[391] Once schools were established and parents were no longer required to teach children at home, selectmen appointed committees to visit the schools, listen to pupils recite, examine their notebooks, and quiz pupils to judge whether they were learning.[392]

In 1721, Boston selectmen appointed a permanent committee on school visitation, and in 1798 Massachusetts required the selectmen of every town to appoint one. At first, towns established separate committees for hiring teachers and approving textbooks. Eventually, these were consolidated into unified school committees and became the first school boards, a model later imitated nationwide.[393]

In 1844, Horace Mann, Massachusetts education secretary, promoted the election of a friend to the Boston School Committee who, upon taking office, developed the first standardized written exam for all Boston 14-year-olds. Testing replaced the previous practice of school board members going to schools to give oral exams to pupils, but it still kept Boston school committee members focused on student performance.[394]

As schools multiplied and municipalities created more school districts, direct supervision of schools and personal examination of pupils became too time consuming for citizen committees.[395] So 19th century school boards began to appoint superintendents to operate the schools – Buffalo and Louisville hired the first in 1837.[396] But it was never clear where superintendents' responsibilities began and school boards' ended – and it is still unclear today. In the 19th and 20th centuries, some school boards continued to hire teachers, choose textbooks, purchase supplies, and determine the curriculum. Few school boards today hire individual teachers, but many continue to carry out administrative, not just policy, functions. Some states still require board members to make school visits – Arkansas, for example, requires board members to visit schools to "encourage pupils in their studies," and Wisconsin requires them to visit and advise administrators regarding the "progress of the pupils" – yet few board members inspect schools for the purpose of systematically ensuring that the schools pursue and achieve the broad goals of public education.[397]

In the early 20th century, reformers ("progressives"[398]) attempted to transform municipal governments, including schools. The reformers were disproportionately upper class and interested in professionalizing public service, ending corruption, and weakening the powers of corporations (and trusts) and immigrant political machines. When it came to school governance, the progressives aimed to prevent ethnic machine bosses from selecting board members who could dispense patronage with public schools' funds. Imitating the American constitutional model with its separation of powers, the progressives insisted that school boards should be only legislative, leaving all executive authority to school superintendents. Progressives said they wanted school boards to establish goals and hold superintendents and staff accountable for achieving them, but refrain from interfering with administration.[399]

To this end, school reformers (Stanford Professor Ellwood Cubberley was the most prominent) campaigned to have urban school boards elected at large, not district-by-district, and to prohibit board members from receiving pay for their volunteer service. This change resulted in boards composed mostly of established businessmen and other wealthy professionals; although working-class and immigrant activists might win election from lower-income and ethnic wards, they could not do so citywide.[400] In New York City, ongoing political struggle between Catholic immigrant-dominated political machines and Protestant elite reformers led to frequent shifts back and forth from locally elected school boards (or central boards elected by ward) to mayoral control or centralized and appointed boards.[401] As the progressives emerged victorious in most parts of the country, labor unions and their academic supporters protested the elite makeup of school boards, claiming that such a governance system led to the teaching of conservative political and social dogma and interfered with the achievement of education's broad goals of academic, social, civic, and personal development.

In 1927, Yale Professor George S. Counts wrote an influential book arguing that the role of school boards is to establish "the basic purposes of education and the relation of the school to the social order." But, Counts observed, this goal-setting is compromised by the composition of school boards: "the more favored economic and social classes," small businessmen, professionals, and business executives, made up 76% of urban school board members, while blue-collar workers accounted for only 8%.[402] A pioneering sociological study of an Indiana town (*Elmtown's Youth* by August Hollingshead) in the early 1940s described how school board nominees were selected by businessmen who were members of the Rotary Club; a vacancy would not be announced to the general public until the club's nominee had filed and the filing deadline had passed.[403] The school board then operated to keep taxes low by ensuring that funds were not wasted on the education of working-class children. Other 20th century studies replicated and reinforced the Counts and Hollingshead conclusion that school boards were so unrepresentative of the public will that they could not be relied upon to hold school administrators accountable for the public's education goals.[404]

In the mid-20th century, there were half a million school board members in the country, many of whom supervised very small, one- or two-school districts. Today, after a century of consolidation of small districts, there are still nearly 100,000 board members. The need to instruct these almost always unpaid volunteers in their duties inspired many 20th century manuals on how to function as a board member. The manuals included great detail about school budgets and personnel management (always with the caution to defer to the superintendent's professional judgment), but little about evaluating outcomes.

One, published in 1927, urged school board members to "occasionally consider what education means" by asking questions like "what are the schools for?" and "do the schools justify themselves?" But it gave no advice about how to go about doing this.[405] Another, in 1929, urged that each school board member visit local schools for one half-day per year, always accompanied by the superintendent.[406] Yet another, published in 1941, recommended that board members should visit schools to gain (unspecified) information but cautioned that such visits should not be considered "inspections."[407]

A manual for board members published in 1946 by the American Association of School Administrators proposed a "board member's creed," including a promise to hire only employees nominated by the superintendent and to vote on policy only after considering the superintendent's recommendation. School board members, the manual asserted, should always serve without pay, because otherwise they "will try to earn the salaries" by interfering with superintendents. The manual specified detailed "legislative" policies that boards should adopt (such as how many square feet a janitor should sweep daily), none of which involved holding executive superintendents or their staffs of educators accountable for student performance.[408] The manual urged that boards approve curricula to ensure outcomes such as civic responsibility, good interpersonal relationships, and health, but said nothing about evaluating whether these curricula were effective.[409]

The progressives believed that, if business leaders dominated school boards, these leaders would behave as corporate boards of directors were said to behave. An advice column in a 1923 issue of the *American School Board Journal* put it this way: a bank director "would never think of buying the ink or typewriter ribbons for the bank....He believes...it is his duty to...select a competent banker... and then hold [him] responsible for results." Yet when the column went on to describe what a board member's duties should be, ratifying administrative decisions and recommendations of the superintendent was the most important. The column mentioned examining "results," or educational outcomes, but offered no explanation of how standardized test scores should be interpreted. And while the column recognized that character and other non-cognitive traits should be important outcomes for schools, it advised board members not to investigate these directly, because students with high academic scores would also likely be developing the appropriate character traits.[410]

The federal government also advised school board members not to interfere in administration or cause problems for school superintendents, yet the government publication said nothing about establishing outcome goals or ensuring that schools were producing them.[411] An influential mid-20th century advocate was former Harvard President James B. Conant, whose book promoting comprehensive high schools said that the most essential characteristic of a modern high school was having a "school board composed of intelligent understanding citizens who realize fully the *distinction between policy-making and administration.*"[412]

Although we teach schoolchildren about the "separation of powers," the pure concept is artificial and unworkable in public education no less than in general government. Candidates for president do not campaign by promoting their administrative skills in carrying out the wishes of Congress; the executive presidency is clearly a policy-making job, and has been since George Washington's time. Congress does not restrict itself to policy making; it not only votes on whether to establish job training programs, but makes administrative decisions such as choosing the towns in which training centers (or army bases) should be located. Likewise, school districts have never successfully distinguished the roles of school boards and superintendents. Superintendents make policy, and school boards meddle in administration, endlessly debating many details that can't reasonably be called policy issues – whether these boards are elected at large or by ward.

A 1962 study calculated that a school board spent virtually none of its time on evaluation of educational outcomes; most was devoted to administrative matters like purchasing school sites or approving insurance policies, housekeeping matters like sending letters of commendation to employees, or non-educational policy matters like whether military service should count toward seniority in a salary schedule.[413] It is today still difficult to attend any school board meeting in the United States without concluding that the board was hopelessly bogged down in administrative detail, ranging from where a new school should be built, to the mapping of bus routes, to the transfer of funds from one tiny account to another, to hearing constituent complaints about particular teachers, counselors, or principals.[414] The National School Boards Association now reports that 97% of board members say they are concerned with student achievement (however narrowly defined), but overwhelming majorities also say they are concerned with budgetary issues, special education, educational technology, teacher quality, parental support, regulations, drug and alcohol use, student discipline, and teacher shortages.[415] When school board members are concerned about everything, they can afford to be truly concerned about nothing.

Forgotten in these debates has been a focus on the goals of education, and a process for monitoring whether the goals are being achieved. This is most disappointing because, as we saw in Chapter 2 (see Table 1), board members overall have sophisticated views of the student outcomes they seek from schools. Their views are consistent with the desires of state legislators, who have the ultimate legal authority for establishing the goals of public education.

School boards could and should concentrate their energies on insisting that these consensus outcomes be met, and in turn delegate administrative decision making to superintendents, their staffs, and their teachers. Boards have mostly not done so, although many now, in conflict with their members' own beliefs, evaluate superintendents by test scores in math and reading rather than by measures balanced among the eight goal areas for which board members state nominal support. And state policies support these practices, again in conflict with the expressed desires of state legislators for public policies that pursue a balanced set of public school outcomes.

School boards' abdication of responsibility for holding educators accountable for achieving the eight goals of education has inspired new reform ideas. Some critics advocate abolishing school districts altogether, expecting school boards to contract with the staffs of individual schools to achieve specified achievement outcomes – in effect, these proposals would make every school a charter school.[416] Yet school boards and other entities (state universities and state education departments) empowered to authorize charter schools have thus far mostly failed to demonstrate an ability or willingness to hold charter school operators accountable for outcomes, even in cases where these outcomes are narrowly defined as basic skills test scores alone. With many studies of charter schools confirming that, on average, their student test scores are about the same as those of regular public schools, the conclusion is inescapable that, although many charter schools may outperform regular public schools, many others underperform them. School boards or other charter authorizers rarely revoke the charters of these underperformers,[417] and there is no reason to think that making every school a charter school would solve this problem.

So despite America's unique potential for democratic school accountability, the failure of school boards to exercise this role makes an alternative accountability system essential.

Regional accreditation agencies

Six regional private agencies now accredit elementary and secondary schools, and they provide a system that could conceivably evolve to hold schools accountable for outcomes. Today, however, there are few consequences, besides embarrassment, for a school that fails to win accreditation, although in some states graduates of accredited high schools can more easily be admitted to state universities or be eligible for state scholarships.[418]

Accreditation is mostly a peer review process and, as such, it is responsible for a largely unheralded culture of continuous improvement in many schools nationwide. But voluntary peer review cannot substitute for democratic accountability. Like school board governance, accreditation as presently practiced is an inadequate vehicle for ensuring that students leave schools with acceptable achievement in the public's eight broad goal areas of education.

The accreditation process began at about the same time as the first school boards were established. In 1870, copying a system used by German universities, the president of the University of Michigan asked his faculty members to visit and inspect high schools throughout the state. The professors examined curriculum and textbooks, and observed instruction. From high schools deemed adequate, graduates were then accepted into the university without question. From schools that failed inspection, graduates still had to take qualifying exams for university admission.[419]

As the number of high schools grew, the university appointed a full-time examiner, replacing the part-time volunteer efforts of faculty members.[420] Other universities, and in some cases state governments, made similar appointments. In a few cases, state governments and universities duplicated each other's school inspections, squabbling about which should predominate.[421]

In 1884, President Charles W. Eliot of Harvard University, hoping to gain agreement on common high school curricular standards prerequisite for college admission, organized the New England Association of Colleges and Secondary Schools. The following year, the chancellor of Vanderbilt University convened the Southern Association for a similar purpose, while in 1896 the University of Michigan president merged the university's own inspection system into a North Central Association. Three other regional associations were subsequently formed, in the West, the Northwest, and the mid-Atlantic.[422]

During the first half of the 20th century, states frequently adopted the associations' standards as legal requirements, and some states made the associations' approval – accreditation – a condition of state funding for high schools.[423]

From the start, however, the accreditation process focused on the quality of high schools' programs and resources, not on the achievement of their students. In the mid-20th century, the associations began to accredit elementary schools as well, also with a focus on programs and resources. Accreditation agencies required schools to offer designated courses; to maintain libraries that owned reference materials and a specified number of books per pupil; to have a minimum number of teachers who were college graduates; to have science laboratories, gymnasiums, assembly halls, and ventilation systems; to be clean (and eventually to have indoor plumbing); to stay below a maximum pupil-teacher ratio; to have guidance counselors; to have a functioning parent-teacher association; to schedule a standard minimum school year and day; and, later, to abide by minimum pay scales for teachers and other staff. Course specifications and other standards continually evolved, also eventually covering the quality of high school educations for students not planning to enter college.[424] In some states, accreditation required providing children with annual dental checkups, health clinics for preschoolers, and referral services for children with emotional problems.[425]

Accreditation as practiced in most regions today has evolved from procedures developed in the 1950s. They consist of a visit by a team of educators, preceded by a year or two of preparation (called a self-study) by the faculty of the school under review. Although some states require schools to undergo the process, in others it is voluntary and the regional associations are membership organizations to which elementary and high schools can choose to belong. In Alabama and Wyoming, for example, all schools participate, but in Texas only 4% do.[426]

Overall, about one-fifth of the nation's 100,000 public elementary and secondary schools are accredited – that proportion includes most secondary schools and a much smaller share of elementary schools. Typically, schools that choose to apply for accreditation undergo comprehensive review from once every three years (in the Western states association) to a maximum of once every 10 years (in New England). In some cases, associations may require follow-up reports between school visits, while in others, schools in danger of losing accreditation may be visited more frequently.

As the accreditation process has evolved, it has continued to focus mostly on improving school programs and practices, not on student achievement of specified goals, although, certainly, fidelity to good programming and practice should lead to good outcomes. The regional associations now claim to base accreditation reviews on outcomes, but what this means is that they expect school faculties to establish their own specific learning goals (usually test scores) and to achieve them; accreditation is then based on whether schools meet their targets and whether curricular practices and other school programs are properly aligned with the specific goals the school faculty itself has set.[427]

This can be very helpful for schools attempting to improve, but it is not an accountability system. Nowhere in the accreditation process are students examined to see if they have acquired appropriate cognitive knowledge and skills, appreciation of the arts, appropriate preparation for skilled employment, citizenship habits, social skills, or physical and emotional health attributes.

The regional associations propose a few broad categories of quality standards –the North Central and Southern associations, for example, have seven categories: vision and purpose; governance and leadership; teaching and learning; documenting and using results; resource and support systems; stakeholder communications and relationships; and commitment to continuous improvement.[428] Standards of the other associations are similar.

In most cases, a year or two prior to a school's accreditation review, its leadership (the principal and usually a committee of faculty) propose goals for improvement in one or more of these areas and establish faculty committees to develop and implement appropriate plans. The goal-setting process is also likely to involve members of the community and parents but, in practice, and especially in communities with low educational levels, school faculties write the mission statements and set goals for improvement. Even in communities with higher educational levels, it is inevitable that full-time professionals (principals and teachers) will have greater influence on the planning process than parent or community volunteers.

An accreditation visit typically lasts three days, during which team members visit classrooms, interview teachers, meet with administrators, look at portfolios of student work, and talk with students and parents. Because these visits are scheduled far in advance, little is random about the observations. Teachers may take care to present their best lessons during the visit; in some regions, school administrators may carefully select students and parents to be interviewed or invited to a group meeting; and teachers may select unrepresentative work to include in the portfolios examined by team members. Nonetheless, trained visitors, and especially the experienced teachers who are members of volunteer visiting teams, can get fairly accurate insights into school quality during three days of observation. Teachers who are not in the practice of inviting student inquiry during a lesson cannot suddenly train their students to ask questions when visitors are present. Students accustomed to direct instruction cannot suddenly learn to work in problem-solving groups when visitors show up.

When an accreditation visit takes place, there is often ambiguity about whether accreditation will be based on a school's progress toward meeting its own goals, or its compliance with minimum standards for facilities and programs that regional associations have developed over the last century.[429]

The regional associations have no tax support and are funded only by membership dues of participating schools. As a result their budgets are small, and the visiting accreditation teams are usually composed only of volunteers. Teams typically consist of five to 10 members for elementary schools and up to 15 for larger high schools. Typically, these volunteers are teachers or administrators from other schools in the region, and an effort is made to include teachers from various subject areas. Some may be retired educators.

Principals of schools in an association may release teachers to participate on visiting teams because their own schools may themselves be visited in the near future, and team members may gain insights that will help their own schools to prepare. The regional associations usually designate one team member as leader, with responsibility for coordinating preparation of the team's written summary of the visit, which may include a recommendation regarding accreditation for the regional association to adopt. Team leaders have usually (but not always) attended summer training sessions conducted by their regional associations. Other team members typically have no formal training for the visits, although some may have participated as volunteers on other teams in the past.

In most cases, team members are highly regarded professional educators, have great insight into issues of school instruction and organization, and may be more competent school evaluators than typical full-time evaluators might be. But the voluntary nature of the role makes quality control to ensure a high degree of competence impossible. Experience and training is as important in school evaluation as it is in any professional activity. Because accreditation team members must usually be released from their regular teaching duties to participate on visiting teams, they can participate only rarely and so don't develop the experience that professional evaluators would have. Being an effective and experienced educator is not the same as being an effective and experienced evaluator. Mentoring and evaluation require different skills from teaching and, although team members may be more insightful than non-educators, they are nonetheless inexperienced in evaluation.

Even when schools receive full accreditation following visitation, reports will normally identify areas for recommended improvement. In some but not all cases, reports propose specific steps schools can take to achieve such improvement. Examples of typical recommendations, taken from recent accreditation reports, include: do better at differentiating instruction for students with distinct ability levels; establish a mentoring program for new teachers; improve students' use of computers for academic research; improve the school climate by improving collaboration between administrators, teachers, and support staff; develop an assessment program for accurate placement of incoming students in academic programs; develop more elective courses; make time for early and late primary grade teachers to meet with each other to coordinate curriculum and instruction; increase parental involvement beyond chaperoning field trips; and disaggregate test scores by socioeconomic subgroups.[430] Accredited schools usually make good faith attempts to implement such recommendations, and so the process results in real ongoing improvement.

But without a serious enforcement mechanism, and because team members who make the recommendations may not be more qualified than those on the receiving end, recommendations may also be ignored. Schools are usually expected to file follow-up reports during their terms of accreditation, documenting progress being made in implementing whatever recommendations have been made. Accreditation agencies may threaten to withdraw accreditation if schools don't report that recommendations are being implemented, but the agencies have limited ability to verify self-reports of compliance.[431]

In the most serious cases (about one-third of those in New England and one-eighth of those in the North Central and Southern regions), schools get formal warnings about areas in which improvements are required.[432] Schools with multiple warnings may be denied unconditional accreditation and placed on probation. In these cases, follow-up visits may take place in subsequent years to confirm that improvement is taking place, and when that is the case full accreditation will be granted. In cases where schools are put on warning status or probation, pressure to improve sometimes leads to dramatic results – warnings, probation, or even loss of accreditation for poor facilities, for example, may be just the evidence that district officials require to get voters to approve new bond issues.[433]

Because membership in the regional associations is voluntary in many states, and the regional associations are dependent on school and district payment of membership dues, associations are somewhat pressured to accredit schools they review. Schools denied accreditation will cease being members of their regional associations, and other schools may also withdraw, fearing similar decisions. Schools that are far from meeting their regional association's standards are unlikely to apply for membership in the first place. Because most members of accreditation teams are from schools that are also subject to visits in the near future, team members are sometimes reluctant to find fault with schools they visit, realizing that too-tough standards might soon be applied to themselves. Accreditation reports are generally not publicized (although they are now generally available on the web), but even this protection against embarrassment is not always sufficient to encourage frank criticism.

And because team members are not experienced professional evaluators, they have difficulty juggling the two somewhat contradictory roles they are asked to fill: as friendly peer advisors, making suggestions to school faculties about how to improve, and as judges, determining whether schools should receive accreditation. The associations counsel that "members of the visiting teams should be seen as equals, not experts."[434] But this advice can undermine team members' resolve to make objective accreditation recommendations.

Even experienced and highly qualified teachers may not be familiar with the full range of reform and staff development programs available to schools desiring to improve. Without additional training, they are not necessarily competent to make recommendations about how other schools and teachers, in circumstances that may be quite different from their own, can make the most effective changes.

The associations' standards themselves are so general that no inferences can be drawn about whether students actually achieve the eight outcome goals for which schools and other institutions should be held accountable. For example, the North Central and Southern associations' teaching and learning category includes whether a school "develops and implements curriculum based on clearly-defined expectations for student learning; promotes active involvement of students in the learning process, including opportunities for them to explore application of higher order thinking skills...; gathers, analyzes, and uses data and research in making curricular and instructional choices; monitors school climate and takes appropriate steps to ensure that it is conducive to student learning."[435] Other regional associations have similar expectations.[436]

The accreditation process today plays an important role in the self-improvement processes of many schools. The requirement for a year or more of self-study prior to an accreditation visit focuses the attention of many schools' teachers and leadership on areas where reform is necessary. The observations and recommendations of visiting teams often reinforce this process and provide useful feedback to school staffs seeking to improve. The more objective judgments of professional peers provide important information and advice to other educators who may be too close to problems in their own schools to see clearly how to solve them. Pressure to meet professional peers' expectations spurs genuine reform in American schools today.

But important though self-improvement and peer review might be, these are not the same as an accountability system, which involves meeting the expectations not of peers but of the American public and its political leaders for satisfactory outcomes in the eight goal areas. Both forms of evaluation are necessary. Formalized peer review through the accreditation process, invaluable though it may be, cannot substitute for public accountability.

Yet the accreditation system includes many elements that could easily be adapted for accountability purposes. Or, because duplicate reviews for self-improvement and accountability purposes would be unwieldy, the accreditation process itself, with some modification, could be transformed into elements of an accountability system. The regional associations' standards would have to be aligned with specific cognitive and behavioral outcomes – the eight goal areas of education – to which we expect schools to contribute. The associations would have to develop measurement tools to assess whether accredited schools actually made the appropriate contributions to outcomes in the eight goal areas. True accountability would make accreditation mandatory, not voluntary; outside intervention would have to accompany serious warnings that might lead to loss of accreditation.

For such adaptation of accreditation for accountability purposes, the associations would require tax support and budgets large enough to conduct school visits more frequently and to employ trained professional evaluators, not volunteers from neighboring schools – although there is no reason why volunteers could not also serve as observers on visiting teams. For accountability reviews, volunteer observers should also include members of the public, such as local business, civic, or political leaders. Exposing the process to public scrutiny in this way would give it much needed credibility.

International models

Other nations use inspections for school accountability, and they manage to overcome the more serious impediments experienced in the U.S. in using the accreditation model for accountability purposes.

An English system, for example, relies upon professional inspectors, not volunteers. The inspection system continually undergoes revision; the following pages describe the English inspectorate as it existed until 2005, when a major revision commenced.

An independent government department, the Office for Standards in Education (Ofsted), oversees education accountability. In the early part of this decade it had a corps of about 6,000 inspectors who visited schools and provided reports on their quality. Most inspectors, usually retired school principals or teachers, were directly employed by a dozen or so firms with which Ofsted contracted to conduct the inspections. An elite group, about 200 of "Her Majesty's Inspectors" (HMIs), were employed directly by Ofsted and oversaw the entire process. Ofsted trained the contracted inspectors, required them to attend annual retrainings, and certified them prior to employment. Ofsted also assured the reliability of judgment by having several inspectors judge the same educational activity and then comparing their ratings. Ofsted monitored the inspectors' work and removed those whose quality was inadequate – for example, those who never found lessons to be unsatisfactory.[437]

To ensure quality, the leader of each team underwent a higher level of training than the other team members, and an HMI sometimes also participated in each larger team of contracted inspectors. Ofsted also required each team to include one lay inspector, often a retiree from another profession, to give the inspections greater credibility with the public. It seemed to have worked out that way in practice; as they gained experience, many lay inspectors came to be highly regarded by educators.[438] Each inspection resulted in a report published on the Internet within three weeks; the report was mailed to every parent, with photocopies also made available to the public.[439] In the case of schools that persistently failed to pass inspection, local governments assumed control and, in the most serious cases, closed them.[440]

Professional inspections are costly. A similar inspection system in the U.S., relative to our larger school system, would require nearly 50,000 professionally trained inspectors. In England, the cost of regular school inspections represented about one-quarter of 1% of all government spending on education in 2003, when inspections were conducted for each school every five to six years (but with more frequent inspections for schools found to be inadequate).[441] In American terms, this model would require an expenditure of about $1.3 billion annually.

The English system continually evolves. HMIs have been inspecting schools since 1839, but prior to 1993 all inspectors were employed directly by the government, there were fewer of them, and inspections were irregular. The inspectors then were concerned both with giving advice about school improvement and with public accountability for school quality, but the emphasis was on advice.[442] In 1993, with greater public concern about accountability, the focus shifted, and inspectors were prohibited from giving advice.[443] After several years the pendulum swung back, and inspectors again played the roles of both advisors and evaluators.[444] But because the inspectors were professionally trained, balancing these roles was less difficult than it is for the volunteer members of American accreditation teams. A typical full-time English inspector may have visited from 15 to 30 schools each year, and part-time inspectors (usually retired principals) may have visited seven or eight.[445] Because of this experience and their training, English inspectors were highly respected by teachers and principals, who were thus more likely to take inspectors' advice seriously and consider inspectors' evaluations as legitimate.

After the system was revised in 1993, Ofsted gave schools a year or more of notice for an upcoming inspection, and, like the American accreditation system, schools then spent the intervening period in self-evaluation and preparation. Ofsted concluded, however, that the lengthy advance notice did more harm than good; although it was useful to have faculties reflect on their own practices, the year-long preparation was stressful and distracting for school staffs.[446] Ofsted inspectors also found themselves observing scripted lessons, prepared especially for the inspection period.[447] In 2000, Ofsted reduced the advance notice period to a maximum of two-and-a-half months, and in 2005 to only two days[448] In 2008, Ofsted announced that it would begin experimenting with no-notice inspections, and this may become the rule for all schools.[449]

Thus, although Ofsted encourages school faculties to continue to engage in ongoing reflection and self-improvement, and it provides them with forms and materials to assist in this process, preparation of elaborate self-study documents in advance of an inspection visit is no longer part of the process.[450] School faculties find this less stressful and distracting, and the inspectors have more confidence that they are seeing typical instruction.

Over time, Ofsted became more flexible about the frequency of inspections. They initially were every six years, and were then mostly reduced to every three.[451] As the system developed, schools with a history of very high ratings were visited less frequently, with smaller teams, and without every classroom and teacher visited. Schools with a history of poor ratings were visited more often and more intensively.[452]

Ofsted inspections have also differed from American accreditation visits in other ways. Until 2005, Ofsted inspectors were required to spend most of their time observing classroom teaching, interviewing students about their understanding, and examining random samples of student work.[453] Ofsted inspectors decided which students to interview and which classrooms to visit at any particular time.[454] Thus, there was less danger of Ofsted inspectors being presented with unrepresentative work, visiting unrepresentative classrooms, or being presented with atypical students to shadow. Unlike American accreditation teams, they spent relatively little time meeting with administrators. Ofsted inspectors did, however, require principals to accompany them on some classroom observations, after which the inspectors asked the principals for their own evaluations of the lessons. In this way, the inspectors were able to make judgments (which became part of their reports) about the competence with which the principals supervised instruction.[455]

English inspections until 2005 also differed from American accreditation in that there was no ambiguity about whether a school's goals were those of the public or of the school's faculty. When English school faculties conduct their own self-evaluations using Ofsted forms, the standard was whether schools met national goals, not faculty-determined ones.[456] There are certainly advocates in England who urge that school faculties should establish, as in the American system, their own expectations of progress, and that inspections should be for the purpose of evaluating whether these expectations are being met and whether schools are pursuing strategies appropriately aligned with their own expectations. But Ofsted has been clear that this is not the purpose of inspection: "a self-selected approach to self-evaluation would fail to give users comparative information about different providers and thus would appear to run counter to the principles of accountability for equity, entitlement and achievement in a publicly-funded education service."[457]

From 1993 to 2005, Ofsted's contracted inspectors observed every teacher in each school, evaluating pupil achievement in all academic as well as in non-cognitive areas.[458] Both academic and non-academic outcomes were also reviewed in inspections prior to 1993, when the government inspected schools directly. Until 2005, Ofsted inspectors rated everything they observed, including teaching skill, student participation, achievement, and academic progress, on a seven-point scale, with supporting paragraphs justifying the ratings. They also wrote reports on student assemblies, playground practice, school cafeteria quality, student behavior in hallways, the range of extracurricular activities, and the quality of physical facilities.[459]

Test scores in math and reading played a role in inspectors' school evaluations, but not the only role. In recent years, Ofsted's focus on broader goals of education has been maintained, and in some ways it has intensified. Ofsted also now inspects early childhood care providers and vocational education programs, and then evaluates how well schools coordinate their own programs with such services. When possible, Ofsted conducts inspections of schools and of other child and welfare services in the same community simultaneously.[460]

Ofsted reports have also evaluated not only how well schools teach academic knowledge and skills but personal development: "the extent to which learners enjoy their work, the acquisition of workplace skills, the development of skills which contribute to the social and economic well-being of the learner, the emotional development of learners, the behaviour of learners, the attendance of learners, the extent to which learners adopt safe practices and a healthy lifestyle, learners' spiritual, moral, social, and cultural development, [and] whether learners make a positive contribution to the community."[461]

Ofsted has made no effort to produce fine rankings of schools by which the public could judge each school in comparison to all others. Rather, Ofsted reports whether schools fall into three categories: those that pass inspection, those in need of fairly modest improvements, and those requiring serious intervention to correct deficiencies.

In addition to regular school inspections, the English system has also included special inspections to evaluate particular problems or curricular areas – for example, music instruction, physical education, the underachievement of minority students, or disparate punishments meted out to them.[462] For these, HMIs visited only a representative group of schools. There were enough of these special inspections, however, that schools were likely to have experienced an inspection for some purpose more frequently than was required by the regular schedule.[463]

As noted, the Ofsted system is in flux, and it is too soon to evaluate recent changes in the inspection system. In 2005, the government began to inspect most elementary schools using only a single inspector and for only a single day, although team inspections of large high schools, lasting several days, continue. Partly, inspections were shortened because of insufficient staff and budget; once Ofsted was assigned the responsibility of inspecting early childhood, after-school, and adult education programs as well as schools in a community, too few inspectors may have been available for multi-day school inspections. In addition, Ofsted apparently concluded that its previous more rigorous process was no longer necessary to assure school quality. Today, only schools requiring serious intervention ("special measures") are visited more extensively. As noted above, Ofsted has reduced the advance notice given to schools, and may soon eliminate it entirely. Beginning in 2009, schools not requiring special measures will again be visited only once every six years, not once every three. Lay inspectors have been eliminated. Training of inspectors has been assigned to the contractors. And self-evaluation has re-emerged in importance, with Ofsted providing lengthy forms for school staffs to complete.[464]

Ofsted will no longer rate a school as satisfactory solely because of exceptional performance on personal development measures if the school's test scores are poor; satisfactory measured academic performance is necessary. But a school with satisfactory academic performance may still be assigned special measures if its personal development indicators are poor. Data on academic performance are risk-adjusted for pupils' socioeconomic background, race, and ethnicity, so Ofsted's standard implicitly varies by the difficulty of the educational task.[465]

Ofsted's published school reports, which previously detailed each school's performance in each subject area and aspect of personal development, now only summarize schools' evaluations and are quite brief. **Figure G** illustrates the standard form

With only a single day or two of inspection by a single inspector, these judgments must necessarily be superficial. Some critics now charge that, because Ofsted no longer devotes the time to investigate a broad range of outcomes and school quality – inspectors can no longer observe even academic lessons in depth – the office has come to rely too heavily on test scores and self-evaluation

FIGURE G Inspection judgments, U.K. Office for Standards in Education (Ofsted)

Key to judgments: grade 1 is outstanding, grade 2 good, grade 3 satisfactory, and grade 4 inadequate.	School overall
Overall effectiveness	
How effective, efficient, and inclusive is the provision of education, integrated care, and any extended services in meeting the needs of learners?	
Effective steps have been taken to promote improvement since the last inspection	Yes/no/ NA
How well does the school work in partnership with others to promote learners' well-being?	
The effectiveness of the foundation stage [early childhood preparation]	
The capacity to make any necessary improvements	
Achievement and standards	
How well do learners achieve?	
The standards reached by learners	
How well learners make progress, taking account of any significant variations between groups of learners	
How well learners with learning difficulties and disabilities make progress	
Personal development and well-being	
How good is the overall personal development and well-being of the learners?	
The extent of learners' spiritual, moral, social, and cultural development	
The extent to which learners adopt healthy lifestyles	
The extent to which learners adopt safe practices	
How well learners enjoy their education	
The attendance of learners	
The behavior of learners	
The extent to which learners make a positive contribution to the community	
How well learners develop workplace and other skills that will contribute to their future economic well-being	

continued on next page

forms to evaluate schools. Consequently, gaming the accountability system by "teaching to the test," the critics say, has become more widespread.[466] Her Majesty's Chief Inspector Christine Gilbert has acknowledged the criticisms and announced that new quantitative measures to supplement test score data are

FIGURE G (cont.) Inspection judgments, U.K. Office for Standards in Education (Ofsted)

Key to judgments: grade 1 is outstanding, grade 2 good, grade 3 satisfactory, and grade 4 inadequate.	School overall
The quality of provision	
How effective are teaching and learning in meeting the full range of learners' needs?	
How well do the curriculum and other activities meet the range of needs and interests of learners?	
How well are learners cared for, guided, and supported?	
Leadership and management	
How effective are leadership and management in raising achievement and supporting all learners?	
How effectively leaders and managers at all levels set clear direction leading to improvement and promote high quality of care and education	
How effectively leaders and managers use challenging targets to raise standards	
The effectiveness of the school's self-evaluation	
How well equality of opportunity is promoted and discrimination tackled so that all learners achieve as well as they can	
How effectively and efficiently resources, including staff, are deployed to achieve value for money	
The extent to which governors and other supervisory boards discharge their responsibilities	
Do procedures for safeguarding learners meet current government requirements?	Yes/No
Does this school require special measures?	Yes/No
Does this school require a notice to improve?	Yes/No

Note: A row relating to private boarding schools has been deleted.

Source: Clark 2008.

being developed on which to base school evaluations. These measures will include data such as the percentage of students who are obese, pregnant, use drugs, or respond to surveys saying they are bored in school.[467]

It is too soon to judge the validity of these recent criticisms, whether Ofsted will be successful in developing additional measures to diminish the importance of testing, or whether the distraction and stress previously associated with the self-evaluation process will reappear. But if the charges of excessive testing turn out to be unfounded, it will have been remarkable that a very tough inspection regime lasting only 12 years (from 1993 to 2005) was sufficient to re-establish the confidence of government leaders and the voting population in the performance of public education in England, thereby making a less intrusive process now politically feasible. Clearly, the American school system does not have that degree of credibility today; we can benefit from study of Ofsted as it operated prior to 2005.

Other nations – Scotland, Wales, and Northern Ireland, as well as the Netherlands, the Czech Republic, Belgium, Portugal, France, and New Zealand – have systems similar to England's.[468] In most cases, inspectors also combine the roles of evaluator and advisor. Other details vary. In the Netherlands, for example, regular school inspections take place more frequently, once a year, but are more superficial, lasting only half a day, with a more intensive, two-day visit every fourth year; schools found to be in need of improvement are visited more frequently and intensively. With this schedule, inspectors can visit only some classes in most schools. Like the English, the Dutch publish a school report after each visit, available on the Internet.[469]

New Zealand has also struggled with the tension between inspections for accountability and inspections for advice and improvement. Until 1993, the national Department of Education sent out school inspectors who combined both roles. Because the inspectors were agents of the department, they could not only evaluate schools but also order additional funds to be allocated if this seemed justified, or even have incompetent teachers dismissed. The inspectors were highly respected former educators whose advice generally seemed to be appreciated by school faculties.[470]

In 1993, however, because political leaders felt that schools were underperforming and the inspectors were too lax, a new Educational Review Office (ERO) was charged with sending teams to evaluate schools, and the teams were prohibited from giving advice. The ERO teams observed classrooms and made public its judgments of school quality. The focus was not on outcomes as such, but on whether schools taught the appropriate nationally mandated curriculum and were organized to deliver this curriculum in an efficient manner.[471] In 2001 the ERO concluded that its prohibition on teams giving advice was a waste of expertise; the advisory function was reinstated.[472]

Although New Zealand has no national standardized tests to inform judgments about school quality, it does have a national assessment, very similar to the early NAEP, which discloses national trends. Called the New Zealand National Education Monitoring Project (NEMP), it covers a broad range of student performance areas, including science, art, data display (graphs, tables, and maps), reading, speaking, music, technology, math, social studies, research skills, writing, listening, viewing, health, and physical education. NEMP administers standardized tests and surveys to nationally representative samples of students, and it employs trained assessors to conduct individual interviews with students in these subject areas. NEMP also videotapes students working collaboratively on projects, creating works of art, or demonstrating physical skills.[473]

But New Zealand authorities have not yet figured out how to merge the information acquired by ERO teams in schools and by the NEMP assessment of national student samples into an integrated accountability system for education.

In the United States, there have been attempts to imitate these foreign inspectorates. In the late 1990s, a student of the English inspection system designed a school visit system for the state of Rhode Island.[474] But with the advent of NCLB, it lost importance as schools came to be judged solely on progress toward universal proficiency levels in math and reading. The Chicago school system hired a former English HMI to design a school review system for the district.[475] New York City hired an Ofsted contractor to visit and evaluate all New York City schools; the evaluations resulting from these visits apparently have credibility with both district administrators and teachers.[476] But these efforts are in conflict with contemporary state and federal accountability standards, which make schools almost exclusively accountable for math and reading test scores. If the accountability judgments of inspectors and the test score requirements are in conflict, it is the test score requirements that now must prevail.

Although England, the Netherlands, New Zealand, and other nations continue to experiment with these approaches to accountability, no nation other than the United States has a school accountability system based exclusively on standardized test scores, nor are the inspection systems of other nations voluntary, as they are here. These international models, however, provide clues about how we can design an American accountability system that tells us whether schools and other institutions of youth development are fulfilling the roles we have assigned to them.

The final chapter brings together such clues, along with elements of early NAEP and contemporary accreditation procedures, to sketch out the design of an accountability system that could ensure that schools and other institutions of youth development perform satisfactorily to achieve the eight broad goals of American education.

CHAPTER 8

An accountability system for schools and other institutions of youth development

This book began by wondering how we can hold schools and other institutions of youth development accountable for fulfilling their public responsibilities. How can we ensure that tax dollars are well-spent to enable young people to achieve the outcome expectations we have established for schools and other public institutions?

It was apparent, however, that first we must ask a prior question – what is it, exactly, that young people should achieve? So the first chapter reviewed the goals of education propounded by thoughtful Americans over the course of two centuries, and concluded that schools and other institutions of youth development should graduate youth with basic academic knowledge and skills, critical thinking ability, an appreciation of the arts and literature, preparation for skilled work, social skills and a good work ethic, good citizenship and community responsibility, and the habits of good physical and emotional health. We surveyed American adults and their elected leaders to confirm that all want these goals to be appropriately balanced. So the question this book proposes became this: how can the public hold schools and other institutions of youth development accountable for this balanced set of outcomes?

We examined contemporary programs, such as state test-based accountability systems and the federal *No Child Left Behind*, that purport to hold educators accountable, and discovered that such programs, based exclusively on test scores of basic skills, corrupt schooling. They create incentives to downgrade many important goals of youth development. They reward schools, and indirectly their teachers, for concentrating only on students whose likely test scores are just below an arbitrary and sometimes fanciful universal proficiency point. They misidentify both failing schools and those that are exemplary.

We found that such corruption is not peculiar to schools and teachers. Other attempts to build accountability systems on quantitative measures alone, whether in health care, labor policy, criminal justice, or the private sector, have been similarly corrupted. If we want to hold any institution accountable for a complex set of outcomes, we need more sophisticated measures than a set of numbers such as test scores.

Chapter 6 showed that this conclusion is not novel. Indeed, when the federal government's National Assessment of Educational Progress was designed in the 1960s and implemented in the 1970s, it embodied many of the characteristics of a sophisticated and balanced accountability system. It combined paper-and-pencil tests with evaluation of youth behavior. It assessed a broad range of goals, similar in scope to the areas that have consistently been important to American citizens and leaders. NAEP later degenerated into a test mainly designed to produce academic test scores largely because Congress, while wanting accountability, was unwilling to appropriate the relatively small sums required to do accountability right.

We also found that, despite frequent calls for schools to be held accountable, a system that is in some respects similar to accountability, but rarely noticed, has slowly developed in most parts of the country over the last 150 years. Called accreditation, its flaws are the opposite of those characteristic of test-based accountability. If standardized testing is too quantitative, accreditation is too subjective. If standardized testing narrows goals only to easily defined basic skills, accreditation broadens them to vague statements of good intentions.

Finally, we learned that other nations have also struggled with accountability for public education. Yet while Americans have relied upon test scores alone – and even worse, cut scores – to judge school quality, others have supplemented standardized testing with school inspection systems that attempt to assess whether students are developing a balanced set of cognitive and non-cognitive knowledge and skills. In particular, Her Majesty's Inspectors in England hold schools and other social welfare institutions accountable for education and youth development.

To fulfill our desire to hold American schools and their supporting public institutions accountable, it makes sense to design a system that draws upon the best elements of standardized testing, early NAEP, school accreditation, and the inspection systems of other nations. So we conclude here by suggesting what such a model might comprehend. It is not our intent to present a fully developed proposal; that is a task for policy makers, public officials, and citizens. We only hope to provoke discussion about accountability that will help to move

American policy beyond the trap into which an exclusive reliance upon narrow standardized testing of basic skills has led.[477]

State- or federally based accountability?

The accountability system we suggest, the mechanism for ensuring that schools produce satisfactory outcomes in the eight goal areas established by democratic decision making, assumes that such accountability should be a state, not federal, responsibility. Not only do we have a constitutional tradition of state control of education, but the failure of *No Child Left Behind* has made it apparent that in this large country, the U.S. Congress and Department of Education are too distant to micromanage school performance. Policy debates in education somehow become more ideologically polarized and less pragmatic when they move from state capitals to Washington. When exchanging ideas about educational improvement, and even when jointly resisting federal blunders, Republicans and Democrats are better able to work together in the National Governors' Association, the Education Commission of the States, and the National Conference of State Legislatures, than in Congress. At the federal level, ideological polarization destroyed attempts in the early 1990s to develop voluntary national standards in American history, mathematics, and reading. Although such polarization has sometimes interfered with standards development at the state level, it has done so less frequently and less consistently across the states. Despite the inability to develop national academic standards, many educators consider the academic standards developed by several states in recent decades to be quite good.[478]

Reliance on state governments, not Washington, to establish specific accountability procedures, and renouncing federal micromanagement of school accountability, will require many advocates of school reform to abandon a cherished myth: that only the federal government can protect disadvantaged minorities from Southern states' indifference. The myth is rooted in an isolated fact: in the decade following the 1954 *Brown v. Board of Education* Supreme Court decision, and then in the decade following Lyndon Johnson's 1964 landslide presidential election, all three branches of the federal government forced states to respect rights not only of African Americans but also of disabled and immigrant children.

But this period was unique. At other times, the federal government has been no defender of the disadvantaged. In the early 20th century, state governments enacted minimum wage, health, and safety laws, only to see them struck down by the Supreme Court. Today, Southern states' attempts to improve education are often impeded by federal policy. In 2007, school integration efforts of a Southern border city like Louisville were prohibited by federal courts; throughout the administration of George W. Bush, administrative agencies blocked local integration efforts. Administration officials argued that the NCLB-granted rights of students to transfer from schools failing to meet the law's targets should trump the school integration orders of federal courts. Civil rights divisions of the Departments of Education and Justice and the federal Civil Rights Commission have often been more interested in protecting the interests of white students denied the benefits of affirmative action than of promoting compensatory programs for disadvantaged students. The rhetoric of *No Child Left Behind* was a conspicuous exception although, as we have seen, by creating incentives for schools to narrow the curriculum for children most at risk of failure, NCLB may have resulted in greater inequality.

Many continue to believe that federal action is necessary to force states of the old Confederacy to advance the interests of disadvantaged children. Yet in recent decades, the Southern Regional Education Board – a consortium of state education officials from the old Confederacy (and border states) – has been a national leader in raising educational standards.[479] Universal pre-kindergarten made its debut in Georgia, where over two-thirds of all 4-year-olds, regardless of family income, are now enrolled.[480] The other state with the highest share of 4-year-olds in pre-kindergarten is Oklahoma. Of the five states guaranteeing pre-kindergarten for all children, four (Florida, Georgia, Oklahoma, and West Virginia) were either Confederate states or, in the cases of Oklahoma and West Virginia, territories claimed by the Confederacy.[481]

Texas has led the way in holding schools accountable for raising the basic skills of minority students, although its testing obsession has distorted the goals of education. And unlike federal policies that claimed to mimic Texas reforms, the state complemented test-based accountability with programs to help disadvantaged students improve their performance. Reforms successfully demanded by Ross Perot and other Texas business leaders in the 1980s included finance reform that made spending of high-poverty and low-poverty school districts more equal; higher qualifications for teachers; the requirement that academic success be a prerequisite for varsity sports; smaller class sizes in the early grades; and subsidized pre-kindergarten for children from low-income families.[482] Although some credible analysts are critical of Texas' educational quality, others – including Achieve, the national organization of governors and corporate executives that advocates higher educational standards – have praised Texas for having among the best educational standards in the nation.[483] We need not determine which group is correct to conclude that Congress will not necessarily improve Texas schools by imposing its own judgment on the quality of Texas school reforms.

North and South Carolina, Tennessee, and Arkansas have had nationally known "education governors" (Jim Hunt and Mike Easley, Richard Riley, Lamar Alexander, and Bill Clinton and Mike Huckabee) who, whatever the merits of their policies, can hardly have been accused of caring less than congressional politicians about the quality of education for minority students. Mississippi is the site of several creative programs to boost the performance of African American children – Robert Moses' Algebra Project, the University of Mississippi's Barksdale Reading Institute, and Mississippi Public Broadcasting's "Between the Lions" programming.[484] These efforts do not require the oversight of federal officials to ensure that attention is paid to disadvantaged children.

The greatest potential for further educational improvement in the South today lies in boosting African American voting participation, not in more federal mandates. At this writing in the summer of 2008 it is too early to say, but one of the lasting impacts of Barack Obama's presidential campaign may be a greater commitment of states with newly mobilized black voting populations to the improvement of their educational and youth development institutions.

We can also be confident that particular states need no federal prod for higher achievement because our survey of the American public demonstrates a remarkable national consensus across every region in support of a balanced set of outcomes for schools and other institutions of youth development. **Table 4** displays the views of a representative sample of American adults in each of nine regions on the relative importance of each of the goals of education. The lack of regional variation is remarkable.

If with the demise of NCLB school accountability again becomes a state, not federal, role, two tasks remain that only the federal government can perform. These are prerequisite to an accountability system that ensures we are raising the performance of disadvantaged children – and of middle-class children as well.

The first federal task: interstate fiscal equalization

The first federal task is making certain that all states have the fiscal capacity to support adequate schools and other institutions of youth development. Consider one of the most extreme cases, Mississippi: no matter how deep the commitment of its leaders may be to improving achievement, its tax base is too small to raise revenues in the way that wealthier states can do, while its challenges – the number of its low-income minority children relative to the size of

TABLE 4 Relative importance of goals of education, national random sample of American adults, by region,* 2005 (in percent)

	New England	Mid-Atlantic	East-North Central	West-North Central	South Atlantic	East-South Central	West-South Central	Moun-tain	Pacific
Basic academic skills	22	20	19	21	20	21	19	21	19
Critical thinking	16	17	16	16	16	16	15	16	16
The arts and literature	9	9	8	8	8	7	8	9	8
Preparation for skilled work	10	11	12	11	11	10	11	9	10
Social skills and work ethic	13	13	15	14	14	13	15	13	14
Citizenship	10	10	10	11	10	12	10	11	10
Physical health	10	10	10	10	11	12	11	10	11
Emotional health	10	10	10	10	10	9	10	9	11
Total	100	100	100	100	100	100	100	100	100

* Samples were not large enough to generate state-level results, nor were they large enough for regional results for school board members, state legislators, or school superintendents. The state components of regions are: New England, CT, MA, ME, NH, RI, VT; Mid-Atlantic, NJ, NY, PA; East North Central, IL, IN, MI, OH, WI, West North Central, IA, KS, MN, MO, ND, NE, SD; South Atlantic, DC, DE, FL, GA, MD, NC, SC, VA, WV; East South Central, AL, KY, MS, TN; West South Central, AR, LA, OK, TX; Mountain, AZ, CO, ID, MT, NM, NV, UT, WY; Pacific, AK, CA, HI, OR, WA.

Source: Jacobsen 2007.

its population – are much greater than those of many states that are considered more progressive.

For the last 30 years, reformers concerned with inadequate resources devoted to the education of disadvantaged children have directed attention almost entirely to intrastate equalization – trying to see that districts serving poor students have as much if not more money to spend as districts serving middle-class children in the same state. These reformers have largely ignored the vast resource inequalities that exist between states. Yet about two-thirds of nationwide spending inequality is between states and only one-third is within them.[485] Efforts to redistribute education funds within states cannot therefore address the most serious fiscal inequalities. In general, fewer dollars are spent on the education of the wealthiest children in Mississippi and Alabama than on the poorest children in New York or New Jersey.

It is politically tough to fix this, because sensible redistribution, with aid given to states in proportion to need and in inverse proportion to capacity, must take tax revenues from states like New Jersey (whose representatives tend to favor federal spending) and direct them to states like Mississippi (whose representatives tend to oppose it).[486] Nonetheless, it is unreasonable to expect states that lack sufficient resources to hold their schools and other institutions of youth development accountable for adequate and equitable performance in each of the eight goal areas.

It is not a novel idea that the federal government's role should be to assist low-wealth states to develop the fiscal capacity to provide adequate education. In a 1948 debate about federal aid to education, Senator Robert A. Taft, then leader of conservative Senate Republicans, asserted that the poor education of children in some states was "not the fault, necessarily, of the States where they lived, but rather, of the financial abilities of the States." Senator Taft proposed "Federal assistance, particularly for those states which today are considered below the average of wealth in the United States."[487] A dozen years later, when Congress was again struggling with a proposal for federal aid to education, a task force commissioned by newly elected President John F. Kennedy proposed a federal grant that would be restricted to those states where per capita personal income was below 70% of the national average.[488]

Yet federal aid to education takes us in the opposite direction. Washington exacerbates inequality in states' fiscal capacities. Federal school aid – to districts serving poor children – is proportional to states' own spending.[489] New Jersey, which needs less aid, gets more aid per poor pupil than Mississippi, which needs more. No attempt to hold schools and other institutions of youth development accountable for better outcomes can be credible unless the federal government does something to address this inequality in fiscal capacity.

The second federal task: gathering valid and reliable state-level information with NAEP

The second critical task for the federal government should be the gathering of valid and reliable information on the relative performance of students in the different states. One helpful aspect of *No Child Left Behind* was the requirement that every state participate in NAEP reading and math assessments for the fourth and eighth grades every two years. Because these are the only assessments administered in common to representative samples of students in all states, they provide a way to compare how each state ensures that its elementary school children gain these two academic skills. In designing state-level accountability systems, legislators and governors can examine these results to compare the effectiveness of their education and youth development policies.

To spur effective state-level accountability, the NAEP state-level sample assessment should be modified and expanded:

Representative student samples should be assessed at the state level and on a regular schedule, not only in math and reading but in other academic subject areas – science, history, other social studies, writing, foreign language – as well as in the arts, citizenship, social skills, and health behavior. As in early NAEP, these assessments should include paper-and-pencil test items, survey questions, and performance observations.

Better demographic data are needed for NAEP samples. NAEP collects background information on students who take its tests, but unsystematically. Some characteristics are collected for some tests and years, other characteristics for others. NAEP has collected systematic demographic data from its samples only for race, Hispanic ethnicity, and free or reduced lunch eligibility. The range of characteristics within these categories is wide. For example, first- and second-generation Hispanic immigrant children are in different circumstances from those who are third generation and beyond, and students eligible for free meals come from families that may be considerably poorer than those in the reduced-price program. Since 2000, NAEP has collected data on maternal educational attainment, and it would be relatively easy to collect a few other critical characteristics – most notably family structure (e.g., single parent) and the country of mother's birth. Such data can be collected by schools upon a child's initial enrollment and become part of a student's permanent record. Adding these demographic characteristics to state-level NAEP may require minimal expansion of sample sizes, but the payoff to this relatively modest expansion would be substantial, and it would facilitate the ability of state leaders to draw valid conclusions about their policy needs.

This seems straightforward, but despite the fact that NAEP reports no student-level data, there is pressure from those (many from the far right-wing) concerned about student privacy to restrict and even eliminate the collection of background information on the NAEP sample. This has led the National Assessment Governing Board (which oversees NAEP) to seek ways to narrow, not expand, such information, although scholars press NAGB in the other direction.[490]

NAEP scores can and should be reported on scales, not achievement levels. Reports of average scale scores at different points in the distribution, such as quartiles, can be published in language easily understandable by the public. State policy makers should then be interested in how the average scale scores of students in each quartile of each relevant demographic subgroup compare with scores of similar students in other states. State officials can then take steps to ensure that their states are not making progress in a distorted fashion – for example, by extraordinary improvement of students in the top quartile but inadequate improvement of students in the bottom one. Successful progress should then be judged by whether such average scores in each achievement quartile make progress toward the scores of comparable students in better-performing states. Because an expanded NAEP would abandon the reporting of ill-considered achievement levels (that were based on fanciful definitions of appropriateness, not feasibility), there would be no all-or-nothing cut scores implied. There would then be no "bubble" of students just below such cut points, and teachers and schools would have no incentive to concentrate instruction only on these students. All students should be expected to make progress.

NAEP should return to age-level, not grade-level, sampling. States vary in the typical ages of students in the same grades. In recent years, many states and districts have changed their policies on social promotion, exacerbating the extent to which grades include children of different ages.[491] States also have changed their eligibility dates for kindergarten, sometimes for pedagogical reasons and sometimes in response to population changes that lead to overcrowding or underutilization of classroom space. Some states and districts permit parents to delay their children's start in school if the parents believe the children are too immature to begin kindergarten at the designated time. And a few students with disabilities are difficult to categorize by grade level.

Early NAEP understood this. It sampled 9-, 13- and 17-year-olds, not fourth, eighth, or 12th graders. Once NAEP randomly identified a school for sampling, it selected the desired number of students of the appropriate ages to be assessed, regardless of the grade to which those students happened to be assigned.

Age-level assessment is the only way to get an accurate reading of the relative effectiveness of state education and youth policies. With the current grade-level assessment, one state's eighth-grade scores may be higher than another's only because more low-performing seventh graders were held back, not because its ultimate outcomes are superior. If 13-year-olds were assessed regardless of grade, this distortion would be avoided. NAEP should return to age-level sampling so that results from states with different promotion and school-age policies can accurately be compared.

A switch back to age-level sampling in NAEP need not mean that states' own tests used for school-level accountability must necessarily be standardized for age, not grade level. Because states, if they choose, can standardize school entry ages and social promotion policies, grade-level test results are less subject to misinterpretation if confined to particular states. States have an interest in using tests to determine if mandated grade-level curricula are being implemented successfully. Provided that NAEP assesses samples of students of the same age, not grade, we will have the data we need to understand if the combination of age-to-grade policies in some states are more effective than they are elsewhere.

In-school samples should be supplemented by out-of-school samples. As early NAEP understood, the best evidence of the quality of our education and youth development policies is the performance of 17-year-olds, for whom states are completing their normal institutional responsibility, and of young adults, to see whether knowledge and skills developed earlier are being retained. To get representative samples of 17-year-olds and young adults, assessments should include an out-of-school household survey. As is the case for 9-, 13- and 17-year-olds who are still in school, these out-of-school assessments should cover each of the eight broad goal areas.

As a measure of state and local policy effects, the young adult assessments should be sufficient. However, if leaders observe that their state is lagging behind in specific outcomes, young adult assessments give insufficient guidance about reforms to be undertaken. If, for example, a state learns that its third-generation Hispanic young adults have higher rates of obesity than those in other states, it can only conclude that its elementary school physical and health education programs may have been inadequate 10 or even 20 years earlier. Or if a state learns that its young adults generally participate in public affairs less often than those in other states, it can also only conclude that its elementary school civics curriculum or cooperative learning pedagogies may have been inadequate many years before. These programs may have improved (or deteriorated) in the meantime. Therefore, to inform an accountability system, states also require information on whether current programs are following best practices, that is, those likely to lead to adequate and equitable outcomes in the eight goal areas. Although good test scores for 9-, 13-, and 17-year-olds don't necessarily guarantee an educational and youth development program that leads to adequate adult outcomes, they are among the best approximate indicators we can develop to that end. Regardless of adult outcomes – which reflect education of a previous generation – the unacceptability of a state's results for young children is an indication that policy reform is in order.

Dramatic expansion of NAEP in this fashion need not have the harmful effects that standardized testing under contemporary state and federal accountability policies has produced. Incentives for teachers to "teach to the test" are avoided because NAEP is a sampled assessment, with particular schools rarely chosen, only a few students in those schools assessed, and those students given only portions of a complete exam. There are no consequences for students or schools who do well or poorly, because results are generated only at the state level; nobody knows how particular students or schools performed. Because an expanded NAEP should assess the full range of cognitive and non-cognitive knowledge and skills encompassed by the eight broad goals of education, NAEP can give state policy makers and educators no incentives to ignore untested curricular areas to concentrate on the tested ones.

NAEP and state policy

With this expanded NAEP, what should governors and state legislators do if they learn that their state's average scale scores, or their scores at particular points in the achievement distribution, in one or all of the eight goal areas, for young adults, students, or some subgroup of these, were below those of comparable young adults or children in other states? State policy makers should examine whether fiscal stress was responsible for their state's relatively poor performance. What matters here is states' comparative taxable wealth and concentration of disadvantaged students. If a state with fiscal capacity and demographic adversity similar to another's had less adequate youth outcomes because the more poorly performing state had made less of a fiscal effort (for example, by having lower tax rates), the governor and legislature should consider whether the mix of policy reforms should include raising revenue to the level of comparable states where outcomes were better.

Next, faced with poorer NAEP average scale scores in one or more goal areas, one or more age groups, and one or more demographic subgroups, state policy makers should consider whether more investment and/or smarter spending (i.e., different policies) are required in the state's various institutions of education and youth development – public elementary and secondary schools; children's health care; early childhood programming; preschool; parental support and education programs; after-school and summer programs;

community redevelopment policies designed to stabilize neighborhoods, promote desegregation, and reduce student mobility; and perhaps others.

No research presently exists by which governors and state legislators can determine what proportion of investment should be directed to each of these institutional areas and, given present levels of spending, where reform is most needed. Some scholars and advocates now believe that early childhood programming should be the priority.[492] Others place the greatest emphasis on downsizing or reform of high schools, or on improving the quality of teachers serving disadvantaged children.[493] Others find that differences in the health of disadvantaged and middle-class children are associated with a substantial part of the achievement gap between them.[494] Until we have better research in this area, governors and state legislators will have to use their best judgment, informed by expert advice, to make decisions about the relative impact of different institutional emphases. Certainly, if some states show improvement in a balanced set of outcomes after particular policy interventions, other states should take notice.

State accountability policies for schools and supporting institutions

An expanded NAEP can tell governors, legislators, and citizens the extent to which their states are doing an adequate job of generating student success in each of the eight goal areas. Then, citizens and state policy makers can use this information for guiding the refinement of state policy. They will want to ensure that particular schools and school districts, children's health care institutions, early childhood and preschool programs, parental support and education programs, after-school and summer programs, and community redevelopment agencies are contributing to, not impeding, the achievement of such success. This requires ways for state government to hold these school districts, schools, and other supporting institutions accountable:

State testing should cover all eight goal areas of public education to avoid the goal distortion that results from accountability only for a few basic skills. The early NAEP and New Zealand's NEMP each provide examples of the types of questions that can be employed to measure individual student performance in all eight goal areas. Many standardized tests in subjects other than math and reading now exist, but few include the kinds of constructed response items, similar to the items found on NAEP exams, that assess critical thinking in these subjects. Certainly higher-quality academic tests in history, writing, the sciences, and other academic areas should be deployed, as should standardized assessment instruments, where possible, in non-academic areas. For example, instruments exist that can assess a student's upper-body strength and, combined with data on the student's weight and height, inform the evaluation of a school's physical education program.[495]

Standardized test scores should be used very cautiously to judge schools, and only in combination with other data. If states tests are improved, as they should be, to include higher-quality items that cannot be machine scored, the precision with which the tests can be scored will decline. Many schools are too small to generate highly reliable results for particular age groups even on existing low-level tests of basic skills. With more complex items included, reliability for precise evaluation will decline further.

Information from standardized tests should be supplemented by expert evaluation of student work. Even the most sophisticated test questions are not fully adequate to reveal students' abilities. NAEP exams include a large number of constructed response items, in which students are not given multiple choices but must work out factual or prose answers on their own. But even these questions are no substitute for expert examination of drafts and redrafts of student essays for evidence of how students respond to critiques of their initial efforts and how they develop themes that are longer than those of a brief constructed response on an exam.

State testing systems should also collect richer background information on students, to make test score comparisons meaningful. As more states develop good student data systems, with unique student identification numbers and maintenance of cumulative records for each student in secure school databases for the student's entire school career, it will become easier to attach richer background information to student assessment results for purposes of analysis. As one example, schools already know which students are eligible for free meals and which are eligible only for reduced-price meals. Yet in their school "report cards," many (but not all) states and school districts combine these categories, rendering them less useful for understanding and comparing student performance. It would be a simple matter for elementary schools to record, upon a student's initial enrollment, not only the student's subsidized lunch eligibility but also the educational attainment of the mother, whether the mother was born in the U.S., and the number of parents or other responsible adults in the student's household.

States should abandon the inherently flawed attempt to establish absolute cut scores, or proficiency-level goals, for student achievement. Goals are valuable, but they should always be feasible, not fanciful. With appropriate controls for background characteristics, states can establish goals based on the performance of other states for students with similar characteristics. Such goals should be established not only for average performance but also for NAEP performance at the higher and lower ends of the student achievement distribution. For example, in a ranking of states (including the District of Columbia) where 51 was the poorest and 1 the best, a state that found itself ranked 40th in the achievement of one of the goals for a particular demographic subgroup might aim to improve achievement for that group so that its level was comparable to that in a state that presently ranked 35th. If all states regularly established and revised such realistic goals, it would result in a permanent process of continuous improvement.

But test scores and evaluation of student work, even for larger schools, and even when connected to more nuanced student background characteristics, are of only partial value. A full accountability system requires evaluation of student performance in areas more difficult to standardize (for example, cooperative behavior) and judgment about whether a school's curriculum and instruction, along with a community's other institutions of youth development, are likely to generate balanced and adequate outcomes in the eight goal areas.

Adapting inspection models to the American context

To supplement test scores and evaluation of student written work, states wanting to hold school districts, schools, and supporting institutions accountable require an accreditation system that is more similar to English school inspections in the first half of this decade than to existing regional accreditation procedures. Perhaps existing accreditation agencies can evolve into ones that hold schools and other institutions of youth development accountable for balanced achievement. Such evolution would require these changes:

Mandatory inspections (or accreditation visits) should be conducted in each school and in each related community institution (children's health care services, early childhood and preschool programs, parental support and education programs, after-school and summer programs, and community development agencies) approximately once every three years. Where feasible, accreditation of all these institutions in a particular community should be coordinated.

School inspections should be designed to determine primarily whether students are achieving adequate outcomes in the eight goal areas of American education, not whether schools are meeting the idiosyncratic goals of their faculties and administrations. Accreditation teams should judge whether schools are achieving in these eight goal areas at levels achieved by higher-performing schools with similar demographic characteristics. Such a standard necessarily will lead to continual improvement by all schools.

Most inspectors on accreditation teams should be professional evaluators, not volunteers, trained to ensure consistency of judgment, and certified as competent by state (or regional) accreditation agencies.

Most school inspectors should be professional educators by background and training, but accreditation teams should also include members of the public, representatives of the business community, or designees of elected officials. Not only would such participation give inspection greater public credibility, but these members, with their varied backgrounds and perspectives, may detect aspects of school quality requiring improvement that may not be apparent to professional educators. Inspection teams reviewing other community institutions of youth development should be similarly constituted with professional and lay members.

School accreditation visits should take place with little or no advance notice, and inspectors should have access to all classrooms for random observation. Likewise, inspectors should choose random students to invite to interview, and whose work to review. An analogy is financial auditing, where accountants have unquestioned access to all supporting documentation.

Accreditation teams should include in their reports an evaluation and interpretation of schools' standardized test scores, but should supplement this by examining student work, listening to student performances, observing student behavior, and interviewing students to gain insight into their knowledge and skills.

Inspectors should make clear recommendations about how curriculum, instruction, or other school practices should be reformed if they find a school's performance to be inadequate in one or more goal areas. Although schools may choose not to follow the specific advice of accreditation inspectors, subsequent inspections (more frequent than once every three years in cases where performance is inadequate) should determine whether performance has improved and, if not, why schools did not follow recommendations for improvement. Inspections of other community institutions should employ similar procedures.

Accreditation reports should be made public, and in a timely fashion. Reports should include responses by administrators or teachers to inspectors' criticisms.

Accreditation should have consequences. States should assume direct control of schools and other public institutions of youth development when improvement does not follow repeated failed accreditation reports. If existing faculty and administration prove incapable of implementing a recommended reform program, states should replace them.

The cost of accountability

This chapter's goal is only to begin a discussion, not set forth a detailed plan. Its theme is that the American public has a right to hold schools and other institutions of youth development accountable for achieving adequate and equitable outcomes in the eight broad goals of American education. This right to accountability can be realized if the federal government ensures that each state has the fiscal capacity to provide adequate education and other youth services, and if the federal government expands NAEP to provide state policy makers with information on the achievement of their states' young adults and 17-, 13-, and 9-year-olds in these eight broad areas.

With this federal support, states can design accountability systems that include academic testing in core subject areas and in those non-academic fields where standardization is possible, such as health awareness and physical fitness. State accountability systems can supplement such testing and provide detailed school-level data by use of accreditation procedures that ensure that adequate performance in each of the eight goal areas is achieved, and that schools and other institutions of youth development implement strategies likely to improve that performance.

Such an accountability system would not be cheap. But neither would it be so expensive that this proposal is unrealistic, as the following "back-of-the-envelope" estimate shows. At present, the federal government spends about $40 million to administer a state-level NAEP exam in math or reading for the fourth, eighth, and 12th grades. Assessing 9- 13- and 17-year-olds in sampled schools rather than fourth, eighth, and 12th graders could add a little but not much to the cost (because, for example, a few 13-year-olds might be found in high schools, not middle schools). Design costs (including substituting new items as old items are rotated out) also add relatively little. Expanding samples so that state-level information can be disaggregated into finer demographic subgroups also adds relatively little. Adding additional academic and non-academic subjects (history, writing, other social studies, science, foreign language, health knowledge, physical fitness, understanding of the arts and vocations) at the state level need not duplicate the full cost for each subject if only paper-and-pencil items are used, because NAEP could use many of the same schools that it samples for math and reading. There would, however, be additional costs for preparing test booklets that included sophisticated multi-color maps or art reproductions. Adding performance and other non-traditional items that can easily be standardized (for example, tests of upper-body strength or identification of musical themes) would incur substantial additional expense. As a very rough estimate, expanding regular state-level NAEP into all eight goal areas and into all subject areas within the academic categories, and administering such assessments every three years, with appropriate subgroup reporting, might cost a total of $500 million annually.

A revived NAEP for young adults and 17-year-olds, requiring an out-of-school household survey conducted once every three years, might cost as much as an additional $20 million annually.

As noted in Chapter 7, England's school inspection system cost about one-quarter of 1% of total elementary and secondary school spending at a time when inspections in each school took place approximately every six years. If we assume a similar ratio for a reformed accreditation system in the U.S., with accreditation teams visiting schools approximately every three years, the annual cost would be about $2.5 billion, or one-half of 1% of current federal, state, and local spending on elementary and secondary education. Additional costs would be incurred for accrediting other institutions of youth development.

Even with the additional costs of an expanded in-school state NAEP, and of a young adult and 17-year-old out-of-school state NAEP, the total cost of the accountability system we have outlined here would still be no more than 1% of total elementary and secondary public school spending in the U.S. This is not an unreasonable price for an accountability system that measured whether schools in every state, in coordination with other institutions of youth development, were preparing young adults to have adequate academic knowledge and skills (basic and critical thinking), appreciation of the arts and literature, preparation for skilled work, social skills and work ethic, citizenship and community responsibility, physical health, and emotional health. If this system succeeded in correcting even some of the incompetent practices in schools and other institutions that do not presently fulfill these goal objectives, the gains in efficiency would more than justify this expenditure. When accountability funds are spent correctly, they eliminate waste and save funds.

But saving money, probable though that might be in the long run, is not the primary purpose of an accountability system. If we truly want to hold institutions accountable for fulfilling the missions to which they have been assigned by the nation, and if we are determined to reverse the corruptions we have visited on schools by narrow test-based accountability policies, we should willingly entertain a system of accountability that might require higher expenditures in the short run.

To sum up

We should get the federal government out of the business of monitoring education at the school or student level. The federal government will have enough to do if it provides states with information about achievement in all eight goal areas, and if it ensures that states have adequate resources to pursue all eight, for all students. With adequate information and resources, states can develop the testing and inspection systems that ensure accountability of schools and other institutions of youth development for achieving these outcomes. Some states will do a better and some a worse job of this. Citizens who want to demand better school performance should direct their attention to state capitals, not to excessively politicized Washington policy makers.

Throughout our history as a nation, Americans have been committed to a broad range of academic and behavioral goals for the public schools. But our ability to achieve these goals was corrupted by *No Child Left Behind* and similar state accountability programs that rely primarily on short-term test score measures of basic skills. Evidence of such corruption should not be surprising. Similar problems have often been documented in other public sectors and in private industries that have attempted to hold their agents accountable for narrow quantitative output alone. Even in education, the shortcomings of such measures were recognized; this is why the early developers of the National Assessment of Educational Progress included student surveys, interviews, and observations of student interaction to supplement quantitative testing. But accountability done right seemed expensive, and funds for these additional measures were cut from the NAEP budget.

For an accountability system that recognizes the broad range of outcomes to which we expect schools to contribute, we can revisit these early NAEP insights. We can also draw inspiration from elements of the voluntary accreditation system that has developed over 150 years here in the United States and from the school inspection systems that have been developed in England and other nations.

Learning from these other experiences with accountability, both here and abroad, in public education and in other sectors, states can develop a new accountability system to provide the public and policy makers with needed information about student growth and progress. The federal government can ensure that states have the fiscal capacity to achieve the goals we set for our youth, and can measure the extent to which states are doing so. By coupling an expanded federal NAEP with state-directed school inspections, we can be sure that all children are making progress in all the goal areas of public education. While such a system of accountability would not be inexpensive, it would be worth every penny.

No Child Left Behind gave accountability a bad name. An alternative program along the lines suggested here can redeem accountability's reputation. And it can give the citizens of this nation a better means to fulfill our responsibilities to provide for our youth and the nation's future.

APPENDIX 1

Schools as scapegoats*

Education is the answer. But what's the question? Simple: what's the cure for any adverse economic condition?

Is your pay stagnant or declining? Quick, get more education.

Are workers failing to share in economic growth? Too bad, they should have gained more skills.

Are you worried about jobs offshored to low-wage countries? Blame schools for workers' lack of creativity.

Is the nation failing to compete globally? Raise education standards across the board.

Education as the cure-all is everywhere around us. But this contention exaggerates the role of schools in the economy, and it conflates two issues: First, how can American firms increase productivity to improve their ability to compete in the world? And second, how have the fruits of U.S. productivity growth been distributed, and what explains rising inequality?

Education can help in the first area, although it is far from a silver bullet. As to the second, education deficits have had little to do with the changes in the distribution of wages. Fortunately, after more than two decades, the education-as-panacea argument is being overwhelmed by contradictory evidence. Perhaps we may now be able to face more clearly the separate challenges of enhancing competitiveness and reconnecting the link between productivity growth and pay.

The modern obsession with schools as the cause and cure of our economic problems began with President Ronald Reagan's 1983 report, *A Nation at Risk*. Increased market shares for Japanese automobiles, German machine tools, and Korean steel, the report charged, reflected the superior education of workers

---

* This appendix, co-authored by Lawrence Mishel and Richard Rothstein, is reproduced with minor modifications from *The American Prospect,* October 12, 2007.

in those nations: "Our once unchallenged preeminence in commerce, industry, science, and technological innovation is being overtaken by competitors
throughout the world....The educational foundations of our society are presently being eroded by a rising tide of mediocrity that threatens our very future
as a Nation...."[496]

In 1990, a group of prominent Democrats and Republicans, calling themselves the National Center on Education and the Economy, followed with
another report, *America's Choice: High Skills or Low Wages.*[497] It saw skills development as virtually the only policy lever for shaping the economy. It charged
that inadequate skills attained at flawed schools had caused industrial productivity to "slow to a crawl" and would, without radical school reform, lead to
permanently low wages for the bottom 70% of all Americans.

Public intellectuals such as Robert Reich focused attention on human capital solutions in a laissez-faire global system. In his book, *The Work of Nations,*
Reich argued that international competition would be won by nations with the
most (and best) "symbolic analysts," not "routine" workers.[498] Lester Thurow's
book, *Head to Head,* forecast that Western Europe would come to dominate
the United States and Japan because European schools were superior.[499] Many
mainstream economists, both liberal and conservative, agreed that rising wage
and income inequality were caused by an acceleration of "skill-biased technological change," meaning that computerization and other advanced technolo-
gies were bidding up the relative value of education, leaving the less-skilled
worse off.

Yet the response of American manufacturers to these analyses was curious.
Automakers moved plants to Mexico, where worker education levels are considerably lower than those in the American Midwest. Japanese manufacturers
pressed their advantage by setting up non-union plants in places like Kentucky
and Alabama, states not known for having the best-educated workers. But high
school graduates in those locations apparently had no difficulty working in
teams and adapting to Japanese just-in-time manufacturing methods.

The ink was barely dry on the *America's Choice* report when Americans'
ability to master technological change generated an extraordinary decade-long
acceleration of productivity in the mid-1990s, exceeding that of other advanced countries. It was accomplished by the very same workforce that the
experts claimed imperiled our future. Productivity advances created new wealth
to support a steady increase in Americans' standard of living.

And for a brief period, standards of living did increase because the fruits
of productivity growth were broadly shared. As **Figure A-1** shows, the late
1990s saw increasing wages for both high school and college graduates.[500]

FIGURE A-1 The productivity-pay gap: hourly productivity and real average wage growth, 1990-2006

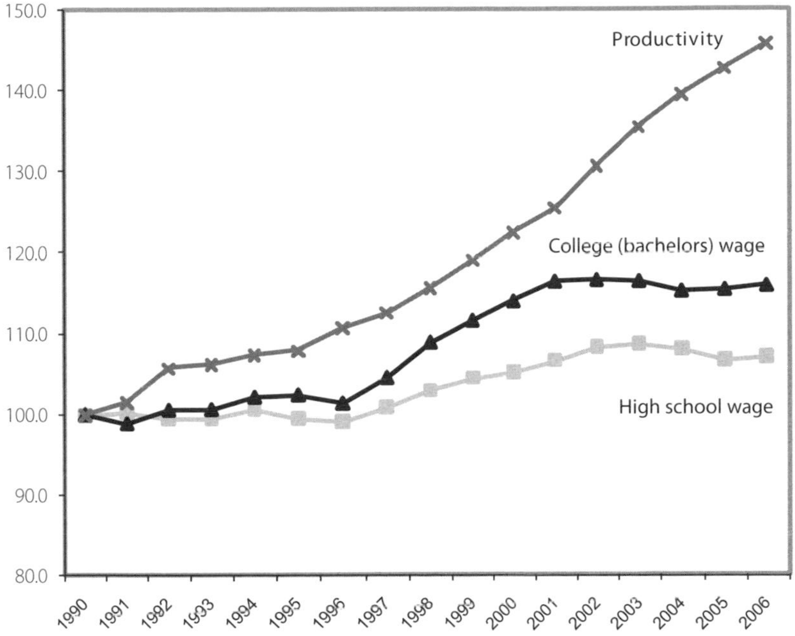

Source: Mishel, Bernstein, and Shierholz 2008.

Even wages of high school dropouts climbed. But no presidential commissions or distinguished experts were praising American education for producing widely shared prosperity. Instead, denunciations of public schools increased in intensity, often tied to calls for their privatization with vouchers.

Then, the collapse of the stock bubble in 2000, the recession of the early 2000s, and the intensification of policies hostile to labor brought wage growth to a halt. Living standards again began to decline and inequality zoomed – at the same time that workforce productivity continued to climb. White-collar offshoring to India, China, and other low-wage countries signaled that globalization was now taking its toll on computer programmers and other symbolic analysts of the information age.

Today, however, a new cast of doomsayers has resuscitated an old storyline, picking up where *A Nation at Risk* left off. Forgetting how wrong such analyses were in the 1980s and 1990s, the contemporary cliché is that however good schools may once have been, the 21st century makes them obsolete. Global competition requires all students to graduate from high school prepared either for academic college or for technical training requiring an equivalent cognitive ability. We can only beat the Asians by being smarter and more creative than they are.

The argument got a boost from *New York Times* columnist Thomas Friedman's 2005 book, *The World Is Flat,* and has been repeated by the same National Center on Education and the Economy in *Tough Choices or Tough Times,* a sequel to its 1990 report.[501] The argument has also garnered support from influential foundations (Gates, for example, and its chairman, Bill Gates) and from education advocacy groups (such as the testing organization ACT).

The *Tough Choices* report bemoans the fact that "Indian engineers make $7,500 a year against $45,000 for an American engineer with the same qualifications" and concludes from this that we can compete with the Indian economy only if our engineers are smarter than theirs. This is silly: no matter how good our schools, American engineers won't be six times as smart as those in the rest of the world. Nonetheless, Marc Tucker, author of *Tough Choices* (and president of the group that produced the 1990 report as well), asserts, "The fact is that education holds the key to personal and national economic well-being, more now than at any time in our history."[502]

Administration officials blame workers' education for the middle-class income stagnation that has occurred on President Bush's watch. Treasury Secretary Henry Paulson contends that "market forces work to provide the greatest rewards to those with the needed skills in the growth areas. This means that those workers with less education and fewer skills will realize fewer rewards and have fewer opportunities to advance."[503] Former Federal Reserve Chairman Alan Greenspan frequently blamed schools for inequality: "We have not been able to keep up the average skill level in our workforce to match the required increases of increasing technology...."[504]

This view can be found on both the Republican right and the Democratic center. The American Enterprise Institute's Frederick Hess and former Clinton White House domestic policy staffer Andrew Rotherham jointly write in an AEI article that "study after study shows an America unprepared to compete in an increasingly global marketplace."[505] They note that the urgent "competitiveness agenda" could be derailed if we focus instead on equity-improving outcomes for disadvantaged students. Avoiding this requires attention to be turned to further improving the technological savvy of those already primed to succeed.

University of Chicago economists Kevin Murphy and Gary Becker (a Nobel laureate) recently wrote that there is an "upside" to income inequality because it encourages more people to go to college. They warn that raising taxes on high-income households and reducing them on low-income households is tantamount to "a tax on going to college and a subsidy for dropping out of high school."[506] In this way of thinking, preserving the Bush tax cuts is the way to stimulate college enrollment.

But these 21st century claims are as misguided as those of the last century. Of course we should work to improve schools for the middle class. And we have an urgent need to help more students from disadvantaged families graduate from good high schools. If those students do so, our society can become more meritocratic, with children from low-income and minority families better able to compete for good jobs with children from more privileged homes. But the biggest threats to the next generation's success come from social and economic policy failures, not schools. And enhancing opportunity requires much more than school improvement.

The misdiagnoses of the early 1990s were understandable. When *America's Choice* was written, when the Reich and Thurow books were best-sellers, American productivity growth had, indeed, stagnated. These authors could not have known that explosive growth was just around the corner. But today's education scolds have no such excuse. Workforce skills continue to generate rising productivity. In the last five years, wages of both high-school- and college-educated workers have been stagnant, while productivity grew by a quite healthy 10.4%.

Rising workforce skills can indeed make American firms more competitive. But better skills, while essential, are not the only source of productivity growth. The honesty of our capital markets, the accountability of our corporations, our fiscal policy and currency management, our national investment in research and development and infrastructure, and the fair play of the trading system (or its absence) also influence whether the U.S. economy reaps the gains of Americans' diligence and ingenuity. The singular obsession with schools deflects political attention from policy failures in those other realms.

But while adequate skills are an essential component of productivity growth, workforce skills cannot determine how the wealth created by national productivity is distributed. That decision is made by policies over which schools have no influence – tax, regulatory, trade, monetary, technology, and labor market policies that modify the market forces affecting how much workers will be paid. Continually upgrading skills and education is essential for sustaining growth as well as for closing historic race and ethnic gaps. It does not, however, guarantee economic success without policies that also reconnect pay with productivity growth.

American middle-class living standards are threatened not because workers lack competitive skills but because the richest among us have seized the fruits of productivity growth, denying fair shares to the working- and middle-class Americans, educated in American schools, who have created the additional national wealth. Over the last few decades, wages of college graduates overall have increased, but some college graduates – managers, executives, white-collar sales workers – have commandeered disproportionate shares, with little left over for scientists, engineers, teachers, computer programmers, and others with high levels of skill. No amount of school reform can undo policies that redirect wealth generated by skilled workers to profits and executive bonuses.

College graduates are, in fact, not in short supply. A background paper for the *Tough Choices* report (but not one publicized in the report itself) acknowledges that "fewer young college graduates have been able to obtain college labor market jobs, and their real wages and annual earnings have declined accordingly due to rising mal-employment."[507] In plain language, many college graduates are now forced to take jobs requiring only a high school education.

In many high school hallways you can find a chart displaying the growing "returns to education" – the ratio of college to high school graduates' wages. The idea is to impress on youths the urgency of going to college and the calamity that will befall those who don't. The data are real – college graduates do earn more than high school graduates, and the gap is substantially greater than it was a few decades ago (see **Figure A-2**).[508] But it is too facile to conclude that this ratio proves a shortage of college graduates.

Statistically, the falling real wages of high school graduates has played a bigger part in boosting the college-to-high-school wage ratio than has an unmet demand for college graduates. Important causes of this decline have been the weakening of labor market institutions, such as the minimum wage and unions, that once boosted the pay of high-school-educated workers.

For the first time in a decade, the minimum wage was recently increased. The curious result will be a statistical decline in "returns to education." But we should not conclude from a minimum wage increase that we need fewer college graduates, any more than we should have concluded from falling wages for high school graduates that college graduates are scarce and schools are failing.

Another too glib canard is that our education system used to be acceptable because students could graduate from high school (or even drop out) and still support families with good manufacturing jobs. Today, those jobs are vanishing,

FIGURE A-2 Returns to education: the college/high school wage premium, 1973-2007*

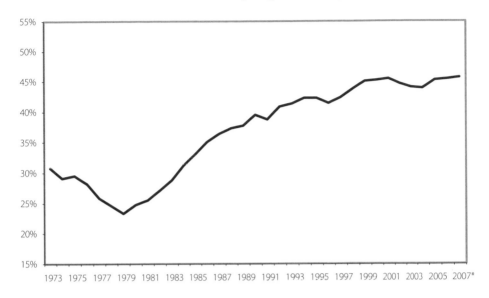

* 2007 first half
Source: Authors' analysis of CPS ORG.

and with them the chance of middle-class incomes for those without a good education.

It's true that many manufacturing jobs have disappeared. But replacements have mostly been equally unskilled or semiskilled jobs in service and retail sectors. There was never anything more inherently valuable in working in a factory assembly line than in changing bed linens in a hotel. What made semiskilled manufacturing jobs desirable was that many (though not most) were protected by unions, provided pensions and health insurance, and were compensated with decent wages. That today's working class doesn't get similar protections has nothing to do with the adequacy of its education. Rather, it has everything to do with policy decisions stemming from the value we place on equality. Hotel jobs that pay $20 an hour, with health and pension benefits (rather than $10 an hour without benefits), typically do so because of union organization, not because maids earned bachelor's degrees.

It is cynical to tell millions of Americans who work (and who will continue to be needed to work) in low-level administrative jobs and in janitorial, food-service, hospitality, transportation, and retail industries that their wages have stagnated because their education is inadequate for international competition. The quality of our civic, cultural, community, and family lives demands school improvement, but barriers to unionization have more to do with low wages than does the quality of education. After all, since 1973 the share of the workforce with college degrees has more than doubled; over 40% of native-born workers now have degrees beyond high school. Additionally, the proportion of native-born workers that has not completed high school or its equivalent has decreased by half to just 7%.

Indeed, Becker's and Murphy's own data confirm what our chart shows: the wage gap between college- and high-school-educated workers was flat from 2001 to 2005. However, inequality surged in this period, a fact that can't be explained by something that didn't change. Moreover, other industrialized countries have seen a more rapid growth in college completion than the United States has, yet those nations accomplished this educational growth without increasing inequality.

Fortunately, the elite consensus on education as a cure-all seems to be collapsing. Offshoring of high-tech jobs has deeply undercut the Clinton-era metaphor of an education-fueled transition to the information age, since it is all too apparent that a college education and computer skills do not insulate Americans from globalization's downsides. Former Clinton economic advisor (and Federal Reserve vice chairman) Alan Blinder has emerged as an establishment voice calling attention to the potentially large-scale impact of continued offshoring. Blinder stresses that the distinction between American jobs likely to be destroyed by international competition and those likely to survive is *not* one of workers' skills or education. "It is unlikely that the services of either taxi drivers or airline pilots will ever be delivered electronically over long distances....Janitors and crane operators are probably immune to foreign competition; accountants and computer programmers are not."[509]

A growing number of other mainstream economists now also caution that blaming inadequate schooling for falling living standards and growing inequality might be too simplistic. In a series of papers, David Autor, Larry Katz, Melissa Kearney, Frank Levy, and Richard Murnane, mainstream Cambridge, Massachusetts-based economists who promoted the story of a technology-based transition to the 21st century, now have revised their account.[510] They assert that, prior to the 1990s, technology increased demand for more-educated workers across the board, but that now there is "polarization," where technology disadvantages middle-skilled workers relative to those with both more and less education. Their finding severely undercuts the suggestion that upgrading human capital is the solution to inequality.

Alan Greenspan's successor as Federal Reserve chairman, Ben Bernanke, has also adopted a less simplistic analysis. While concurring that skills matter, Bernanke also observes that a poorly educated workforce cannot explain "why the wages of workers in the middle of the distribution have grown more slowly in recent years than those of workers at the lower end of the distribution, even though, of the two groups, workers in the middle of the distribution are typically the better educated."[511]

Prominent free-trade economists now also acknowledge that education reform cannot address Americans' economic insecurity nor solve globalization's political problems. In a recent analysis prepared for the financial services industry, two prominent former Bush administration economists (Grant Aldonas and Matthew Slaughter) and one from the Clinton administration (Robert Z. Lawrence) wrote that, since 2000, "only a small share of workers at the very high end has enjoyed strong growth in incomes. The strong U.S. productivity growth of the past several years has not been reflected in wage and salary earnings, and instead has accrued largely to the earnings of very high-end Americans and to corporate profits. The bottom line is that today, many American workers feel anxious – about change and about their paychecks. Their concerns are real, widespread, and legitimate....For college graduates and those with non-professional master's degrees, this poor income performance is a new and presumably unwelcome development."[512]

And Robert Reich no longer believes that being a symbolic analyst is adequate income protection. He now blogs, "The only people who are getting much out of this economy are in the top one percent – earning over $800 grand a year. They're taking home almost 20% of total income. Back in 1980, the top one percent took home 8% of total income."[513]

In a paper recently posted on the National Bureau of Economic Research's website, Massachusetts Institute of Technology economists Frank Levy and Peter Temin wrote, "The current trend toward greater inequality in America is primarily the result of a change in economic policy that took place in the late 1970s and early 1980s." They went on to say that "the recent impacts of technology and trade have been amplified by the collapse of these institutions," by which they mean the suppression of unions and the abandonment of the norm of equality.[514]

These are not problems that can be solved by charter schools, teacher accountability, or any other school intervention. A balanced human capital policy would involve schools, but would require tax, regulatory, and labor market reforms as well. To take only one example, in the daze of college-for-all, what used to be called "vocational" or "career" education has been discredited. It should be brought back. We recently analyzed a group of 21st century occupations not requiring a college education that, at least for the time being, still provide middle-class incomes. These include firefighters, electricians, machinists, aircraft engine mechanics, electronic technicians, licensed practical nurses, and clinical laboratory technicians. We found that white non-college youth were 50% more likely to land one of these "good" jobs than black non-college youth. Equalizing this access will require a combination of stepped up antidiscrimination efforts, job placement services, and skills training directed at schools serving minority youth.

In their paper posted on the website of the National Bureau of Economic Research, Levy and Temin conclude, "No rebalancing of the labor force can restore a more equal distribution of productivity gains without government intervention and changes in private sector behavior."

We agree.

APPENDIX 2

A Broader, Bolder Approach to Education*

The *No Child Left Behind* law, passed with bipartisan support in 2002 and now up for reauthorization, assumes that ineffective schools are *the* major reason for low student achievement. It also presumes that higher standards for students and teachers, frequent testing, better teacher training, and accountability can eliminate achievement gaps between disadvantaged and advantaged students.

Some schools have demonstrated unusual effectiveness. But even they cannot, by themselves, close the entire gap between students from different backgrounds in a substantial, consistent, and sustainable manner on the full range of academic and non-academic measures by which we judge student success.

Reducing social and economic disadvantages can also improve achievement. But national and state policy has mostly failed to act on this understanding.

As the limitations of a "schools-only" approach become more obvious, it is time to rethink our assumptions. We propose a **Broader, Bolder Approach** that can realistically boost disadvantaged students' achievement.

While continuing to press for school improvement, our proposed **Broader, Bolder Approach** also promotes high-quality early childhood programs and preschool, after-school and summer opportunities. Along with improving test scores, it also emphasizes physical health, character, social development, and non-academic skills. It prizes traits needed for effective citizenship, creativity, and the ability to work in diverse environments.

A **Broader, Bolder Approach** is built around four pillars:

Pursue an aggressive school improvement strategy, including ensuring smaller classes in early grades for disadvantaged children; attracting high-quality teachers

---

* This statement appeared as a paid advertisement in the *New York Times* and *Washington Post*, June 10, 2008 and remains available at www.boldapproach.org.

to hard-to-staff schools; improving teacher and school leadership training; making a college preparatory curriculum accessible to all; and paying special attention to recent immigrants.

Provide developmentally appropriate and high-quality early childhood, preschool and kindergarten care and education that promotes not just academic readiness but positive lifetime social, economic, and behavioral outcomes for low-income children.

Address children's health, including routine pediatric, dental, hearing, and vision care for all infants, toddlers, and schoolchildren to minimize health problems that impede school success. Full-service school clinics can overcome the absence of primary care physicians in low-income areas and address poor parents' inability to miss work for children's routine health services.

Improve the quality of out-of-school time. Low-income students learn rapidly in school but often lose ground after school and during summers. Successful out-of-school and extended day programs not only focus on remediation but also provide cultural, organizational, athletic, and academic enrichment that middle-class children routinely enjoy.

This **Broader, Bolder Approach** applies equally to federal, state, and local policy.

Test scores alone should not define school effectiveness. New and broader accountability systems are needed to promote more effective school programs. These new systems will be considerably more expensive than the tests currently employed, many of which are seriously flawed.

America's education policy can continue to focus on schools alone and on narrow, test-based accountability – and be content with modest improvements. Or we can ratchet up our ambitions and adopt a broad new strategy to enable all our children to pursue the American dream.

We urge policy makers to embrace this **Broader, Bolder Approach to Education**.

Co-Chairs:

Helen F. "Sunny" Ladd, Duke University

Dr. Pedro Noguera, New York University

Tom Payzant, Harvard Graduate School of Education; former San Diego and Boston schools superintendent., U.S. Assistant Secretary of Education (1993-95)

Task Force Members & Signers:

Paul E. Barton* - Education Testing Service

Julian Bond - Chairman, NAACP

Barbara T. Bowman - Co-Founder, The Erikson Institute

T. Berry Brazelton M.D. - Pediatrician and Author

Richard H. Carmona M.D. - University of Arizona; U.S. Surgeon General (2002-06)

James Comer M.D.* - Yale University

Ernesto Cortes Jr.* - Director, Southwest Industrial Areas Foundation

Mark E. Courtney - Executive Director, Partners for Our Children

Rudolph F. Crew* - Superintendent, Miami-Dade Public Schools

Linda Darling - Hammond Stanford University; Executive Director, National Commission on Teaching and America's Future

John DiIulio - University of Pennsylvania; White House Director, Office of Faith-Based and Community Initiatives (2001)

Jan Harp Domene - President, National PTA

Arne Duncan - Superintendent, Chicago Public Schools

Peter Edelman - Georgetown University Law Center; Assistant Secretary, U.S. Department of Health and Human Services (1993-96)

Joycelyn Elders M.D.* - University of Arkansas; U.S. Surgeon General (1993-94)

Edward B. Fiske* - Journalist; Education Editor, *New York Times* (1974-91)

Milt Goldberg - Policy Consultant; Executive Director, A Nation At Risk commission (1983); Director, Office of Research, U.S. Department of Education (1989-92)

John I. Goodlad - President, Institute for Educational Inquiry

David Grissmer* - University of Virginia

Beverly L. Hall - Superintendent, Atlanta Public Schools

James Heckman - University of Chicago; Recipient, Nobel Prize in Economics (2000)

John H. Jackson* - President, The Schott Foundation; Chief Policy Officer, NAACP (2005-07)

Christopher Jencks* - Harvard University

Sharon Lynn Kagan* - Columbia University; Yale University

Richard Kazis* - Vice President, Jobs for the Future

Henry Kelly - President, Federation of American Scientists

Rev. Dr. Michael Kinnamon - General Secretary, National Council of Churches

Lloyd Kolbe - Indiana University; Director, Division of Adolescent and School Health, U.S. Centers for Disease Control and Prevention (1988-2003)

Karen Lashman* - Vice President of Policy, Children's Defense Fund

Arthur Levine* - President, Woodrow Wilson Foundation

Michael Levine - Executive Director, Joan Ganz Cooney Center at Sesame Workshop

Glenn C. Loury* - Brown University

Robert L. Lynch - President and CEO, Americans for the Arts

Julianne Malveaux - President, Bennett College for Women

Ray Marshall* - University of Texas; U.S. Secretary of Labor (1977-81)

Deborah Meier - Founder, Central Park East Schools

Richard J. Mouw - President, Fuller Theological Seminary

Susan B. Neuman - University of Michigan; Assistant Secretary, U.S. Department of Education (2001-03)

Joseph M. O'Keefe S.J. - Dean, Lynch School of Education, Boston College

Hugh Price* - The Brookings Institution; President, National Urban League (1994-2003)

William Raspberry - Former Columnist, *Washington Post*

Diane Ravitch - New York University; Assistant Secretary, U.S. Department of Education (1991-93)

Janet Reno - U.S. Attorney General (1993-2001)

Norman Rice - Enterprise Community Partners; Mayor, Seattle (1990-98); President, U.S. Conference of Mayors (1995-96)

Julius B. Richmond M.D. - Harvard Medical School; U.S. Surgeon General (1977-81)

Bella Rosenberg* - Policy Consultant; Assistant to Albert Shanker, President of the American Federation of Teachers (1983-97)

Richard Rothstein* - Economic Policy Institute; Education Columnist, *New York Times* (1999-2002)

Robert B. Schwartz* - Harvard Graduate School of Education; President, Achieve (1997-2002)

Ted Sizer - Chairman Emeritus, Coalition of Essential Schools

Marshall S. Smith - Under Secretary, U.S. Department of Education (1993-2001); Dean, School of Education, Stanford University (1986-93)

James Gustave Speth - Dean, School of Environmental Studies, Yale University

William Spriggs* - Chair, Department of Economics, Howard University

Carola Suarez-Orozco* - New York University

Marcelo Suarez-Orozco* - New York University

Mary Catherine Swanson - Founder, AVID (Advancement Via Individual Determination)

Rachel B. Tompkins* - President, Rural School and Community Trust

Jane Waldfogel* - Columbia University

William Julius Wilson - Harvard University

Alan Wolfe - Director, Boisi Center for Religion and American Public Life, Boston College

* Members of the task force who drafted this statement. The task force was convened by:

Lawrence Mishel
President, Economic Policy Institute

A longer version of the statement, also endorsed by the above-listed signers, along with information about how you can join this effort, is available at:

www.BoldApproach.org

APPENDIX 3

Goals survey methodology[*]

Online polling

To administer a poll to representative samples of the four groups (adults over the age of 18, school board members, state legislators, and school superintendents), we commissioned Knowledge Networks (KN), an online polling firm that maintains a nationally representative panel of the American public, accessible via the Internet. KN develops its panel using a conventional random-digit dial (RDD) telephone survey of all U.S. households. Because of the reliance on RDD to develop the panel, cellphone-only households and those without a landline were excluded from the sampling frame. The resulting sampling error is generally the same as those conducted through a more conventional telephone poll.[515]

Knowledge Networks makes an initial contact, and verified telephone numbers are dialed a minimum of 10 times over a 90-day period. Extensive refusal conversion is also completed to ensure that the sample is representative of the country.[516] In this initial contact, interviewers invite households to participate in the online panel. Approximately 56% of contacted households agree to become members of the panel. If the respondent advises the interviewer during the initial recruitment telephone call that the household has a computer and Internet access, the interviewer invites the respondent to participate in a panel to take surveys on the household's own equipment. For households that do not have Internet access, KN installs WebTV hardware to provide Internet access free of charge. Provision of WebTV not only ensures that all contacted households are able to participate, but also is an incentive for respondents.

To maintain panel participation, Knowledge Networks also uses an incentive system that awards points for survey participation, with the points redeemable

---

[*] This appendix is drawn from Jacobsen 2007.

for prizes. For our goals of education survey, however, additional points were not awarded.

The KN panel is representative of the adult U.S. population, with a slight overrepresentation of those in the middle-income categories and slight underrepresentation of those in the upper-income categories. Those over 64 are also somewhat underrepresented. The final sample from the panel was weighted using CPS weights to correct for this underrepresentation.

For our goals of education poll, the KN online panel was used to draw a simple random sample of the general public.

In addition to surveying the general public, we also surveyed samples of state legislators, school board members, and school superintendents. To draw simple random samples, we used membership databases from the National Conference of State Legislators (NCSL), the National School Boards Association (NSBA), and the American Association of School Administrators (AASA). We are grateful to these organizations for making their memberships lists available to us. These database lists became the universe from which to sample.

Final sample sizes were as follows for the questions used in this analysis:

- KN panel of the general public – n = 1,297

- State legislators – n = 191

- School board members – n = 377

- Superintendents – n = 830

Instrument construction

Respondents were presented with eight goals of public education, derived from the authors' analysis of historical documents about the goals of public education. The goals were presented to respondents in random order.

Each goal description was tested in cognitive interviews. Seven members of the Knowledge Networks adult panel and three members of the National School Boards Association population agreed to participate in a one-hour interview. These respondents completed a draft version of the online poll and then provided feedback regarding the clarity of the instrument as well as their understandings of the goal descriptions. This was followed with the fielding of 300 pretests. In addition to the full survey instrument, additional open-ended questions were added to the survey to elicit responses regarding the clarity of the instrument. Eighty pretests from the general public were completed and only three offered a critique of the goal wording. Fifty-five pretests were completed by state legislators and school board members, and three of these respondents also offered critical feedback regarding the goal descriptions. This feedback influenced revisions of the final instrument.

Method – constant sum allocation exercise

The calculations draw upon data obtained through a constant sum allocation exercise where respondents were asked to allocate 100 points across the eight goals. Exact question wording was as follows: "We would now like you to think about how important you feel the following goals are. In this question we would like you to allocate a total of 100 points across the eight goals based on the level of importance you feel each should receive." The online mode supported respondents' accurate completion of this task by alerting respondents if their sums did not total 100. This enabled respondents to revise their responses and resubmit so that errors in addition did not result in the loss of valid responses. The computer system would allow a respondent to move on even if the allocation exceeded 100 points after the respondent clicked "enter" two times. This allowed respondents to complete other portions of the survey even if this section was completed incorrectly. Fewer than 0.1% of all respondents allocated more or fewer than 100 points.

APPENDIX 4

Teacher accounts of goal distortion

For this book, teachers were interviewed teachers about their experiences with goal distortion under federal and state accountability systems. A few of these interviews are summarized in the following pages. The experiences or opinions expressed in these interviews do not purport to be representative, either of teachers in the schools where our interviewees work, of teachers in their districts and states, or of teachers nationwide. The teachers whose interviews we report were self-selected because their experiences illustrate the goal distortion that this book describes. As interview respondents themselves note, some of their colleagues are more favorably disposed toward contemporary accountability.

For representative data, see the report by the Center on Education Policy, described in Chapter 3.[517] The summaries that follow provide anecdotal illustrations of goal distortion documented in the CEP report. The interviews selected for summary below offer particularly vivid examples of the abandonment of non-tested subjects and an unreasonable shift of instruction toward basic skills for disadvantaged students.

Because the writing and research team involved in the preparation of this book had previously written about goal distortion under NCLB,[518] our interpretations were well known. To identify teachers for interviews, we requested referrals from colleagues who were in contact with teachers whose accounts would likely illustrate these interpretations. In some cases, teachers had complained about goal distortion to the National Education Association and, at our request, NEA officials referred them to us. These interviews were mostly conducted during the 2006-07 school year by Jessica Salute, a teacher at P.S. 161 in Manhattan, the Don Pedro Albizu Campos Elementary School. Although we edited our interview notes for space and relevance, each of the interview subjects has approved what follows as an accurate account of his or her interview.

Shari Adams *is an elementary school art education teacher in Prince Freder-*
ick, Calvert County, Md. Over two-thirds of her students are low income;
nearly two-thirds of her students are African American and one-third are
white. She has 14 years of teaching experience.

Many times, kids are removed from art for testing. As far as being an art teacher, I used to see them for an hour a week; now, it's just 45 minutes, and they are
getting pulled out for reading and math because of the increased accountability. Some are hardly getting any access to the arts. They are supposed to
have art 45 minutes each week, but the remedial students are allowed to miss
art, as far as the district policies go. Sometimes I am concerned because the
visual and kinesthetic students are being forced to use only paper and pencil to
show what they know. If you are like that, it won't be revealed in a paper-and-
pencil test. The district is now thinking of starting a written art exam. Doesn't
that leave a lot of learners behind? If there is therapeutic value in art, does a
paper-and-pencil test reveal that? What about reflecting on how it feels? Those
are the immeasurable or intrinsic aspects of art education. They need to touch
the materials, and share. They don't just need to know who painted a famous
painting for the test.

　When they are pulled out of art class, they miss out on learning about tolerance, taking turns, being responsible to clean up and help as a team. I focus on
those lessons more than the art technique every day. They learn as a community,
they learn the give and take, the life skills, the self-expression part. The piece of
paper that we do art with eventually will fall into the trash, but if you felt good
about who you were while you were doing it, and remember and share with others, that's the important lesson. Those are the emotional, social, and functional
skills that I teach.

Missy Beach *is an elementary school teacher in Beaumont, Texas. About half*
her students are African American, and additional students are Hispanic.
Most are low income. She has 20 years of teaching experience.

In the early and mid-nineties, our school had amazing challenge classes and
really neat activities going on all the time. That's why I chose to put my own
children in that school.

　We were studying the parts of the eye when I taught third grade. I got real
deer eyes from a taxidermist and the kids dissected them. When I taught first
grade, I used to do a play on "The Legend of the Blue Bonnet" when we studied
Native Americans. It is an award-winning book that combines the study of Na-

tive Americans and Texas history. The bluebonnet is the Texas state flower. In the last hour of the day we would practice a play based on the book.

We don't do that anymore. Recently, I found some old pictures of a class six years ago putting on the play, and it reminded me of all the things like that we used to do; they took time, but you can't really show a test outcome for them, so we can't do them.

I have been using a classroom management program called "Workshop Way." It has a lot of stuff like jobs or centers around the room, with certain tasks for which the children get a partner.

But when Texas began its standardized test program, we started to have testing every six weeks, and everything got so rigid that we couldn't do any of the neat stuff anymore – there just wasn't any time. We tried to keep doing what we knew was good, but we would get in trouble for not following exactly what we were told to do. I continued to do Workshop Way for a while, but had to hide it from my principal.

There are no art or the novel projects we used to do– we don't have time any more for anything that can't be tested or be put on a scantron [a multiple choice test that can be scored automatically by a scanner]. Even our second graders have to use scantrons.

We used to sit in the lounge to cut out things and laminate, the teachers would visit, the older teachers would help the younger teachers. Teachers don't collaborate now, it's more isolated.

We used to make cute things and celebrate everything – Ground Hog Day, St. Patrick's Day, but not anymore. It made school fun and exciting for children. They learned the rhythm of the seasons and so much social studies and it was creative. No more.

Now, there are daily announcements in the morning: "15 instructional days until TAKS [the Texas standardized test]," "14 instructional days until TAKS," and so on. There is almost nothing left of arts and crafts, especially past first grade. Every day is chock full of TAKS practice books, TAKS blitzes, TAKS tutorials.

History, civics, and fine arts go by the wayside because we are frantically spending their entire day doing drills in the tested areas. In our school, gifted programs have been minimized or done away with, because the main focus of school is now on students at risk of failing the test. Everything is micromanaged and tracked. Across-the-board curriculums are being adopted and everyone must be on the same page, doing the same thing at the same time. Increasingly, the curriculum comes to you in a large box with the exact words you are to say, scripted in the teacher's guide. This is supposedly to guard against the chance of students being "trapped" in a class with an inadequate teacher. My experience has been it makes us all inadequate.

I feel this type of implementation of NCLB is common in schools that deal with minority populations. I had a girlfriend who taught in a rich suburb of Dallas and they did not do all this rigid stuff. They just had to teach TAKS strategies a month or so before the test.

I do think that there needs to be accountability of some sort. It's probably like any profession, you have one or two teachers coasting and who wouldn't show growth. Those teachers, they weren't popular. They ended up with not many kids in their class. It seemed like it worked out. We probably did need some accountability. If they said, "We are going to look at the achievement test at the end of the year and look for growth," that would have been good enough. We did not need to throw out everything else that was going on in schools; so much of it was so good. I am glad my own children have graduated.

Casey Bilger *is a third-grade teacher in Phoenix, Ariz. His students are overwhelmingly low income and Hispanic. He has seven years of teaching experience.*

They don't specifically say, "Don't do science or social studies," but there is no emphasis in those areas. There are strict blocks of time for reading, 90 minutes, each day. Then 60 minutes of writing and 60 minutes of math. In reality, there is no time leftover for anything else. I feel like they are missing out on a lot. I used to teach social studies more my first few years. But as we got closer and closer to being labeled underperforming we had to cut back. Basically, the kids just aren't learning stuff they are supposed to. They aren't learning about government, communities, people, or places. They just aren't getting it in science either. In science, they miss out on group work and hands-on learning. I can't imagine that it won't have effects on them. There are science and social studies materials, but no training on how to use them. However, with reading and math, they just cram training down our throats on how to use it and when to use it. But science and social studies aren't even mentioned.

As far as our state test goes, there is a lot I think kids should know. They kind of are helping the teachers to see their students' progress. In some ways, it whips you into shape. But on the other hand, there is nothing about inquiry, independence, or creativity on the test. It's not important even in reading, writing, or math. They are not learning skills like decision making, independence, or creativity. They don't really get to do art, projects, group work over time, where they have to make decisions together about how to do it. It just doesn't happen anymore. What they want you to do instead is cram one standard after another down their throats. There are too many standards in too short a time. Anything that is interactive, like write a summary about a book or draw a picture, takes too much time. The answer is we don't have time for that anymore.

I notice a change in kids' behavior when the work is really boring. They don't understand the NCLB legislation obviously, so to them it's just boring. Basically, with our kids, I can't even teach it in a fun way, I just have to show them exactly how it will be on the test, what it will look on the test. Boring curriculum becomes behavior problems.

Johanna Brekke-Brownell is a third-grade teacher at an elementary school in Oakland, Calif. She has 19 years of teaching experience. African American and Hispanic students make up less than half of her school's enrollment; Asian students are the largest subgroup. Her school's acceptable test scores do not subject it to sanctions under NCLB, but she previously taught at a school that had not made "adequate yearly progress" for four years. She refers to that school, where over 80% of students were Hispanic or African American, and over 90% were low income, as a "year-4 school."

I have only been at Laurel School two years. It's wonderful because we aren't in trouble. The year before that I was at a year-4 school. The year-4 school had more lower-income students, and more recent Spanish-speaking immigrants. Most of the parents did not have a high school education. The greatest contrast between the two schools was in the way I was treated as an educator by the site and downtown administrators. The biggest problem at the year-4 school was that reading and math were the only things that counted as education. That's according to what the administrators thought. It was a very stilted, recipe-driven instruction. Not that it had any better chance to leading to any success. It led to a lot of fear of the administration; the only way administrators chose to grapple with the task of educating students and leading a school was to try to standardize everything. As the school year progressed, all efforts were focused on creating something new: The first efforts were to do away with the public school and create a charter school. There was no discussion with parents, administrators, and staff about what could make a difference. In isolation, a plan was concocted to dissolve the school and start a new charter. The teachers needed to approve this concept by signing a petition. Only a handful of teachers signed, so then they (site and downtown administrators) essentially got rid of most of us. The next year many first-year teachers were hired for our positions.

On the other hand, I think NCLB has allowed some schools to have a focus. Even though testing is a minimal way of judging, at least it gave a common way of moving forward and encouraging each other. But at the year-4 school, I couldn't truthfully say I was teaching in all the content areas; science and social studies were set aside, because those subjects were not being tested then. This year, at my new school, I have had a lot more flexibility, we – the teachers and site administrators – aren't under so much scrutiny.

When I look back through the years, teachers were accountable for the academic areas in general. But now teachers in Oakland are being directed to teach reading first thing in the day for two-and-a-half hours, and then come back to it after math. You can't change your schedule to allow what your class needs. For instance, if your class has a behavior problem, and you feel like your class needs a community meeting first thing in the morning, you really can't do it.

At the year-4 school, I squeezed in a couple books to read aloud to the class, but I wasn't able to read literature very often. The children are missing out on real literature. The students aren't really reading on their own. They read an Open Court story two or three times but never alone. If you do it that way, your students miss the joy of reading a book for enjoyment. Students are rarely finding out for themselves what a story is all about; they are not experiencing the struggle of understanding the written word. We are feeding them so much; my fear is that that's what they think education is. They aren't going to know that you can just sit and think, "What do I want to find out about? How could I do it?" They are treated like little sponges waiting for us, or not waiting.

And then, as teachers, we are humans, and become creatures of habit as well. We get used to our little pattern, and we stop thinking creatively. Teachers won't think anymore, "Oh it could be done differently." I think this is a problem that's going to really influence teachers in the future and change education for the worse.

As far as field trips, at the year-4 school we could only go on a trip if it tied into the reading theme at that point in the year. A lot of the after-school programs were focused on reading, math, and homework. Maybe the last half hour would be enrichment, art or physical education. I didn't even see a science fair. As rich as the multi-cultural environment was, we didn't do anything multicultural.

Certainly when you aren't building themes, there is a lot less collaboration between teachers. The focus of teacher meetings, particularly in the year-4 school, was always focused on content with a coach. It was always thinking about the basic curriculum and its impact on testing. It was not the bigger picture. We didn't spend time thinking about what our kids should really be walking away with, from elementary school. Or what would make our school a better place. I do feel this year at the new school, we looked at new ways of doing each subject or ways we could bring parents or the community into our school more. In the year-4 school, it seemed teachers and parents felt intimidated, angry, and frightened.

Samantha Cleaver *taught in Washington, D.C. for two years with an alternative certification program, the D.C. Teaching Fellows. She taught special education (a pull-out class of fourth to sixth graders) in a school that was 99% African American, and a kindergarten/first-grade class in a school with a majority of Hispanic students. In both schools, most students were low income.*

Because the focus is on testing and test prep, the purpose of my school was not comprehension or full understanding and expanding students' minds, but how they performed during one week of the year. Though I find standards to be helpful, there doesn't seem to be a lot of wiggle room in what students are taught, especially when it comes to supporting children who are struggling. Some of the students that I taught didn't need as much special education services as we provided; instead, they were in my class because they couldn't keep up with the curriculum, and their teachers didn't have the time to give them special attention. Because it's all about the paper test, my students, who were often talented in other areas, weren't appropriately assessed for their strengths and needs, which left them frustrated.

Science and social studies, art, technology, and music didn't get enough time, and I have yet to see a drama class in a D.C. public elementary school. I think that including those courses could keep kids more interested in their core classes; I know that I was very interested in social studies growing up, and that piqued and maintained my interest in reading.

Paula Dennis *teaches math at a newly constructed middle school in North Portland, Ore. She has taught for 11 years. Nearly half or her students are black (including some African immigrants), about a quarter are Hispanic. Nearly all her students are low income.*

Our school was not built with a gym. Instead we have drama and dance. These two classes are aligned with the reading curriculum to assist students with understanding and comprehension of the stories in their reading program. Teachers are restricted in what and how they can teach – not to say we are told to teach to the test, but we end up teaching to the test, as we want to feel successful, we want our students and their families to feel successful, too, and for our district and school we also have a responsibility. So teachers are leaving out the fluff. We no longer have a morning and afternoon recess, and students come to school stressed with all the testing.

There was once a time when students had time to draw and make collages, and create art projects. Our days are almost planned out for us now. We have minimum math and reading lessons that pretty much take care of our mornings. We have drama and dance in the afternoons. We no longer have the option of teaching geography. Our science is taught for the test and not a specialty area (like rocks, or space, or electricity) that interests the teacher. Having students create art projects that relate to their reading programs would enhance the comprehension and make reading more enjoyable.

One of the benefits of NCLB is just the name. It's powerful to say that no child will be left behind! There are teachers out there, like in any profession, that are not fulfilling their obligations to teach the students what they need to know to be successful. It also has cut some of the fluff from the administration programs and geared more funds towards the front lines – the children.

But besides reading and math, other subjects get less school or district support; the copyright on our encyclopedias is 1992. We don't even have access to the last few presidents. There is a huge push to purchase reading and math programs – however, leisure reading and good-quality children's literature is not deemed as that important.

Social studies and science get a push prior to state testing in those subjects, but throughout the week, our main focus is on reading and math. Some of our fifth-grade students don't even know if Portland is a state or city!

Mary Pat Eul *teaches high school math in Arizona. Three-fourths of her school's students are Hispanic, black, or Native American, and almost half are low income. She has been teaching for 30 years.*

No Child Left Behind has made the math curriculum a mile wide and an inch deep. There are so many requirements put on by the state and NCLB. In Arizona, there are now 143 performance standards. There is no time, you have to keep plowing through because you have to "cover it all." The students might be able to pass the test, but it doesn't sink in, long term.

We don't get to do any of the fun activities anymore. I love math, I couldn't have taught math for 30 years if I didn't, but it's hard to teach the kids to love math now, or make them really learn or retain the material. I have a whole file cabinet of math activities and projects that I call "Fun Stuff." I can't tell you how long it's been since I got to use them.

For example, there is one activity I used to teach trigonometry. The students measure their shadows and use it to measure other things outside. But now, I don't have time to do it. Those kinds of activities may only take a day, but that's too much time. You can't take a day for an activity like that and still cover everything you need to. It's projects that I have to take out of my curriculum. You have to prove that you taught every single standard to each kid. There is no flexibility any more and that's sad as sad can be.

Kids have to pass tests, and if they don't, they are put in an extra math class, instead of getting an elective like art, music, band, marketing, or computer applications. These are courses that all students should take before they leave school. Now they miss out on those subjects because they have to take an extra English or math class. That's where it affects other subjects the most.

Ruth Gregory *teaches in special programs for gifted children at two magnet schools in St. Louis, Mo. About two-thirds of the schools' students are black, and nearly three-fourths are low income. She has been teaching for 18 years.*

No Child Left Behind has completely destroyed everything I ever worked for. I had taught in the gifted program for many years; it was extremely successful and attracted kids to the magnet school. We did Shakespeare plays, science projects – it was a rich, rich program. We won honors trophies, ribbons. Everything changed when NCLB came on board; the school district positioned itself to get Reading First funding and brought in Open Court. When they brought Open Court in, they brought in consultants with it. We now have an enforced 90-minute reading block. Before, we always had that much reading in our schedule, but the difference now is that it's 90 minutes of uninterrupted time. It's impossible to schedule a lot of the things that we had been able to do before.

Each magnet school had its own focus and specialty to attract kids and to desegregate. Now the program is direct instruction, and direct instruction is incompatible with these specialties. It didn't take parents long to figure that out. The magnet schools lost enrollment. If you take 90 minutes of time, and say no kids can come out at that time, you can't fit the drama, band, and other specialized programs in. The strings program at one of my schools was closed. All the violins are in storage. All band instruments are in storage at the other school. There are fewer choices.

I have worked in good schools, but our reading scores have gone down since Open Court. Open Court teaches you how to repeat, not to comprehend. There is a ridiculous emphasis on fluency – reading is now about who can talk the fastest. Even the gifted kids don't read for meaning; they just go as fast as they possibly can. Their vocabulary is nothing like it used to be. We used to do Shakespeare, and half the words were unknown, but they could figure it out from the context. They are now very focused on phonics of the words and the mechanics of the words, even the very bright kids are.

I have seen highly trained special ed teachers who have worked miracles with children, but now they are not allowed to work with their students in small groups for reading. Instead, they have to go into the whole class and become a teacher's assistant to the Open Court program.

The schools do have some science, because we have a standardized state science test. If social studies gets taught, it's a miracle. Every teacher writes it in on their lesson plan, because you have to. But it takes way more than 90 minutes to do the reading activities that are required, so other things have to be cut.

Teachers feel isolated. It used to be different. There was more team teaching. They would say, "Can you take so-and-so for reading because he is lower?" That's not happening. The teachers are incredibly frustrated. The only feedback they get is from consultants who say, "Do you have the poster on the left wall?" or "I noticed on paragraph 3 you said 'was' instead of 'is.'" Teachers feel like they have no support. For each unit assessment, you need the scores of the kids. Teachers take home garbage bags of workbooks each night to grade them because the consultants need all this stuff.

Teachers are as frustrated as I've ever seen them. The kids haven't stopped wetting pants, or coming to school with no socks, or having arguments and fights at recess. They haven't stopped doing what children do but the teachers don't have time to deal with it. They don't have time to talk to their class, and help the children figure out how to resolve things without violence. Teachable moments to help the schools and children function are gone. But the kids need this kind of teaching, especially inner-city kids and especially at the elementary levels.

Nancy Hoffman *is an elementary and middle-school music teacher in Sparks, Nev. Half of her schools' students are Hispanic, and half are low income. She teaches beginning strings in the sixth grade and string orchestra to seventh and eighth graders. She has been teaching for 29 years.*

When the sixth-grade block music program was first started, the students were given 120 minutes of instruction a week, typically three 40-minute classes. When NCLB was implemented, we were told that we could not have that much music at the elementary schools. So at my elementary schools, instrumental music classes were reduced from 120 to 90 minutes a week.

At my middle school different reading programs were introduced to focus on tested subjects and to expose the students to more reading and writing time. The elective offerings have changed dramatically. We used to have a full complement of foreign languages offered. All of those are gone. The drama program was very good – it's gone. We used to have industrial arts – that is gone. The only remaining electives are the choir, band, string, and home and careers classes, but the number of students in the programs has fallen. I used to have as many as 100 students in my music classes and now I am lucky if I have 40 students.

A counselor came into my classroom one day during my string orchestra class to see one of my students. The young man was apparently deficient in math. As a result, he was permanently removed from my class and required to take an extra math class instead of music.

I believe in the importance of reading and math classes, but if students don't also have what speaks to their souls and their hearts, they won't succeed. I have had so many kids come back during or after high school saying they would have dropped out of school if they hadn't had music. The only reason they stayed in school was because they could look forward to going to orchestra everyday and playing their violas.

Joan Lo Curto *teaches in kindergarten and first grade in a high-poverty elementary school in Buffalo, N.Y. Her students are mostly African American, with some Hispanic and immigrant students from Somalia and other countries. Almost all of her school's students are low income. She has 16 years of teaching experience.*

I have an M.A. in teaching reading. I used to use a balanced literacy approach: you do reading and writing and choice reading and comprehension every day. It was very successful. But since NCLB, not only are their reading levels worse, but so is the atmosphere.

The way I used to teach, it was a human way to teach. It was not ability-grouped; everyone was writing and reading everyday. The students felt successful everyday. How they feel about themselves makes a difference in their lives. I was told I am no longer to teach that way. We have purchased a reading program, which is heavily scripted, from Harcourt. For instance, in the first grade, we have to be on the same page on the same day. The district has chosen a very heavily phonics-based philosophy. I have a handful of children who read on second-grade level. I have to cheat to give them more advanced stuff. But the administrators walk around watching you, to make sure you are on the same page for all children.

There used to be a whole block of time for writing. I would model the writing process, I would do a "think-aloud," talk about spelling, grammar, and then the children had time to write themselves. They would develop their own way of using phonics, they were stretching their words. A lot of learning was going on. But now we are really not doing much writing.

And we are not doing science or social studies at all. Teachers take classes here in Buffalo, at the science museum, and we get these wonderful classroom kits that fit the New York State science curriculum. My kits have not even been opened this year! I don't know anyone whose kits are opened. The required block of time is two-and-a-half hours of phonics and remediation and 60 minutes of math. In kindergarten, we literally sent the rugs home, there was no nap time for the kids! I told the principal I thought it was child abuse.

Now, all the children who do poorly on the test have to go on "direct instruction," which has no literature. I don't believe children know what reading is anymore. You aren't even allowed to have read-aloud time. I have to sneak it in.

They are not immersed anymore in any poems, rhymes, or songs. They don't come in knowing about Jack and Jill on their own, so they never get that stuff. We used to teach them to have fun with language first, so they would want to read.

They would never stand for this in the suburbs. My kids have hard lives already, many live with their great grandma, or with parents with two or three jobs just to pay the bills. They are being doubly punished by a society that has allowed them to become this poor, and then having this federal management, which is the worst thing for their love of reading.

We no longer have playtime. There are no field trips unless they have objectives connected to the reading curriculum. So there are certainly no more fun field trips. There is no social studies. There was a big African American history program for years in Buffalo. But we can't teach it anymore. There is no teaching about holidays or themes. We cannot come off the reading page we are supposed to be on. My kids in first-grade get art, physical education, and music once every six days. And each of those are only 30-minute periods.

What's upsetting to me is that they aren't experiencing a love of reading. There is no choice in reading. I have 40 books on tape that I have collected over the years, and we had to take everything like that home. The kids can only listen to books from Harcourt.

They are missing cooperative learning opportunities because they have to work independently so much. They are sitting in their seats for two hours each day and can't get up out of their seats. My principal was observing a kindergarten teacher with a small reading group and a little kid came running up to ask about a spilled glue bottle; the next night the principal reamed her out about not engaging with other kids while she is in a small group, unless it's an emergency. The children are stressed; to a kindergartener, spilled glue is an emergency.

The only collaboration we have with other teachers now is, every six days we have a grade-level meeting. You are told to bring your number 2s up to 3s. [In the New York State accountability system, "number 2s" are children just below the proficiency point, and "number 3s" are children just above. See the discussion about "bubble kids" in Chapter 4.] Everything is about that. They are kind of letting the lowest kids go.

Heather Mildon *teaches kindergarten in Anchorage, Alaska. Her school is integrated – about three-fourths of its students are white, with blacks the largest minority. One-third of the school's students are low income. She has taught for 13 years.*

Over the past few years, the Anchorage School District has implemented the Houghton Mifflin reading program to have every school in the district on the same schedule. Administrators were seeking to provide some consistency for students who move between schools during a given year. It was also a decision based on giving administrators more control over what is taught and how, because of accountability requirements of NCLB.

I personally believe that this scripted reading curriculum has crippled my creativity and ability to teach and connect with my students. I have heard the same from plenty of other teachers, but do know of some who seem to be having a more positive experience with the program.

Prior to adoption of the Houghton Mifflin program, classroom teachers were able to use state and district grade-level expectations as the centerpiece around which to plan instruction, largely as they deemed appropriate, based on their knowledge of students and best instructional practices. Our district had a group of reading specialists who visited our buildings to share model lessons, and to observe and critique teachers. They also planned grade-level training for teachers that was often centered on recent literacy research. I credit this training with helping to bring me to the level of understanding I presently possess regarding best teaching practices for young children.

Prior to NCLB, there was no formal end-of-the-year evaluation of kindergarten students, save for what teachers conducted themselves to complete report cards for parents. As NCLB took hold, we were required to assess our kindergartners at the end of the year on a standardized test. To be "proficient" – to be on track to pass the third-grade test, which counts – our students must reach a level 2 on this test, as well as meet certain qualifications for letter and sound ID on a letter-identification assessment. When we were first told to score our kindergartners as "proficient" or "non-proficient" in reading, we expressed our dismay to the reading specialists. I was asked in reply, "Don't you teach reading?" or something similar to that, which felt like a slap in the face. I replied that of course we teach reading, but in no way should we panic or label students if they aren't reading independently by age 5-and-a-half at the end of kindergarten!

Once Houghton Mifflin was adopted, we had regular visits from the reading specialist assigned to our building to tell us to "teach the program with fidelity." That meant to maintain the pacing schedule so we were on course with the district. We were told to teach the target skills above all else, noted in the manuals with a bull's eye. These specialists no longer modeled lessons – after all, what is to be modeled when all one must to do "teach" this curriculum is read the blue highlighted print? The responses students are to supply are also often provided! Instead the specialists were reduced to supporting teachers by cutting and laminating phonics boards for us to use. Ludicrous.

Teaching the Houghton Mifflin program "with fidelity" has devastated my classroom practices. My children memorize high-frequency words now, and boy, can most write and read them! But they once wrote lengthy, creative, detailed sentences with their "kid writing" spelling, and now they write, "I like my dog" or "I see a cow" with no personal relevance and little joy. Instead of writing and reading our own experience-based class books, they fill in the blanks on work pages – with four sentences about Nan and Dan who have a van.

I no longer can do the things I loved about teaching kindergarten – our annual holiday play based on nursery rhymes the children had memorized, our hatching of chicks and caterpillars, our regular cooking center, and Friday paint day.

I can't say for sure the cause, of course, but I had parents say this year that their children don't like school anymore. Sharp, creative thinkers – interested learners – wishing to stay home and not come to school? I can't recall that happening in the past with kindergartners. I have seen capable kids in tears because they didn't know how to read the words on the page. It is wrong to put that type of pressure on a 5-year-old.

In addition to students under stress, boredom, less enthusiasm for school, and stifled writing, one significant loss has been a noticeable decrease in read-aloud time. I spend so much time running through workbook pages or phonics drills that I read far fewer books aloud to my kids than ever in the past.

Yet with all of these negatives, I believe I still see the same variance in student achievement. Some kids are guessing as they read the few words they should know from sight word lists or randomly write those same words in mixed-up order on assigned pages. Others breeze through it all, are finished quickly and then are awaiting challenging material. Others' literacy skills are slowly developing, but are getting there.

I believe our present focus on test scores and not students is harmful. I believe children's school experiences should be meaningful, memorable, and motivational so that kids' natural curiosity is sparked and they are inspired to seek further learning opportunities throughout life.

John Perry teaches fourth grade reading and writing in Tampa, Fla. He has been teaching for 11 years. His school's students are about evenly divided between whites, blacks, and Hispanics, with a few other minorities as well; three-quarters of its students are low income. Many of his students have come from Puerto Rico; others have immigrated from Latin American or Asian nations.

The district has a number of FCAT [Florida Comprehensive Assessment Test] practice tests it gives to the students. Our assistant principal is giving us one practice test every two weeks for reading, and then they take a math practice test on the other weeks. So they are taking a practice test every week. Those tests take at least one reading block to take the test and then you have to go over it with them, that eats up a couple of days every two weeks – it's an absurd amount of FCAT practice.

Any regular reading instruction gets cut during practice tests. If you are going to do any social studies, there isn't time for it, so you have to integrate it in your reading block. You lose out on social studies content. The district's plan to deal with our low practice scores was that before the FCAT, the third grade wasn't going to teach writing, just reading, and the fourth grade was told not to teach science, because in third grade there is no FCAT writing test, and in fourth grade there is no science test.

A couple of summers ago, a team member and I worked hard to integrate social studies into our language arts teaching. But our principal said, "We won't be focusing on social studics, we will focus only on the FCAT test content."

Field trips have definitely been affected. They tell us, no field trips are allowed for grades 3, 4, and 5 before the FCAT. We just got finished with tests and now we have nine weeks left to go on trips. We have to do them now. In other words the kids get no variety, no enriching activities, like trips. I used to take the fifth grade to Tallahassee, the state capital, from Tampa. But my principal said we aren't going to do that again, and I don't know why. We took that trip after the FCAT during the time when the legislative session starts. We went to the Supreme Court, they acted out mock oral arguments, and watched the House in session. They met their legislators. That was a great experience, especially for low-income kids. Government is a real abstraction for those students. Taking them to Tallahassee, where they would see the Supreme Court and see the legislature in action, to meet legislators, it's a chance to make it real for the students. It might be a chance for them to make the connection that they might be participating citizens. I don't think anything could be more important for them. It's an opportunity they would never otherwise have. A lot of these kids have never been outside of Tampa.

I can't say why she said we weren't going to do the Tallahassee trip again. Now at our school, literally nothing [like that] goes on anymore. It's hard to pinpoint why – is it the pressure from testing? Is it a result of the administration not wanting to bother with it?

There are also fewer teachers taking kids out to recess, especially in third, fourth, and fifth grades. And my kids really need that and they don't get it. I try to give it to them in the room, but a lot of them don't get it in order to perform better on FCAT. The school grade and NCLB AYP [adequate yearly progress, the annual requirement for improved test scores under NCLB] is attached to it. The teacher pay-for-performance program is attached to it. I don't know, maybe teachers are nervous. They want to be in the class and not be seen as wasting time on the playground. No one tells you not to, but they feel the pressure.

Cooperative learning where children learn social skills they need also goes by the wayside, if you are prepping for a test.

I teach a lot of English-as-a-second-language students. I have two students who have only lived here one year, and they are taking a test on a fourth-grade reading level in English, which is absurd, they can't read it. Their scores count against our school grade. Special education students are expected to make the same standards as the general population, but if you are in a special ed program, it's because you scored low on tests in the first place! You are still expected to take the FCAT, and you might get accommodations, but that doesn't make up for it. I don't think we find out anything from the FCAT that we wouldn't know anyway. We have a lot of different assessments we can use; I find out way more by observing them in the class. I don't think the FCAT tells parents any more than they could learn from a good teacher. High-stakes tests only really corrupt the school system.

Jim Sando teaches fifth grade at an elementary school in suburban Philadelphia, Pa. Three-fourths of the school's students are white; about one-sixth of the school's students are black and about one-sixth are low income. He has been teaching for 29 years.

I can no longer do many of the classroom activities that I would have done in the past. There is no time left to do those. If I do these other things, the time has to come from somewhere. I was at a bar mitzvah and saw a parent of a student from a class about 12 years ago. He asked if I still do the Revolutionary War activity I used to do, or a science activity I did with his child. That is the kind of thing students and parents remember, but I can't do that stuff anymore. Most of the science hands-on stuff we do is very structured – you have to follow a set script. There is a little bit of latitude but not nearly the latitude we used to have.

Language arts and math are the two areas that are focused on the most – even the books that are now being used are designed around what is tested. That is the entire curriculum. We have a professional development program, and someone has the title of staff developer, and what it turns out to be is, "here is the new strategy to teach this test question and that test question." The entire staff development program is about this.

There used to be a reasonable amount of field trips, especially considering we live in Philadelphia. We are teaching about government and the development of North America in fifth grade, and there are so many great places we could visit, whether it's Valley Forge or Washington's Crossing. Now we are limited to two field trips a year, and the kids have to pay for the entire field trip. The district isn't spending any of its own money on it. It's all about focusing classroom time and resources on testing.

Social studies is *the* subject that gets the most shortchanged. In the Revolutionary War activity, we used to take a week and model the types of battles. The kids would really begin to understand what happened with Washington when they crossed the Delaware and surprised the troops. We also used to take two weeks and divide up the branches of government and the students would research their branch in groups and then go through the process of creating three laws that went through all the different branches. For example, the judicial branch would figure out if a new law would be acceptable to the school constitution. Because of this kind of activity, when they leave here, and hear news about a Supreme Court decision, it makes sense to them because they were involved in more authentic learning, as opposed to just learning for the test.

If we combine all of the time that is there for science and social studies, it's maybe 80 minutes a day. You can't do justice to both of those subjects with that amount of time.[519]

It's a good thing to look at what students need in math or language arts. To the extent that this has shined a light on where students are, on a year-to-year basis, that is not a bad thing. But it is not applied in a way that is going to really help kids. It's much more of a focus on the test, not a focus on the child.

Anita Yarbrough *teaches middle-school math in Kansas City, Kan. Her school's students are almost all white, with few low-income students. She has been teaching for 13 years.*

No Child Left Behind has impacted me the most. I teach an extra math class for students that didn't do well on the state assessment. So this is an extra math class in addition to their regular math class. When they are in this class, they miss art, PE, or one of their other "explo" [exploratory] classes. It's a semester or quarter class, depending on how they do. They might stay in the class all year.

It's beneficial; the only thing that is going to make them better at math is practicing more math, just as athletes practice to get better at their skills. It has a negative connotation because they are missing a "fun" class, so I try to make it as fun as possible. From the data it does look like there has been some improvement.

Testing takes so much time. We try to give the kids other tests to help them with state tests, so that's three times a year. Every time you turn around we are testing again. Testing, testing, testing – that has to be bad for the students. The testing schedule for math goes on for two weeks. We also test in other core areas – reading, social studies. Eventually we will be testing in all core classes – math, communication arts, science, social studies.

Endnotes

1. In 2003-04, public funds for elementary and secondary schools totaled $462 billion (Snyder, Dillow, and Hoffman 2007, Table 159). In that year, the U.S. defense budget was $380 billion, not including nuclear weapons development outside the Department of Defense, and not including over $100 billion for the Iraq war (DOD 2003, Table 1.1). In fiscal year 2004, total federal, state, and local tax revenues totaled $3.029 trillion (OECD 2007).

2. Helen F. Ladd (2007) distinguishes market-based accountability (parent satisfaction) from political accountability (to elected leaders) and administrative accountability (to government agencies). In a representative democracy, however, government agencies themselves are accountable to elected leaders, so the accountability discussed in this book requires participation of both elected leaders and administrative agencies. Accountability of professionals to their peers for carrying out professional norms is another important aspect, but not a topic of this book. For discussions, see Abelmann et al. 1999, O'Day 2004, and Meier 2002.

3. I use the term goal "distortion," rather than the term more common in accountability literature, goal "displacement," because test-based accountability systems not only result in displacement – the substitution of some goals for others (e.g., substituting drill in math for arts or physical education) – but also in corrupting the nature of instruction in the tested skills themselves.

4. The conclusions of many researchers and policy experts on this point are summarized in my book, *Class and Schools* (Rothstein 2004).

5. A few states include other subject area tests in their accountability systems. NCLB requires states to test students in science, but science test scores are not counted in the NCLB accountability system.

6. Chapter 3 and Appendix 4 describe this shift in teacher attention in greater detail.

7. Franklin 1749, p. 10 (with punctuation modernized). Franklin, here, was quoting with approval the chaplain to the Prince of Wales (Americans were, of course, still loyal colonial subjects at this time).

8. Quoted in Pangle and Pangle 2000, p. 30.

9. Franklin 1749, pp. 22-23 (with punctuation modernized).

10. Franklin 1728, p. 56.

11. Members of the Democratic-Republican Party. They were then termed Jeffersonian Republicans.

12. Cremin 1951, p. 29.

13. Washington 1790, p. 3.

14. Washington 1796, p. 25.

15. Ellis 2001, p. 154. Alexander Hamilton, Washington's speechwriter, considered Washington's public university proposal a distraction from his main themes and did not include it in the final draft of the farewell address.

16. Cited in Wagoner 1991, pp. 25-26.

17. Cited in Wagoner 2004, p. 30.

18. Thorpe 1909, Vol. 3, p. 1907 (Constitution or Form of Government for the Commonwealth of Massachusetts, 1780, Chapter 5, Section 2).

19. Thorpe 1909, Vol. 2, pp. 960-61 (Northwest Ordinance, 1787, Sec. 14, and Sec. 14, Article 3).

20. Mitchell 1830. Also quoted in Cremin 1951, pp. 34-35.

21. Mann 1845, p. 117.

22. Mann 1844, p. 23.

23. Mann 1848, pp. 52-53.

24. Goldin and Katz 2003, p. 25.

25. Mann 1848, p. 77.

26. Mann 1845, pp. 135-36.

27. Mann 1848, p.123.

28. In the 1960s, with the growth of teacher unionism, the NEA began to lose teacher-members to the American Federation of Teachers (AFT). NEA leaders came to believe that their organization could not compete with the AFT if NEA teachers and administrators, who sat on opposite sides of the collective bargaining table, remained in the same organization. The NEA then evolved into a teachers union, with administrators and researchers splitting off into separate organizations (Robinson 1983; Urban 1998).

29. Committee of Ten 1893, p. 3.

30. Committee of Ten 1893, Table 1, pp. 34-35.

31. Committee of Ten 1893, p. 48.

32. Committee of Fifteen 1895.

33. Committee of Ten 1893, p. 17.

34. For example, Committee of Ten 1893, p. 110.

35. Committee of Ten 1893, p. 22.

36. The Committee of Ten report asserted that "only an insignificant percentage" of graduates of secondary schools go on to college (Committee of Ten 1893, p. 51). However, this claim is contradicted by Census and enrollment data from that period. Calculations of enrollment and graduate rates in this paragraph by the author are available from the author upon request.

37. Cardinal Principles 1918, pp. 11-12.

38. Horace Mann was a Whig, not a Jacksonian Democrat. But from the perspective of 180 years later, the educational philosophies of Whigs and Democrats are not easily distinguished.

39. Cardinal Principles 1918, pp. 11-16.

40. Kelly et al. 1937, p. 34.

41. Kelly et al. 1937, p. 45.

42. Kelly et al. 1937, p. 47.

43. Kelly et al. 1937, p. 44.

44. Kelly et al. 1937, pp. 52-53.

45. Kelly et al. 1937, pp. 64, 79, 116.

46. Kelly et al. 1937, p. 122.

47. EPC 1938, p. 16.

48. EPC 1938, pp. 77, 31-32, 34.

49. EPC 1938, p. 123.

50. EPC 1938, pp. 153-54.

51. McElroy 1956, p. 9.

52. McElroy 1956, pp. 5-7. The conference supported the statement unanimously, except for two disagreements: whether schools' obligation "to foster moral, ethical, and spiritual values" could be accomplished without unconstitutional involvement with religion, and how rapidly schools should be desegregated.

53. Rockefeller Brothers Fund 1958, pp. 14, 16.

54. Rockefeller Brothers Fund 1958, p. 29.

55. The performance contracting fad was abandoned after it became apparent that the firms' test scores were not markedly better than those in traditionally run schools and after publicity about firms that cheated on tests to produce higher scores and maximize financial rewards. (See Tyack and Cuban 1995, 117-120.)

56. Dyer 1970, p. 211.

57. Dyer 1970, p. 208.

58. Nixon 1970; see also Finn 1977.

59. Gallagher 1970, p. 3

60. Nation at Risk, p. 24.

61. Nation at Risk, p. 20.

62. Nation at Risk, p. 20.

63. Nation at Risk, pp. 5-7

64. Goodlad 1979, pp. 46-52.

65. Fiske 1983.

66. NAE was established in 1965 by John Gardner and James B. Conant and includes, by invitation only, leading education researchers and scholars in the nation.

67. NAE 1987, p. 51.

68. Morgan et al. 1991, p. 64.

69. Morgan et al. 1991, p. 19.

70. Peternick et al. 1999.

71. M. Smith 2006.

72. Burke 1774 (spelling has been modernized), paragraph 4.1.22.

73. Johnson and Immerwahr 1994, pp. 10-13, 41.

74. Downey 1960.

75. Krumboltz et al. 1987.

76. Krumboltz et al. 1987, Tables 3 and 4.

77. Krumboltz et al. 1987, pp. 20-21.

78. Rose and Gallup 2005, question 39.

79. Bushaw and Gallup 2008, question 36.

80. Choy et al. 1993, Tables 6.1 and 6.2.

81. Hart 1998.

82. Marzano, Kendall, and Cicchinelli 1999.

83. See, for example, Converse and Presser 1986; Schuman and Presser 1996; Dillman 2000.

84. SSRC 2005. The Scripps-Howard poll presented emotional health as "student self-confidence," social skills and work ethic as "reliable work habits and the ability to work in teams," appreciation of the arts and literature as "arts and music," and physical health as "health and physical education."

85. http://www.knowledgenetworks.com/

86. For more detail on this poll, see Appendix 3 and Jacobsen 2007.

87. On a number of occasions, we have administered a similar survey to audiences to whom we have lectured. Often, these are university audiences, mostly in schools of education. These audiences' judgments are similar to those of the public and elected officials, except that university audiences almost always give a higher rating to "appreciation of the arts and literature," with other goals reduced proportionally.

88. The weights in Table 2 reflect only the judgment of Rebecca Jacobsen, Richard Rothstein, and Tamara Wilder. Readers may interpret the findings of Chapters 1 and 2 somewhat differently.

89. For additional examples, see Nichols and Berliner 2007, pp. 122 ff. For a more general discussion of "score inflation" that results from instruction that stresses the unrepresentative skills that happen to be assessed by a particular test, see Koretz 2008, chapter 10.

90. CDC 2003.

91. Ogden et al. 2006, Table 2 (overweight data are for 6-11-year-olds); MMWR 2003, Table 1 (daily physical activity data are for 9-13-year-olds).

92. Eaton et al. 2006, Table 52. Recommended physical activity "increases your heart rate and makes you breathe hard some of the time." The CDC has illustrated such recommended activity as "playing basketball or soccer, running, swimming laps, fast bicycling, fast dancing, or similar aerobic activities" (Eaton 2006; Grunbaum et al. 2004).

93. For brief reviews of recent research, see Vail 2008 and Viadero 2006.

94. Dillon 2005.

95. Campaign 2006.

96. Schiesel 2008.

97. Carnegie-Knight Task Force. 2007.

98. Obama 2008.

99. Toch 2006, p. 17.

100. Koretz et al. 1996, Table 6.

101. McNeil 2000, pp 242-43, and passim.

102. Clarke et al. 2003, pp. 50-52.

103. Clarke et al. 2003, pp. 54-56.

104. Clarke et al. 2003, p. 64.

105. Ladd and Zelli 2002, Figures 5 and 11.

106. Von Zastrow with Janc 2004, Figure 17.

107. Von Zastrow 2005.

108. McMurrer 2007, Table 3; McMurrer 2008.

109. Sandholtz, Ogawa, and Scribner 2004.

110. Taylor et al. 2001, p. 30.

111. Duran 2005.

112. Schwartz 2004, p. 26.

113. Finn and Ravitch 2007a.

114. Finn and Ravitch, 2007b, p. 6

115. Darling-Hammond and Wise 1985, p. 320.

116. Nation at Risk 1983, p. 10.

117. Nation at Risk 1983, p. 20.

118. A "margin of error" is the maximum amount by which, in most cases, a reported score might differ from the true score, if the test had been repeated a sufficient number of times. Frequently, "most cases" means 95% of the time. In political polling based on surveying a random sample of the voting population, for example, if a candidate is reported to have the support of 45%, with a margin of error of 3%, this means that in 95% of the samples drawn, the candidate's true support might be anywhere from 42% to 48%. The larger the sample of voters polled, the smaller will be the margin of error. An alternative way of describing this is to say that the 95% confidence interval is 6 percentage points. The confidence interval is twice the margin of error. Although most informed citizens are familiar with the "margin of error" concept from newspaper reports, the U.S. Department of Education decided to use the less familiar term, "confidence interval," to describe the uncertainty surrounding test scores.

119. We sometimes describe this variation in terms of 'I.Q.' and say that the normal range is from 85 to 115, with an average of 100. However, I.Q. is not entirely determined by genetic potential, because genes interact with environment to express human ability. Even in the

best environments, there will be a range of I.Q. scores, although with better environments the range would be narrower than it is today. Disadvantaged groups now have lower average I.Q. scores because these groups are afflicted with social circumstances that affect measured I.Q. Black children, for example, are more likely to live in deteriorated neighborhoods where they are more likely to contract lead poisoning, and lead poisoning is known to lower cognitive ability. Disadvantaged children are also raised in environments that interact with genetic potential in ways that are less likely to stimulate that potential (see Shonkoff and Phillips 2000). Claims that the lower average I.Q. scores of black students have genetic as opposed to environmental bases have been persuasively refuted. For one review, see Dickens 2005.

120. For a further discussion, see Koretz 2008, p. 169.

121. Kane and Staiger 2002. (This is the published version of the paper that was circulated to Washington policy makers in the summer of 2001.) For a more recent and comprehensive explanation of the unreliability of single and relatively brief tests as indicators of school quality, see Koretz 2008, especially Chapter 7.

122. Carey 2006.

123. Perie, Grigg, and Dion, p. 2; Education Week 2006.

124. For detail on how these comparisons were calculated, see Rothstein, Jacobsen, and Wilder 2006, pp.8-9, 11, 18. See also Phillips 2007 for similar calculations.

125. In actuality only about 99%, not all, students are expected to reach proficiency under NCLB. The law exempted the most severely disabled 1% of children from the proficiency demand, but in practice this means, for example, that U.S. children with mental retardation must be as proficient in math as the best-performing students in Taiwan and Singapore!

126. Hess and Finn 2007. The Education Trust proposes federal review and approval of state standards, a process that would be indistinguishable from national standards (Education Trust 2007). The Aspen Institute's Commission on No Child Left Behind proposes "model national standards," with the federal government evaluating and reporting on whether state standards conformed to these (Aspen Commission 2007).

127. Typical is a Washington State Department of Education website with "frequently asked questions" about the state's testing and accountability program: "Think of the [state test] like the test you take to earn a driver's license. It doesn't matter what the average score on the test is or whether some drivers scored above or below you. What matters is whether you can show you have the driving skills and knowledge of traffic laws to 'meet the standard' and get a license" (WOPI 2008). A parent involvement program promoted by the U.S. Department of Education describes NCLB's testing requirements like this: "If teachers cover the subject matter required by the standards and teach it well, students should do well on the test. It's like taking a driver's test. The instructor covers all the important content the state wants you to know and much more" (Project Appleseed 2006).

128. In part, they eventually pass because their skills improve with more study. In part, test takers become familiar with the specific questions asked by the test, even if they don't become better at understanding traffic rules overall. And in part, they eventually pass because there is an element of chance involved in selecting the answer to any multiple choice question, and both the first failing score and the later passing score may be statistically indistinguishable. In these respects, a driver's exam does shed some light on school achievement tests.

129. Glass 1978.

130. In a large enough national sample, the median (mid-point) and mean (average) score should be nearly identical.

131. In technical language, the score of 600 was designed to be one standard deviation above the mean. In a normal distribution, a standard deviation is about equal to about 34 percentile points above or below the mean.

132. NAEP scales for higher grade levels use a higher but overlapping series of numbers. This unfortunate complication leads to a misunderstanding that the scales can be combined into a continuous series, and that a fourth grader, for example, who achieves a score equal to that of the typical eighth grader, is capable of doing eighth-grade work. Such a conclusion, however, is unwarranted. Fourth graders who achieve such a score are not answering the same kinds of questions as typical eighth graders.

133. NCES 2006

134. Vinovskis 1998, p. 42.

135. Vinovskis 1998, p. 42.

136. Vinovskis 1998, p. 43.

137. Lapointe and Koffler 1982, p. 4. Wirtz and Lapointe 1982, p. x.

138. Wirtz and Lapointe 1982, pp. 32, 33, 38, 33.

139. Vinovskis 1998, p. 44.

140. Vinovskis 1998, pp. 44-45.

141. NCES 2004, Table 8. In 2001, the 1991 cohort of 17-year-olds would have been 27 years of age. In 2001, 29% of the 25-29-year-old age group had earned a bachelor's degree).

142. In the psychometric literature, this is referred to as the "Angoff method." Another way to pose the same question is to ask judges to imagine a group of 100 barely proficient test takers, and to estimate how many of them will answer the particular question correctly.

143. Livingston and Zieky 1982; GAO 1993; or see pp. 1-3 of Loomis and Bourque 2001a or Loomis and Bourque 2001b.

144. Finley and Berdie 1970, pp. 57-58.

145. Glass 1978, p. 244.

146. Rothman 1991.

147. Rothman 1991.

148. Finn 2004, p. 261.

149. Popham 2000, p. 164.

150. Loomis and Bourque 2001a or 2001b, p. 2.

151. The statisticians were Daniel L. Stufflebeam, Michael Scriven, and Richard M. Jaeger.

152. Vinovskis 1998, pp. 46-47.

153. GAO 1993, pp. 31-32.

154. GAO 1993, p. 38.

155. GAO 1993, p. 57.

156. The panel was chaired by Robert Glaser and Robert Linn, and its investigation conducted by Lorrie Shepard.

157. NAE 1993, pp. xxii, 148.

158. NAE 1993, p. xxiv.

159. Pelligrino, Jones, and Mitchell 1999, p. 7. I have previously recounted some of this history in Rothstein 1998, pp. 70ff, and in Rothstein 2004, pp. 88ff.

160. Vinovskis 1998, p. 56.

161. Contemporary NAEP reports include a caution, buried in the text, defending the use of achievement levels only for observing trends (changes in the percent of students who achieve proficiency over time) but not for validating the percentages at any given point in time. The caution concludes by offering no defense of achievement level definitions other than the fact that government officials continue to use them:

     As provided by law, NCES, upon review of congressionally mandated evaluations of NAEP, has determined that achievement levels are to be used on a trial basis and should be interpreted with caution. However, NCES and NAGB have affirmed the usefulness of these performance standards for understanding *trends* in achievement. NAEP achievement levels have been widely used by national and state officials (Grigg, Lauko and Brockway 2006, p. 5, emphasis added).

162. Popham 2000, p. 176.

163. Of eight states whose fourth-grade reading standards were examined by the Northwest Evaluation Association, four (California, Colorado, Iowa, and Montana) have proficiency cut scores that are below NAEP's basic cut score (see Table 4 in Kingsbury et al. 2003 vs. Table 1 in Perie, Grigg, and Donahue 2005. This conclusion, arrived at by comparing data from two separate reports, must be tentative because data in the two reports are from close but not identical years.)

164. Kingsbury et al. 2003.

165. Linn 2006.

166. Linn 2000, Fig. 6, p. 10.

167. Lee 2006, Table B-1, p. 68.

168. Horn et al. 2000, pp 24-25.

169. Hoff 2002.

170. Evidence that incentives lead teachers to ignore students both above and far below the proficiency cut score comes from Neal and Schanzenbach 2007; Booher-Jennings 2006; Ballou and Springer 2007; Hamilton et al. 2007; UFT 2007; and Rubin 2004. In an article in the Winter 2008 issue of *Education Next*, Matthew Springer claimed that evidence from one unnamed state (apparently, Idaho) showed that accountability testing did not cause teachers to ignore students at the bottom of the distribution. However, this claim was not repeated in Ballou and Springer 2007, a more recent paper. Because states vary widely in the difficulty of their proficiency cut points, analyses of the "bubble" will be affected by the states chosen. In states with very low cut scores, few students at the bottom of the distribution can be ignored, but in such states the share of students above the cut score will be much more numerous.

171. Neal and Schanzenbach 2007.

172. Jacob and Levitt 2003.

173. Zehr 2007; TEA 2007.

174. Figlio 2006.

175. Figlio and Getzler 2002.

176. For a discussion of how difficult it is to monitor the appropriateness of accommodations for special education test takers, see Koretz 2008, chapter 12.

177. Figlio and Getzler 2002; Jacob 2005.

178. Kantrowitz and Springen 1997; Zlatos 1994. Although there are no nationally representative data confirming the extent of such gaming, Martha Thurlow, Ph. D., director of the National Center on Education Outcomes, states, regarding research in the early 1990s on inclusion and exclusion of students from testing: "As I presented our early findings about exclusion, teachers and parents came up to me afterward to describe what had happened to them – a principal called to suggest keeping a child home on the test day so that the child would not suffer anxiety when it was unnecessary (parent of a learning-disabled student), special education teachers talking about test day being designated as the day that they went on field trips – usually to the zoo. We had person after person relate these stories to us when we presented our data on inclusion and exclusions" (Thurlow 2007).

179. Jacob 2005.

180. Lee 2006, pp. 21-22, 47-51.

181. I have discussed these problems at length in Rothstein 2004, Chapter 1. Neuman 2008a and 2008b are more recent and eloquent treatments of these issues.

182. For estimate of effect of mobility: Hanushek, Kain, and Rivkin 2004; for estimate of effect of child and maternal health: Currie 2005.

183. Aspen Commission 2007.

184. Kane and Staiger 2002.

185. CAP et al. 2007; Cohen 2007; Spellings 2007.

186. Simon 1978, p. 352, 366.

187. Ridley and Simon 1938, 1943, p. vii.

188. Ridley and Simon 1938, 1943, p. 2.

189. Ridley and Simon 1938, 1943, pp. 47-48.

190. Ridley and Simon 1938, 1943, p. 26.

191. Ridley and Simon 1938, 1943, p. 43.

192. Ridley and Simon 1938, 1943, p. 45.

193. D. Campbell 1979, p. 85.

194. Wilson 1989, p. 117.

195. Nove 1964, p. 294.

196. Nove 1964, p. 289.

197. Mullen 1985, p. 165.

198. Mullen 1985, p. 165.

199. Mullen 1985, p. 165.

200. This book is not the first, or only, discussion of the applicability of Campbell's law to contemporary test-based educational accountability policies. Nichols and Berliner 2007 and Koretz 2007, 2008 have made similar observations.

201. West 2007, p. 57.

202. D. Campbell 1979, p. 86.

203. Murray 2005.

204. Deming 1986, p. 104; Uhlig 1987; Jackman 2004; Moore 2007.

205. Skolnick 1966, p. 164.

206. Farhi 1996.

207. Hoyt 2007.

208. Jaschik 2007.

209. Finder 2007.

210. Skolnick 1966, pp. 176, 181.

211. Seidman and Couzens 1974.

212. Seidman and Couzens 1974, p. 462.

213. Morrissey 1972; Twigg 1972.

214. D. Campbell 1979, p. 85 (citations in text omitted).

215. Johnson, Reiley, and Munoz 2006.

216. Green, Passman, and Wintfeld 1991, p. 1853.

217. P. Smith 1993, pp. 141-42.

218. P. Smith 1993, pp.146-47.

219. Goddard, Mannion, and Smith 2000, pp. 141-142, 149.

220. P. Smith 1995, p. 291.

221. Lu 2007.

222. GAO 1994, p. 55.

223. Carnoy et al. 2005.

224. Ridley and Simon 1938, 1943, p. 3.

225. Ridley and Simon 1938, 1943, p. 10.

226. Ridley and Simon 1938, 1943, p. 17.

227. Ridley and Simon 1938, 1943, p. 28.

228. Iezzoni 1994, p. 4.

229. Schick 2001, p. 41.

230. Casalino et al. 2007, p. 495.

231. Santora 2005; Casalino et al. 2007, p. 496.

232. Altman 1990.

233. McKee 1996, p. 430.

234. Iezzoni et al. 1995.

235. Associated Press 1993.

236. Kassirer 1994.

237. GAO 1994, pp 5-6.

238. GAO 1994, p. 26.

239. GAO 1994, p. 42.

240. P. Smith 1993, p. 149.

241. Bird et al. 2005, p. 20.

242. Bevan and Hood 2006, p. 531.

243. Bevan and Hood 2006, p. 523.

244. Timmins 2005.

245. GAO 1994, p. 38.

246. McKee and Hunter 1994, p. 112; P. Smith 1993, p. 148.

247. Green and Wintfeld 1995, Table 1.

248. Green and Wintfeld 1995; Epstein 1995.

249. Dranove et al. 2003, pp. 555-56, 577.

250. Dranove et al. 2003, pp. 583-85.

251. Harris 2007.

252. Steinbrook 2006.

253. Blau 1955, pp. 38-42, 45-46.

254. Courty, Heinrich, and Marschke 2005, p. 338.

255. Stecher and Kirby 2004, p. 54, citing Courty and Marschke 1997, p. 384.

256. Barnow and Smith 2004, p. 258-59.

257. Barnow and Smith 2004, p. 249.

258. Heckman, Heinrich, and Smith 2002, p. 808. See also Blalock and Barnow 2001, p. 505.

259. Barnow and Smith 2004, pp. 269-70.

260. Barnow and Smith 2004, pp. 269-70; GAO 2002, p. 17.

261. Barnow and Smith 2004, pp. 271-72, citing Courty and Marschke 1997.

262. Courty, Heinrich and Marschke 2005, pp. 331, 341-42.

263. Heinrich and Choi 2007, p. 418 and Appendix.

264. Heinrich and Marschke 2007, pp. 21-23.

265. Wiseman 2007. In congressional testimony regarding TANF reauthorization in 2005, Assistant Secretary of Health and Human Services Wade Horn proposed that the performance

incentive program be cut in half, and used only to reward employment outcomes (Horn 2005). However, even this reduced program was not implemented.

266. Courty, Heinrich, and Marschke 2005, pp. 340, 342, 336-37; Heinrich 2004; GAO 2002, pp. 9, 14.

267. GAO 2002, p. 28.

268. Courty, Heinrich, and Marschke 2005, pp. 328, 338; see also Anderson et al. 1991, pp. 33, 37, 39.

269. GAO 2002, pp. 14-15.

270. Dranove et al. 2003, p. 581.

271. Gootman 2007.

272. Bloomberg 2007.

273. Adams and Heywood 2007, Tables 2 and 7.

274. This discussion considers "quantitative" measures to be those, such as test scores or employee production, where the raw data are in numerical form. "Qualitative" evaluations can also be converted to numerical indicators. Thus, a supervisor's evaluation, although based on judgment rather than an employee's measurable output, can be expressed as a numerical rating. Accountability systems that combine quantitative and qualitative measures can still rank employees or institutions in numerical order, and many do so.

275. P. Smith 1990, p. 70.

276. Healy 1985; Jaworski and Young 1992, p. 20.; P. Smith 1990, p. 68; Schiff 1966.

277. Jaworski and Young 1992, p. 20.

278. Kaplan and Atkinson 1998, pp. 692-93.

279. Rothstein 2000a.

280. Ittner, Larcker, and Meyer 1997, p. 9. That labor market success seems to be correlated with employees' physical attractiveness confirms that supervisory evaluations are flawed tools for objective evaluations of performance. See Hamermesh and Biddle, 1994.

281. Bommer et al. 1995, p. 602.

282. Baker 2002, p. 750.

283. Rothstein 2000a.

284. Deming 1986, pp. 76, 101-02. See also Pfeffer 1998 and Deming Institute 2007. Deming was not hostile to quantitative analysis where he thought it appropriate. He advocated analysis of factors that contribute to quality and performance through statistical modeling.

285. Kaplan and Atkinson 1998, p. 368.

286. Schick 2001, p. 50.

287. The influential work (Kaplan and Norton, 1996) describing the balanced scorecard approach relies on descriptions of illustrative firms, including Rockwater (an undersea construction company that is a division of Brown and Root, now a subsidiary of Haliburton), Analog Devices, FMC Corporation, and five pseudonymous firms in the banking, retail, petroleum, and insurance industries. Other balanced scorecard case studies are included in Kaplan and Atkinson, 1998, pp. 380-441.

288. Kaplan and Norton 1996, p. 220.

289. For a discussion, see Stecher and Kirby 2004.

290. BNQP 2007a.

291. BNQP 2007b.

292. BNQP 2007c.

293. Epperson 2007.

294. GAO 1994, p. 56.

295. Kelman and Friedman 2007.

296. Goddard, Mannion, and Smith 2000, p. 141; Bevan and Hood 2006, pp. 526-27.

297. Kelman and Friedman 2007.

298. Kerr 1975.

299. Vinovskis 1998, p. 4.

300. Viscusi 1964, p. 1; Thorndike 1964, p. 1; Finley and Berdie 1970, p. 1.

301. Vinovskis 1998, p. 6.

302. Tyler 1936.

303. Tyler 1949, p. 106.

304. Tyler 1949, pp. 108, 112.

305. Tyler 1949, pp. 108, 115.

306. Hazlett 1974, pp. 26-29.

307. Hazlett 1974, pp. 132, 154-56, 186-90.

308. Hazlett 1974, pp. 12-14; Chromy, Finkner, and Horvitz 2004, p. 390.

309. Viscusi 1964, pp. 12-13.

310. Hazlett 1974, p. 91.

311. Hazlett 1974, p. 90; Tyler 1972, p. 4.

312. Merwin and Womer 1969, p. 315.

313. Hazlett 1974, pp. 105, 8, 83, 87-88, 91, 172.

314. Morrissett 2004, p. 128.

315. V. Campbell and Nichols 2004, p. 344.

316. Rossi 1964.

317. Hazlett 1974, p. 124

318. Thorndike 1964, p. 4.

319. Greenbaum, Garet, and Solomon 1977, p. 10; Hazlett 1974, p. 36; Mosher 2004, p. 101; V. Campbell and Nichols 2004, p. 344.

320. Thorndike 1964, p. 1; Goslin 1964, p. D1; Viscusi 1964, p. 6.

321. Cronbach 2004, p. 141; Finley 1972.

322. ECAPE would have preferred to define young adults to be sampled as those 30 years old or, according to another account, 27 years old. It chose a broader age span because the costs would have been too great to sample the number of households necessary to locate a sufficient number of adults who were exactly 30 years of age. For similar reasons, 17-year-olds were defined as those between 16 ½ and 18 ½ years old, provided they were no longer in school by age 17. NAEP used a single household survey to locate both young adults and out-of-school "17-year-olds" (Chromy, Finkner, and Horvitz 2004, p. 386, 390; Jones 1996, n. 3, p. 21).

323. Vinovskis 1998, p. 11; Jones 2004, p. 15.

324. Chromy, Finkner, and Horvitz 2004, pp. 424-25; NAEP 1979, p. i; Messick 1985.

325. Jones 2004, p. 20.

326. Carr 2004, p. viii.

327. Messick 1985.

328. Koretz 1991; Jones 1996.

329. DOE 2008.

330. Ravitch 2003b, pp. 14-17.

331. Ravitch 2008.

332. Vinovskis 1998, p. 40.

333. NCLB 2002, §411(b)(5)(A); Schlafly 2001.

334. NCLB 2002, §412(e)(4).

335. Mann 1848, p. 89.

336. For other discussion of the Wirtz-Lapointe report, see the Chapter 4 topic, "Arbitrariness of proficiency definitions."

337. Wirtz and Lapointe 1982, pp. 22, 14, 16, 17, 61.

338. Alexander 1987, pp. 8, 16, 20-24.

339. NAE 1987, p. 51. For other discussion of this NAE report, see the Chapter 1 topic, "Accountability demands and reactions in the late 20th century: *A Nation at Risk*."

340. Cited in Persky, Sandene, and Askew 1998, p. i.

341. Persky, Sandene, and Askew 1998, p. ii.

342. Persky, Sandene, and Askew 1998. The assessment also included theater and dance, but NAEP did not assess a representative sample of eighth graders in these topics because, nationally, too few students had exposure to them in school. Items covering drama were administered only to students who attended schools where drama was part of the arts curriculum; items covering dance were not administered anywhere, but the CD-ROM includes examples of dance performance items that would have been administered if sufficient students had been available to sample (Persky, Sandene, and Askew 1998, pp. i-ii). The CD-ROM remains available from the National Center for Education Statistics at http://nces.ed.gov/pubsearch/pubsinfo.asp?pubid=1999485.

For theater, NAEP gave eighth graders a portion of a script and asked whether they could describe where special lighting would be necessary, what sound effects would be needed, which objects were essential to the set, and what the actress should communicate through her body, face, and voice (Persky, Sandene, and Askew 1998, pp. 49-63). Survey questions asked whether students had acted or had otherwise participated in live productions, and whether they had attended out-of-school dramatic productions (Persky, Sandene, and Askew 1998, p. 67). NAEP gave sampled students a character to play in a brief scene, and evaluated them on their abilities to combine dialogue, action, and expression to communicate to an audience (Persky, Sandene, and Askew 1998, p. 78).

For dance, NAEP developed items that asked students to analyze videotaped performances of various ethnic folk dances, jazz, and modern dance. An instructor was to teach a sequence of jazz steps, with students then videotaped as they performed what they had just learned, to be rated later by NAEP judges (Persky, Sandene, and Askew 1998, p. 122).

343. Persky, Sandene, and Askew 1998, pp. 80-117.

344. Rivas 1974a, pp. 24-28; Rivas 1974b, p. 11.

345. Rivas 1974a, pp. 24-28; Rivas 1974b, p. 11.

346. Rivas 1974b, p. 21.

347. Persky, Sandene, and Askew 1998, pp. 15-16; Rivas 1974a, pp. 17ff.

348. Persky, Sandene, and Askew 1998, pp. 27-28.

349. Rivas 1974a, pp. 31-35; Rivas 1974c; Persky, Sandene, and Askew 1998, p. 33.

350. Rivas 1974a, p. 8; Rivas 1974b, pp. 4-5.

351. Rivas 1974b, p. 3

352. Persky, Sandene, and Askew 1998, pp. 12, 20.

353. Katz et al. 1977, p. 2.

354. V. Campbell et al. 1970, pp. 108-09; ECS 1976, pp. xv, 5; Katz et al., p. 5c.

355. ECS 1976, p. 43.

356. ECS 1976, p. xv.

357. ECS 1976, p. 6, Katz et al. 1977, pp.85ff.

358. ECS 1976, p. 7.

359. ECS 1976, p. 9; Katz et al. 1977, pp. 5k, 5p, 122-3.

360. Katz et al. 1977, p. 199.

361. Rothstein 2004, pp. 151-52.

362. Katz et al. 1977, pp. 2-3.

363. Katz et al. 1977, p. 5aa.

364. V. Campbell et al. 1970, pp. 61-62, 79-80.

365. V. Campbell et al. 1970, pp. 61-62, 81-83. As noted, this was the form in which NAEP reported all results – the percent of students who either answered a specific question or whose observed behavior could be categorized in specific ways. NAEP considered that it was up to the public to decide what percentage of 13-year-olds, for example, should be expected to defend a position in the face of opposition if their school programs were developing this trait appropriately.

366. ECS 1976, p. 11.

367. V. Campbell et al. 1970, pp. 111-12; ECS 1976, pp. 9, 14.

368. V. Campbell et al. 1970, pp. 113-14.

369. V. Campbell et al. 1970, pp. 18-19.

370. V. Campbell et al. 1970, p. 20. One large unidentified state and two unidentified school districts prohibited NAEP from asking these questions about racial discrimination within their jurisdictions.

371. V. Campbell et al. 1970, pp. 16-17.

372. V. Campbell et al. 1970, p. 35.

373. V. Campbell et al. 1970, p. 36.

374. V. Campbell et al. 1970, p. 47.

375. V. Campbell et al. 1970, p. 63.

376. V. Campbell et al. 1970, p. 66.

377. V. Campbell et al. 1970, pp. 69-73.

378. V. Campbell et al. 1970, p. 102.

379. V. Campbell et al. 1970, p. 103.

380. V. Campbell et al. 1970, pp. 76-77.

381. NAEP 1979, pp. 6-7.

382. NAEP 1979, pp. 36, 17.

383. NAEP 1979, pp. 32, 46, 42.

384. NAEP 1979, pp. 97-98.

385. NAEP 1979, pp. 104-05.

386. V. Campbell et al. 1970, p. 116.

387. NAEP 1979, p. 28.

388. NAEP 1979, p. 30.

389. NAEP 1979, pp. 8-10.

390. Womer and Mastie 1972, p. 28.

391. Cubberley 1920, p. 364.

392. AASA 1946, p. 10.

393. NSBA 1967, p. 2.

394. Callahan 1975, p. 22.

395. Almack 1927, pp. 46-47.

396. Crawford 2004, p. 15.

397. Goldhammer 1964, pp. 50, 57-58; Villani 2008; C. Smith 2008.

398. The term "progressive" can be confusing, because it is used to describe two distinct groups. One comprised the municipal and social reformers of the late 19th and early 20th centuries, described here. The other comprised the education reformers with a more child-centered

approach who heavily influenced education policy from about 1920 to 1950. Some members of the first group were also in the second.

399. Ravitch 1974; Kirst 1991.

400. Callahan 1975, pp. 35-38.

401. Ravitch 1974.

402. Counts 1927, pp. 3, 82, 70.

403. Hollingshead 1949, p. 123.

404. Goldhammer 1964, pp. 89-91; White 1962, Table 11, Figure 2.

405. Almack 1927, p. 246.

406. Mendenhall 1929, p. 4.

407. Hagman 1941, p. 15.

408. AASA 1946, pp. 62, 49-52, 123.

409. AASA 1946, p. 178.

410. Ronalson 1923.

411. White 1962, p. 40.

412. Conant 1959, p. 43 (italics in the original).

413. Cunningham 1962.

414. For example, McAdams 2000, chapter 4.

415. Hess 2001a, Table 2.

416. Hill 2003; NCEE, 2006.

417. Hess 2001b; Carnoy et al. 2005, pp. 109-16.

418. CSAC 2004.

419. Hill 1930, p. 9.

420. McVey 1942, p. 21.

421. McVey 1942, pp.117-18, 195; Huitt 1964, pp. 14ff.

422. Harcleroad 1980, p. 10; Simmons 1976, pp. 2-3.

423. McVey 1942, pp. 7-9, 17, 20, 25, 142, 202, and passim.

424. McVey 1942, pp. 31-35, 71; Huitt 1964, pp. 22ff.

425. Huitt 1964, p. 89 and passim.

426. Calculated from AdvancEd 2008 and NCES 2008, Table 94; Hawley 2008.

427. Gray-Bennett 2003; DeLucia 2000; Hurst 2008.

428. AdvancEd 2007.

429. Author Rothstein observed a meeting of the Commission on Public Secondary Schools of the New England Association of Schools and Colleges (NEASC) on March 18, 2001. In 2007, co-author Jacobsen participated as a member of a NEASC elementary school accreditation team and, in 2008, she participated in two North Central Association charter school accreditation teams. Professor Jacobsen's undergraduate research assistant, Sarah

Winchell, also participated in one of these. In 2007, co-author Wilder participated as a member of a NEASC secondary school accreditation team. Where sources for conclusions in this chapter are not provided, they are the authors' conclusions from this participation.

430. Hawley 2008.

431. Hawley 2008.

432. Gray-Bennett 2008; Hawley 2008.

433. In a Massachusetts accreditation, in which one of the authors was a team member, probationary accreditation status due to inadequate science laboratories and gym facilities was successfully publicized to get a bond issue passed, resulting in construction of a new high school. See also Hollingshead 1949, p. 132ff., where even loss of accreditation was not sufficient to get a bond issue passed.

434. Pence 2006, p. 168.

435. AdvancEd 2007, p. 15.

436. NEASC-CPSS 2008; WASC 2008.

437. Matthews and Sammons 2004, pp. 83-84.

438. Matthews and Sammons 2004, pp. 80, 82; Brighouse 2008.

439. Matthews and Sammons 2004, p. 9; Wilson 1996, p. 134; Ofsted 2008.

440. Grubb 2000, p. 709.

441. Matthews and Sammons 2004, p. 141, Table 18; p. 16.

442. Grubb 2000, pp. 699, 703.

443. Wilson 1996, pp. 161, 168, 172, 184.

444. Matthews and Sammons 2004, pp. 18, 19; Ofsted 2008.

445. Brighouse 2008.

446. Matthews and Sammons 2004, pp. 28; Grubb 2000, pp. 702-03.

447. Matthews and Sammons 2004, pp. 22, 128-31, 159-60.

448. Matthews and Sammons 2004, p. 43; Brighouse 2008; Ofsted 2008.

449. Brighouse 2008; Ofsted 2008.

450. Matthews and Sammons 2004, p. 43.

451. Ofsted 2008.

452. Brighouse 2008.

453. Grubb 2000, pp. 701, 703; Wilson 1996, p. 127.

454. Grubb 2000, pp. 703; Wilson 1996, p. 71.

455. Brighouse 2008.

456. Ofsted 2008.

457. Matthews and Sammons 2004, p. 78.

458. Matthews and Sammons 2004, pp. 14, 34; Grubb 2000, p. 701.

459. Grubb 2000, p. 701; Brighouse 2008.

460. Ofsted 2008, p. 9

461. Ofsted 2008, pp. 22.

462. Matthews and Sammons 2004, pp.112, 108; Smithers 2001.

463. Matthews and Sammons 2004, p. 150; Smithers 2001; Ofsted 2008.

464. Bubb et al. 2007.

465. Clark 2008.

466. Curtis 2007; BBC 2007.

467. Hayes 2008.

468. Ehren and Visscher 2008, p. 206.

469. Matthews and Sammons 2004, p. 19; Ehren, Leeuw, and Scheerens 2005, pp. 60-61, 69; Ehren and Visscher 2008, pp. 206, 210.

470. Fiske and Ladd 2000, pp. 117ff.

471. Fiske and Ladd 2000, pp. 117ff.

472. Crooks 2002, p. 239.

473. Crooks 2002, pp. 251-52.

474. The system was designed, and then implemented, by Thomas A. Wilson, whose study (Wilson 1996) of the English system prior to the 1993 reforms made it familiar to American education experts. See RIDE 2008.

475. Grubb 2000, p. 718.

476. Weingarten 2008.

477. Others are also helping to provoke this discussion. The proposal set forth here joins a conversation in which Ladd 2007, Nichols and Berliner 2007, and Dorn 2007 have engaged. Jones (2006) and Fruchter and Mediratta (2006) envision an accountability system with clements similar to those proposed here, but where accountability is primarily to local governing bodies (school boards or parent councils), not state government.

478. The Thomas B. Fordham Foundation has published a series of reports denouncing the quality of many, though not all, state academic standards, but its conclusions are not uniformly supported by curricular experts (Finn, Julian, and Petrilli 2006; Achieve Inc. 2002b). Nonetheless, having good academic standards as guides to curriculum and teaching does not mean that tests are written actually to assess the curriculum required by the standards, nor does it mean that states have set passing scores on tests to reflect accurately whether students are meeting those standards. As Chapter 4 described, state political manipulation of cut scores has been widespread under the pressure of flawed accountability systems, particularly the federal NCLB. States can simultaneously have very low cut scores and very high standards, with the latter ignored in practice (Rothstein 2002).

479. SREB 2008.

480. Raden 1999; Maeroff 2003.

481. New York adopted a similar guarantee, but did not fund it. Kirp 2007, pp. 4, 180-98.

482. McNeil 2000, chapter 5; Grissmer et al. 2000, p 82, n6; Kirp 2007, pp. 198-207.

483. McNeil 2000; Achieve Inc. 2002a.

484. Moses and Cobb 2001; BRI 2008; WGBH 2008.

485. Murray, Evans, and Schwab 1998, p. 808.

486. Rothstein 2000b and Liu 2006 offer proposals for interstate finance equalization. They differ in that Liu proposes an adjustment for state tax effort, and Rothstein does not.

487. Cited in Cross 2004, p. 6.

488. Cited in Cross 2004, p. 6.

489. Liu 2008.

490. NAGB 2003; *Education Reporter* 2003; Viadero 2003a, 2003b; Schemo 2003.

491. Social promotion is the practice of keeping students together with their age cohort by promoting them for the next year to the next grade, even if they have not mastered the minimally expected curriculum of their present grade.

492. For example, Knudson et al. 2006.

493. For example, various essays in Ravitch 2003a (high schools) and Ravitch 2004 (teacher quality).

494. Currie 2005.

495. Cooper Institute 2008.

496. Nation at Risk, p. 5.

497. NCEE 1990.

498. Reich 1991.

499. Thurow 1992.

500. For similar estimates, see Mishel, Bernstein, and Shierholz 2008, chapter 3.

501. Friedman 2005; NCEE 2006.

502. Tucker 2007.

503. Paulson 2006.

504. Greenspan 2004.

505. Hess and Rotherham 2007.

506. Becker and Murphy 2007.

507. Sum et al. 2006.

508. For similar estimates, see Mishel, Bernstein, and Shierholz 2008, chapter 3.

509. Blinder 2006.

510. For example, Levy and Temin 2007.

511. Bernanke 2007.

512. Aldonas, Lawrence, and Slaughter 2007.

513. Reich 2006.

514. Levy and Temin 2007.

515. Schonlau, Fricker, and Elliott 2002.

516. Pineau and Dennis 2004.

517. McMurrer 2007.

518. For example, Rothstein and Jacobsen 2006.

519. The interview with Mr. Sando was conducted in 2007. In August 2008, as this book was going to press, Mr. Sando wrote: "We are about to start a new schedule that reduces science and social studies to a combined total of 45 minutes per day. So much for a well-rounded curriculum."

Bibliography

In each case where an Internet address (URL) is given, the citation was accessed and rechecked on August 15, 2008 to confirm its accuracy as of that date. In cases where URLs given are no longer valid, readers are invited to contact the author to obtain a copy of the document.

AASA (American Association of School Administrators). 1946. *School Boards in Action.* Twenty-Fourth Yearbook. Arlington, Va.: Commission on School Boards in Action (Omer Carmichael, Chairman), AASA, February.

Abelmann, Charles, et al. (Richard Elmore, with Johanna Even, Susan Kenyon, and Joanne Marshall). 1999. "When Accountability Knocks, Will Anyone Answer?" CPRE-RR-42. Philadelphia, Pa.: Consortium for Policy Research in Education. http://eric.ed.gov/ERICDocs/data/ericdocs2sql/content_storage_01/0000019b/80/17/72/01.pdf

Achieve Inc. 2002a. *Aiming Higher. Meeting the Challenges of Education Reform in Texas.* Washington, D.C.: Achieve, June. http://www.achieve.org/files/Aiming_Higher_Texas.pdf

Achieve Inc. 2002b. *Staying on Course. Standards-Based Reform in America's Schools: Progress and Prospects.* Washington, D.C.: Achieve, November. http://www.achieve.org/files/5YearReportfinal.pdf

Adams, Scott J., and John S. Heywood. 2007. "Performance Pay in the U.S.: Concepts, Measurement and Trends." 2nd Draft. Washington, D.C.: Economic Policy Institute, November 19.

AdvancEd. 2007. *AdvanceEd Accreditation Standards for Quality Schools. For Schools Seeking NCA CASI or SACS CASI Accreditation.* Schaumburg, Ill.: AdvancED.

AdvancEd. 2008. "Accredited Schools." Schaumburg, Ill.: AdvancED.

Aldonas, Grant D., Robert Z. Lawrence, and Matthew J. Slaughter. 2007. "A New Policy Agenda for the American Worker." Washington, D.C.: Financial Services Forum, June 26. http://www.financialservicesforum.org/atf/cf/%7B95F7C378-E3F0-4073-AB67-ED043F25DBB7%7D/REPORT%20-%20Succeeding%20in%20the%20Global%20Economy.pdf

Alexander, Lamar (chair). 1987. *The Nation's Report Card. Improving the Assessment of Student Achievement. Report of the Study Group. With a Review of the Report by a Committee of the National Academy of Education. Robert Glaser*, Chairman. Washington, D.C.: Office of Educational Research and Improvement, U.S. Department of Education and the National Academy of Education.

Almack, John C. 1927. *The School Board Member*. New York. N.Y.: Macmillan.

Altman, Lawrence K. 1990. "Heart-Surgery Death Rates Decline in New York." New York Times, December 5.

Anderson, Kathryn H., et al. (Richard V. Burkhauser, Jennie E. Raymond, and Clifford S. Russell). 1991. "Mixed Signals in the Job Training Partnership Act." Growth & Change 22(3): 32-48.

Aspen Commission (Thompson, Tommy G., and Roy E. Barnes, co-chairs). 2007. Beyond NCLB. Fulfilling the Promise to Our Nation's Children. The Commission on No Child Left Behind. Aspen, Colo.: Aspen Institute. http://www.aspeninstitute.org/atf/cf/%7BDEB6F227-659B-4EC8-8F84-8DF23CA704F5%7D/NCLB_Book.pdf

Associated Press. 1993. "Rating of Hospitals Is Delayed on Ground of Flaws in Data." New York Times, June 23.

Baker, George. 2002. "Distortion and Risk in Optimal Performance Contracts." Journal of Human Resources 37(4): 728-51.

Ballou, Dale, and Matthew G. Springer. 2007. "Achievement Trade-Offs and No Child Left Behind." Prepared for panel "The Intended or Unintended Consequences of NCLB Accountability, Autonomy, and Choice Mechanisms on Student Academic Achievement." Annual Meeting of the American Education Research Association, April 7.

Barnow, Burt S., and Jeffrey A. Smith. 2004. "Performance Management of U.S. Job Training Programs: Lessons From the Job Training Partnership Act." Public Finance & Management 4(3): 247-87.

BBC (British Broadcasting Corporation). 2008. "Ofsted Says Tests Narrow Learning." BBC News, July 21. http://news.bbc.co.uk/2/hi/uk_news/education/7518200.stm.

Becker, Gary S., and Kevin M. Murphy. 2007. "The Upside of Income Inequality." The American, May/June. http://www.american.com/archive/2007/may-june-magazine-contents/the-upside-of-income-inequality

Bernanke, Ben S. 2007. "The Level and Distribution of Economic Well-Being." Speech Before the Greater Omaha Chamber of Commerce, Omaha, Nebraska, February 6. http://www.federal-reserve.gov/newsevents/speech/Bernanke20070206a.htm

Bevan, Gwyn, and Christopher Hood. 2006. "What's Measured Is What Matters: Targets and Gaming in the English Public Health Care System." Public Administration 84(3): 517-38.

Bird, Sheila M., et al. (Sir David Cox, Vern T. Farewell, Harvey Goldstein, Tim Holt, and Peter C. Smith). 2005. "Performance Indicators: Good, Bad, and Ugly." Journal of the Royal Statistical Society, Series A 168(1): 1-27.

Blalock, Ann, and Burt Barnow. 2001. "Is the New Obsession With 'Performance Management' Masking the Truth About Social Programs?" In Dall W. Forsythe, ed., Quicker; Better; Cheaper: Managing Performance in American Government. Albany, N.Y.: Rockefeller Institute Press.

Blau, Peter Michael. 1955 (rev. 1963). The Dynamics of Bureaucracy; A Study of Interpersonal Relations in Two Government Agencies. Chicago, Ill.: University of Chicago Press.

Blinder, Alan S. 2006. "Offshoring: The Next Industrial Revolution?" *Foreign Affairs* 85(2). www.foreignaffairs.org/20060301faessay85209/alan-s-blinder/offshoring-the-next-industrial-revolution.html

Bloomberg, Michael. 2007. "Mayor's Press Release." No. 375, New York, N.Y., October 17.

BNQP (Baldrige National Quality Program). 2007a. "Criteria for Performance Excellence." Washington, D.C.: Baldrige National Quality Program, National Institute of Standards and Technology, Technology Administration, U.S. Department of Commerce. http://www.quality.nist.gov/PDF_files/2007_Business_Nonprofit_Criteria.pdf

BNQP (Baldrige National Quality Program). 2007b. "Education Criteria for Performance Excellence." Washington, D.C.: Baldrige National Quality Program, National Institute of Standards and Technology, Technology Administration, U.S. Department of Commerce. http://www.quality.nist.gov/PDF_files/2007_Education_Criteria.pdf.

BNQP (Baldrige National Quality Program). 2007c. "2005 Award Winner." Washington, D.C.: Baldrige National Quality Program, National Institute of Standards and Technology, Technology Administration, U.S. Department of Commerce. http://www.quality.nist.gov/PDF_files/Jenks_Public_Schools_Profile.pdf

Bommer, William H., et al. (Jonathan L. Johnson, Gregory A. Rich, Philip M. Podsakoff, and Scott B. McKenzie). 1995. "On the Interchangeability of Objective and Subjective Measures of Employee Performance: A Meta-Analysis." *Personnel Psychology* 48(3): 587-605.

Booher-Jennings, Jennifer. 2006. "Rationing Education in an Era of Accountability." *Phi Delta Kappan* 87(10), June: 756-61.

Brighouse, Tim (visiting professor of education at the Institute of Education, London University, and formerly chief adviser to London Schools and chief education officer for Birmingham). 2008. Personal correspondence and telephone interview with author (various dates, and May 8).

BRI (Barksdale Reading Institute). 2008. "BRI at a Glance." Oxford, Miss.: BRI. http://www.msreads.org/glance/glance.html

Bubb, Sara, et al. (Peter Earley, Elpida Ahtaridou, Jeff Jones, and Chris Taylor). 2007. "The Self-Evaluation Form: Is the SEF Aiding School Improvement." *Management in Education* 21(3): 32-36.

Burke, Edmund. 1774. "Speech to the Electors of Bristol, November 3." In E. J. Payne and Francis Canavan, eds., 1999. *Select Works of Edmund Burke, and Miscellaneous Writings.* Indianapolis, Ind.: Liberty Fund Inc. Library of Economics and Liberty. http://www.econlib.org/library/LF-Books/Burke/brkSWv4c1.html

Bushaw, William J., and Alec M. Gallup. 2008. "Americans Speak Out – Are Educators and Policy Makers Listening? The 40th Annual Phi Delta Kappa/Gallup Poll of the Public's Attitudes Toward the Public Schools." *Phi Delta Kappan* 90(1): 9-20.

Callahan, Raymond E. 1975. "The American Board of Education, 1789-1960." In Peter J. Cistone, ed., *Understanding School Boards; Problems and Prospects*. Lexington, Mass.: Lexington Books.

Campaign (Campaign for the Civic Mission of Schools). 2006. *Call to Action*. Silver Spring, Md., April 17. http://www.civicmissionofschools.org/

Campbell, Donald T. 1979. "Assessing the Impact of Planned Social Change." *Evaluation and Program Planning* 2: 67-90. (Reprinted, with minor revisions and additions, from Gene M. Lyons, ed., 1975. *Social Research and Public Policies*. Hanover, N.H.: University Press of New England.)

Campbell, Vincent, and Daryl Nichols. 2004. "Assessing Citizenship." In Lyle V. Jones and Ingram Olkin, eds., *The Nation's Report Card. Evolution and Perspectives*. Bloomington, Ind.: Phi Delta Kappa Educational Foundation.

Campbell, Vincent N., et al. (Daryl G. Nichols, Manford J. Ferris, Susan F. Sawyer, and Richard A. Bond). 1970. *National Assessment of Educational Progress. A Project of the Education Commission of the States. Report 2. Citizenship: National Results*. Washington, D.C.: U.S. Government Printing Office, November.

CAP (Center for American Progress) et al. (Citizens Commission for Civil Rights, Education Trust, Lawyers Committee for Civil Rights Under Law, and National Council of La Raza). 2007. "Letter to Chairman Miller and Ranking Member McKeon." Washington, D.C.: CAP, July 13. http://blogs.edweek.org/edweek/thisweekineducation/2007/07/dem_groups_concerned_about_mil.html

Cardinal Principles (Commission on the Reorganization of Secondary Education). 1918. *Cardinal Principles of Secondary Education. Department of the Interior, Bureau of Education*, Bulletin No. 35. Washington, D.C.: U.S. Government Printing Office.

Carey, Kevin. 2006. *Hot Air: How States Inflate Their Educational Progress Under NCLB*. EducationSector, May. http://www.educationsector.org/analysis/analysis_show.htm?doc_id=373044

Carnegie-Knight Task Force. 2007. *Mandatory Testing and News in the Schools. Implications for Civic Education*. Cambridge, Mass.: Carnegie-Knight Task Force on the Future of Journalism Education. http://www.ksg.harvard.edu/presspol/carnegie_knight/news_in_schools_web.pdf

Carnoy, Martin, et al. (Rebecca Jacobsen, Lawrence Mishel, and Richard Rothstein). 2005. *The Charter School Dust-Up. Examining the Evidence on Enrollment and Achievement*. Washington, D.C.: Economic Policy Institute.

Carr, Peggy G. 2004. "Preface." In Lyle V. Jones and Ingram Olkin, eds., *The Nation's Report Card. Evolution and Perspectives*. Bloomington, Ind.: Phi Delta Kappa Educational Foundation.

Casalino, Lawrence P., et al. (G. Caleb Alexander, Lei Jin, and R. Tamara Konetzka). 2007. "General Internists' Views on Pay-for-Performance and Public Reporting of Quality Scores: A National Survey." *Health Affairs* 26(2): 492-99.

CDC (National Center for Chronic Disease Prevention and Health Promotion). 2003. National Diabetes Fact Sheet. Atlanta, Ga.: CDC. http://www.cdc.gov/diabetes/pubs/pdf/ndfs_2003.pdf

Choy, Susan P., et. al. (Robin R. Henke, Martha Naomi Alt, Elliott A. Medrich, and Sharon A. Bobbitt). 1993. *Schools and Staffing in the United States: A Statistical Profile 1990-91* (SASS). Washington, D.C.: U.S. Department of Education, National Center for Education Statistics, July. http://nces.ed.gov/pubs93/93146.pdf

Chromy, James R., Alva L. Finkner, and Daniel G. Horvitz. 2004. "Survey Design Issues." In Lyle V. Jones and Ingram Olkin, eds., *The Nation's Report Card. Evolution and Perspectives.* Bloomington, Ind.: Phi Delta Kappa Educational Foundation.

Clark, Joseph (Ofsted inspector). 2008. Personal correspondence with author, June.

Clarke, Marguerite, et. al. (Arnold Shore, Kathleen Rhoades, Lisa Abrams, Jing Miao, and Jie Li). 2003. *Perceived Effects of State-Mandated Testing Programs on Teaching and Learning: Findings From Interviews With Educators in Low-, Medium-, and High-Stakes States.* Lynch School of Education, Boston College, Mass.: National Board on Educational Testing and Public Policy. January.

Cohen, Michael. 2007. "Testimony, Hearing on No Child Left Behind, House Committee on Education and the Workforce." September 10. http://edlabor.house.gov/testimony/091007Mike CohenTestimony.pdf

Committee of Fifteen. 1895. *Report of the Committee of Fifteen on Elementary Education.* National Education Association of the United States. New York, N.Y.: American Book Company.

Committee of Ten. 1893. *Report of the Committee on Secondary School Studies Appointed at the Meeting of the National Educational Association.* Washington, D.C.: U.S. Government Printing Office.

Conant, James Bryant. 1959. *The American High School Today. A First Report to Interested Citizens. (The Conant Report).* New York, N.Y.: McGraw Hill.

Converse, Jean M., and Stanley Presser. 1986. *Survey Questions: Handcrafting the Standardized Questionnaire.* London: Sage Publications.

Cooper Institute. 2008. *Fitnessgram/Activitygram.* Dallas, Texas: Cooper Institute. http://www. fitnessgram.net/files/FGBrochure2-08.pdf

Counts, George S. 1927. *The Social Composition of Boards of Education. A Study in the Social Control of Public Education.* University of Chicago, July.

Courty, Pascal, Carolyn Heinrich, and Gerald Marschke. 2005. "Setting the Standard in Performance Measurement Systems." *International Public Management Journal* 8(3): 321-47.

Courty, Pascal, and Gerald Marschke. 1997. "Measuring Government Performance: Lessons From a Federal Job-Training Program." *American Economic Review* 87(2): 383-88.

Crawford, David L. 2004. "School Boards: Issues of Good Governance in Public Education." *AASA Professor* 26(3): 15-18.

Cremin, Lawrence A. 1951. *The American Common School. An Historic Conception.* New York, N.Y.: Bureau of Publications, Teachers College, Columbia University.

Cronbach, Lee J. 2004. "An Interview with Lee J. Cronbach." In Lyle V. Jones and Ingram Olkin, eds., *The Nation's Report Card. Evolution and Perspectives.* Bloomington, Ind.: Phi Delta Kappa Educational Foundation.

Crooks, Terry J. 2002. "Educational Assessment in New Zealand Schools." *Assessment in Education* 9(2): 237-53.

Cross, Christopher T. 2004. *Political Education. National Policy Comes of Age.* New York, N.Y.: Teachers College Press.

CSAC (California Student Aid Commission). 2004. *The Cal Grant Application Process.* Rancho Cordova, Calif.: CSAC, July. http://www.csac.ca.gov/cgm/Chap04.pdf

Cubberley, Ellwood P. 1920. *The History of Education. Educational Practice and Progress Considered as a Phase of the Development and Spread of Western Civilization.* Boston, Mass.: Houghton Mifflin.

Cunningham, Luvern L. 1962. "Decision-Making Behavior of School Boards." *American School Board Journal* 144: 13-16.

Currie, Janet. 2005. "Health Disparities and Gaps in School Readiness." *The Future of Children* 15(1): 117-38.

Curtis, Polly. 2007. "Who Watches the Watchdog?: As Ofsted's Remit Expands, Some Critics Fear Its Power Could Be Getting out of Control." *The Guardian* (London), March 27.

Darling-Hammond, Linda, and Arthur E. Wise. 1985. "Beyond Standardization: State Standards and School Improvement." *Elementary School Journal* 85(3): 315-36.

DeLucia, Joseph J. (Executive Director, Commission on Secondary Schools, Middle States Association of Colleges and Schools). 2000. Personal correspondence with author, May 24.

Deming, W. Edwards. 1986. Out of the Crisis. Cambridge: Massachusetts Institute of Technology, Center for Advanced Engineering Study.

Deming Institute (The W. Edwards Deming Institute). 2007. "Teachings." Palos Verdes Estates, Calif.: Deming Institute. http://deming.org/index.cfm?content=66

Dickens, William. 2005. "Genetic Differences and School Readiness." *The Future of Children* 15(1): 55-69.

Dillman, Don A. 2000. *Mail and Internet Surveys: The Tailored Design Method.* New York, N.Y.: John Wiley and Sons.

Dillon, Sam. 2005. "From Yale to Cosmetology School, Americans Brush Up on History and Government." *New York Times*, September 16.

DOD (U.S. Department of Defense, Office of the Under Secretary of Defense [Comptroller]). 2003. "National Defense Budget Estimates for FY 2004." Washington, D.C.: DOD, March. http://www.defenselink.mil/comptroller/defbudget/fy2004/fy2004_greenbook.pdf

DOE (U. S. Department of Education). 2008. "Department of Education Fiscal Year 2009 President's Budget." Washington, D.C.: DOE, January 23. http://www.ed.gov/about/overview/budget/budget09/summary/appendix4.pdf

Dorn, Sherman. 2007. *Accountability Frankenstein: Understanding and Taming the Monster.* Charlotte, N.C.: Information Age Publishing.

Downey, Lawrence William. 1960. *The Task of Public Education. The Perceptions of People.* Chicago, Ill.: Midwest Administration Center, University of Chicago.

Dranove, David, et al. (Daniel Kessler, Mark McClellan, and Mark Satterthwaite). 2003. "Is More Information Better? The Effects of 'Report Cards' on Health Care Providers," *Journal of Political Economy* 111(3): 555-88.

Duran, Jacquelyn. 2005. "An Adequate Teacher: What Would the System Look Like?" Term Paper. New York, N.Y.: Teachers College, Course ITSF 4151, December 23.

Dyer, Henry S. 1970. "Toward Objective Criteria of Professional Accountability in the Schools of New York City." *Phi Delta Kappan* 52(4): 206-11.

Eaton, Danice K., et al. 2006. *Youth Risk Behavior Surveillance – United States, 2005.* MMWR (Morbidity and Mortality Weekly Report) 55 (SS-5), June 9: 1-108. Atlanta, Ga.: National Center for Chronic Disease Prevention and Health Promotion. http://www.cdc.gov/mmwr/PDF/SS/SS5505.pdf

ECS (Education Commission of the States). 1976. *The First National Assessment of Career and Occupational Development: An Overview.* Denver, Colo.: National Assessment of Educational Progress. Career and Occupational Development Report No. 05-COD-00, November.

Education Reporter. 2003. "Feds Clamp Down on Nosy Questions." *Education Reporter* (Eagle Forum) 213, October. http://www.eagleforum.org/educate/2003/oct03/nosy-questions.html

Education Trust. 2007. Education Trust Recommendations for No Child Left Behind Reauthorization. http://www2.edtrust.org/NR/rdonlyres/5A150FED-85FD-4535-8DF6-737A536EB0FB/0/EdTrust-NCLBRecommendations41607.pdf

Education Week. 2006. "Chat Wrap Up: The Changing Federal Role in Education." *Education Week* 26(10): 33.

Ehren, Melanie C.M., Frans L. Leeuw, and Jaap Scheerens. 2005. "On the Impact of the Dutch Educational Supervision Act: Analyzing Assumptions Concerning the Inspection of Primary Education." *American Journal of Evaluation* 26(1): 60-76.

Ehren, Melanie C.M., and A.J. Visscher. 2008. "The Relationships Between School Inspections, School Characteristics, and School Improvement." *British Journal of Educational Studies* 56(2): 205-27.

Ellis, Joseph J. 2001. *Founding Brothers. The Revolutionary Generation.* New York, N.Y.: Alfred A. Knopf.

EPC (Educational Policies Commission). 1938. *The Purposes of Education in American Democracy.* Washington, D.C.: National Education Association of the United States and the American Association of School Administrators.

Epperson, Shaun. 2007. "Jenks School Misses NCLB Standard." *Tulsa World,* November 14.

Epstein, Arnold. 1995. "Performance Reports on Quality – Prototypes, Problems, and Prospects." *New England Journal of Medicine* 333(1): 57-61.

Farhi, Paul. 1996. "Television 'Sweeps' Stakes." *Washington Post,* November 17.

Figlio, David, 2006. "Testing, Crime and Punishment." *Journal of Public Economics* 90(4-5): 837-51.

Figlio, David N., and Lawrence S. Getzler. 2002. "Accountability, Ability, and Disability: Gaming the System." Working Paper No. W9307. Cambridge, Mass.: National Bureau of Economic Research, November.

Finder, Alan. 2007. "College Ratings Race Roars on Despite Concerns." *New York Times,* August 17.

Finley, Carmen J. 1972. "Not Just Another Standardized Test." *Compact* 6(1), February: 9-12. Denver, Colo.: Education Commission of the States.

Finley, Carmen J., and Frances S. Berdie. 1970. *The National Assessment Approach to Exercise Development.* Ann Arbor, Mich. and Denver, Colo.: National Assessment of Educational Progress.

Finn, Chester E., Jr. 2004. "An Interview With Chester E. Finn Jr." In Lyle V. Jones and Ingram Olkin, eds., *The Nation's Report Card. Evolution and Perspectives.* Bloomington, Ind.: Phi Delta Kappa Educational Foundation.

Finn, Chester E., Jr. 1977. *Education and the Presidency.* Lexington, Mass.: D.C. Heath and Company.

Finn, Chester E., Jr., Liam Julian, and Michael J. Petrilli. 2006. *The State of State Standards,* 2006. Washington, D.C.: Thomas B. Fordham Foundation, August.

Finn, Chester E., Jr., and Diane Ravitch. 2007a. "Not by Geeks Alone." *Wall Street Journal,* August 8.

Finn, Chester E., Jr., and Diane Ravitch, eds. 2007b. *Beyond the Basics: Achieving a Liberal Education for All Children.* Washington, D.C.: Thomas B. Fordham Institute.

Fiske, Edward B. 1983. "Education: An Expert Urges Multiple Reforms." *New York Times,* July 26.

Fiske, Edward B., and Helen F. Ladd. 2000. *When Schools Compete: A Cautionary Tale.* Washington, D.C.: Brookings Institution.

Franklin, Benjamin. 1728. "The Busy-Body, No. 3. On Virtue." In John Hardin Best, ed. 1962. *Benjamin Franklin on Education.* New York, N.Y.: Bureau of Publications, Teachers College, Columbia University.

Franklin, Benjamin. 1749. *Proposals Relating to the Education of Youth in Pensilvania.* Facsimile Reprint. Philadelphia: University of Pennsylvania Press (1931).

Friedman, Thomas L. 2005. *The World Is Flat. A Brief History of the Twenty-First Century.* New York, N.Y.: Farrar, Straus and Giroux.

Fruchter, Norm, and Kavitha Mediratta. 2006. "Thinking Ahead." In Ken Jones, ed., *Democratic School Accountability.* Lanham, Md.: Rowman and Littlefield Education.

Gallagher, James J. 1970. "Conference on Issues Relating to a National Institute of Education. Summary and Related Proposed Legislation." May 4. ED 044-352. Washington, D.C.: U.S. Office of Education, Department of Health, Education, and Welfare.

GAO (U.S. General Accounting Office). 1993. *Educational Achievement Standards. NAGB's Approach Yields Misleading Interpretations.* Washington, D.C.: General Accounting Office. http://www.gao.gov/docdblite/info.php?rptno=PEMD-93-12

GAO (U.S. General Accounting Office). 1994. *Health Care Reform. "Report Cards" Are Useful but Significant Issues Need to Be Addressed.* Washington, D.C.: General Accounting Office, September.

GAO (U.S. General Accounting Office). 2002. *Workforce Investment Act: Improvements Needed in Performance Measures to Provide a More Accurate Picture of WIA's Effectiveness.* Washington, D.C.: General Accounting Office, February.

Glass, Gene, 1978. "Standards and Criteria." *Journal of Educational Measurement* 15(4): 237-61.

Goddard, Maria, Russell Mannion, and Peter C. Smith. 2000. "The Performance Framework: Taking Account of Economic Behaviour." In P.C. Smith, ed., *Reforming Markets in Health Care.* Buckingham, England: Open University Press.

Goldhammer, Keith. 1964. *The School Board.* New York, N.Y.: Center for Applied Research in Education.

Goldin, Claudia, and Lawrence F. Katz. 2003. "The 'Virtues' of the Past: Education in the First Hundred Years of the New Republic." Working Paper No. W9958. Cambridge, Mass.: National Bureau of Economic Research, September.

Goodlad, John I. 1979, 1994. *What Schools Are For.* 2nd ed. Bloomington, Ind.: Phil Delta Kappa Educational Foundation.

Gootman, Elissa. 2007. "Teachers Agree to Bonus Pay Tied to Scores." *New York Times*, October 18.

Goslin, David A. 1964. *Summary Report: Two Conferences on a National Assessment of Educational Attainment, December 18/19, 1963; January 27/28, 1964.* Reprinted as Appendix J in Lyle V. Jones and Ingram Olkin, eds. 2004. *The Nation's Report Card. Evolution and Perspectives.* Bloomington, Ind.: Phi Delta Kappa Educational Foundation.

Gray-Bennett, Pamela. 2003. "Focused Thinking: Aiming Accreditation Toward Improved Learning." In Joseph DiMartino, John Clarke, and Denise Wolk, eds., *Personalized Learning.* Lanham, Md.: Rowman and Littlefield, Scarecrow Press.

Gray-Bennett, Pamela (director, Commission on Public Secondary Schools, New England Association of Schools and Colleges). 2008. Personal correspondence with author (various dates).

Green, Jesse, Leigh J. Passman, and Neil Wintfeld. 1991. "Analyzing Hospital Mortality: The Consequences of Diversity in Patient Mix." *Journal of the American Medical Association* 265:1849-53.

Green, Jesse, and Neil Wintfeld. 1995. "Report Cards on Cardiac Surgeons: Assessing New York State's Approach." *New England Journal of Medicine* 332(18): 1229-33.

Greenbaum, William, Michael S. Garet, and Ellen R. Solomon. 1977. *Measuring Educational Progress: A Study of the National Assessment. Including a Response From the Staff of the National Assessment of Educational Progress.* New York, N.Y.: McGraw Hill.

Greenspan, Alan. 2004. "Testimony, July 20." Hearing of the Senate Banking, Housing, and Urban Affairs Committee. Federal News Service.

Grigg, W., M. Lauko, and D. Brockway. 2006. *The Nation's Report Card: Science 2005.* Washington, D.C.: U.S. Department of Education, National Center for Education Statistics, May. NCES 2006-466.

Grissmer, David W., et al. (Ann Flanagan, Jennifer Kawata, and Stephanie Williamson). 2000. Improving Student Achievement: *What State NAEP Test Scores Tell Us*. Santa Monica, Calif.: RAND.

Grubb, W. Norton. 2000. "Opening Classrooms and Improving Teaching: Lessons From School Inspections in England." *Teachers College Record* 102(4): 696-723.

Grunbaum, Jo Anne, et al. (Laura Kann, Steve Kinchen, James Ross, Joseph Hawkins, Richard Lowry, William A. Harris, Tim McManus, David Chyen, and Janet Collins), 2004. "Youth Risk Behavior Surveillance – United States, 2003." *In Surveillance Summaries, Morbidity and Mortality Weekly Report (MMWR)* 2004-53 (SS-2): 1-96, May 21.

Hagman, Harlan L. 1941. *A Handbook for the School Board Member.* Topeka, Kan.: School Activities Publishing Company.

Hamermesh, Daniel S., and Jeff E. Biddle. 1994. "Beauty and the Labor Market." *American Economic Review* 84(5): 1174-94.

Hamilton, Laura S., et al. (Brian M. Stecher, Georges Vernez, and Ron Zimmer). 2007. "Passing or Failing? A Midterm Report Card for 'No Child Left Behind.'" *RAND Review*, Fall. http://rand.org/publications/randreview/issues/fall2007/passing1.html

Hanushek, Eric A., John F. Kain, and Steven G. Rivkin. 2004. "Disruption Versus Tiebout Improvement: The Costs and Benefits of Switching Schools." *Journal of Public Economics* 88(9-10): 1721-46

Harcleroad, Fred F. 1980. *Accreditation: History, Process, and Problems*. Clearinghouse on Higher Education and the American Association for Higher Education. AAHE-ERIC Higher Education Research Report No. 6, ERIC No. ED198774.

Harris, Gardiner. 2007. "Report Rates Hospitals on Their Heart Treatment." *New York Times*, June 22.

Hart (Peter D. Hart Research Associates). 1998. *Survey by Shell Oil Company and Peter D. Hart Research Associates, July 17-July 20, 1998*. Retrieved January 1, 2006 from the iPOLL Databank, Roper Center for Public Opinion Research, University of Connecticut. http://www.ropercenter.uconn.edu/ipoll.html

Hawley, Jill (executive vice president, AdvancEd). 2008. Personal correspondence with author (various dates).

Hayes, Dominic. 2008. "Schools Could Be Failed if Children Are Fat or Bored." *Evening Standard* (London), May 19, p. B4.

Hazlett, James A. 1974. *A History of the National Assessment of Educational Progress, 1963-1973: A Look at Some Conflicting Ideas and Issues in Contemporary American Education*. Ed.D. Dissertation, University of Kansas.

Healy, Paul M. 1985. "The Effect of Bonus Schemes on Accounting Decisions." *Journal of Accounting and Economics* 7: 85-107.

Heckman, James J., Carolyn Heinrich, and Jeffrey Smith. 2002. "The Performance of Performance Standards." *Journal of Human Resources* 37(4): 778-811.

Heinrich, Carolyn J. 2004. "Improving Public-Sector Performance Management: One Step Forward, Two Steps Back?" *Public Finance and Management* 4(3): 317-51.

Heinrich, Carolyn J., and Youseok Choi. 2007. "Performance-Based Contracting in Social Welfare Programs." American Review of Public Administration 37(4): 409-35.

Heinrich, Carolyn J., and Gerald Marschke. 2007. "Dynamics in Performance Measurement System Design and Implementation." July (draft).

Hess, Frederick M. 2001a. *School Boards at the Dawn of the 21st Century*. Alexandria, Va.: National School Boards Association.

Hess, Frederick M. 2001b. "Whaddya Mean You Want to Close My School? The Politics of Regulatory Accountability in Charter Schooling." *Education and Urban Society* 33(2): 141-56.

Hess, Frederick M., and Chester E. Finn, Jr. 2007. "Conclusion. Can This Law Be Fixed? A Hard Look at the NCLB Remedies." In Frederick M. Hess and Chester E. Finn, eds., *No Remedy Left Behind*. Washington, D.C.: American Enterprise Institute.

Hess, Frederick M., and Andrew J. Rotherham. 2007. "Can NCLB Survive the Competitiveness Competition?" *Education Outlook 2*, June. American Enterprise Institute for Public Policy Research. http://www.aei.org/publications/pubID.26339/pub_detail.asp

Hill, Henry H. 1930. "State High School Standardization." *Bulletin of the Bureau of School Service* II(3). Lexington: University of Kentucky.

Hill, Paul T. 2003. *School Boards. Focus on School Performance, Not Money and Patronage*. Washington, D.C.: Progressive Policy Institute.

Hoff, David J. 2002. "States Revise the Meaning of 'Proficient.'" *Education Week* 22(6): 1, 24-25.

Hollingshead, August B. 1949. *Elmtown's Youth. The Impact of Social Classes on Adolescents*. New York, N.Y.: John Wiley & Sons.

Horn, Catherine, et al. (Miguel Ramos, Irwin Blumer, and George Madaus). 2000. *Cut Scores: Results May Vary*. Boston College, Mass.: National Board on Educational Testing and Public Policy Monograph 1(1).

Horn, Wade F. 2005. "Welfare Reform Reauthorization Proposals." Testimony before the Subcommittee on Human Resources, House Ways and Means Committee, February 10. http://www.acf.dhhs.gov/programs/olab/legislative/testimony/2005/welfare_reform_testimony.html

Hoyt, Clark. 2007. "Books for the Ages, if Not for the Best-Seller List." *New York Times*, October 21.

Huitt, Raymond Edgar. 1964. *A Survey of Elementary School Accreditation Practices and Standards in the United States*. Ph.D. Dissertation, University of Nebraska.

Hurst, David (vice president for professional services, AdvancEd). 2008. Personal correspondence with author (various dates).

Iezzoni, Lisa I. 1994. "Risk and Outcomes." In Lisa I. Iezzoni, ed., *Risk Adjustment for Measuring Health Care Outcomes*. Ann Arbor, Mich.: Health Administration Press.

Iezzoni, Lisa I. et al. (Michael Shwartz, Arlene S. Ash, John S. Hughes, Jennifer Daley, and Yevgenia D. Mackiernan). 1995. "Using Severity-Adjusted Stroke Mortality Rates to Judge Hospitals." *International Journal for Quality in Health Care* 7(2): 81-94.

Ittner, Christopher D., David F. Larcker, and Marshall W. Meyer. 1997. "Performance, Compensation, and the Balanced Scorecard." Philadelphia: Wharton School, University of Pennsylvania, November 1. http://knowledge.wharton.upenn.edu/papers/405.pdf

Jackman, Tom. 2004. "Falls Church Police Must Meet Quota For Tickets." *Washington Post*, August 8.

Jacob, Brian A., and Steven D. Levitt. 2003. "Rotten Apples: An Investigation of the Prevalence and Predictors of Teacher Cheating." *Quarterly Journal of Economics* 118(3): 843-77.

Jacob, Brian A. 2005. "Accountability, Incentives, and Behavior: The Impact of High-Stakes Testing in the Chicago Public Schools." *Journal of Public Economics* 89: 761-96.

Jacobsen, Rebecca J. 2007. *Priorities for Public Schools: An Analysis of Elite and Popular Opinion on the Goals of Public Education*. Ph.D. Dissertation, Columbia University. ProQuest Digital Dissertations database (Publication No. AAT 3285094).

Jaschik, Scott. 2007. "Should U.S. News Make Presidents Rich?" *Inside Higher Ed* (Inside-highered.com), March 19. http://www.insidehighered.com/news/2007/03/19/usnews

Jaworski, Bernard J., and S. Mark Young. 1992. "Dysfunctional Behavior and Management Control: An Empirical Study of Marketing Managers." *Accounting, Organizations, and Society* 17(1): 17-35.

Jefferson, Thomas, et al. 1818. "Report of the Commissioners Appointed to Fix the Site of the University of Virginia, etc." In Roy J. Honeywell, 1964. *The Educational Work of Thomas Jefferson*. New York, N.Y.: Russell and Russell; Appendix J.

Johnson, Jean, and John Immerwahr. 1994. *First Things First. What Americans Expect From the Public Schools. A Report From Public Agenda*. New York, N.Y.: Public Agenda.

Johnson, Ryan M., David H. Reiley, and Juan Carlos Munoz. 2006. "'The War for the Fare.' How Driver Compensation Affects Bus System Performance." August (draft). http://www.u.arizona.edu/~dreiley/papers/WarForTheFare.pdf

Jones, Ken. 2006. "Thinking Ahead." In Ken Jones, ed., *Democratic School Accountability.* Lanham, Md.: Rowman and Littlefield Education.

Jones, Lyle V. 1996. "A History of the National Assessment of Educational Progress and Some Questions About Its Future." *Educational Researcher* 25(7): 15-22.

Jones, Lyle V. 2004. "Chronology, 1963-2003." In Lyle V. Jones and Ingram Olkin, eds., *The Nation's Report Card. Evolution and Perspectives.* Bloomington, Ind.: Phi Delta Kappa Educational Foundation.

Kane, Thomas J., and Douglas O. Staiger. 2002. "The Promise and Pitfalls of Using Imprecise School Accountability Measures." Journal of Economic Perspectives 16(4).

Kantrowitz, Barbara, and Karen Springen. 1997. "Why Johnny Stayed Home." *Newsweek*, October 6.

Kaplan, Robert S., and Anthony A. Atkinson. 1998. Advanced Management Accounting. Third Edition. Englewood Cliffs, N.J.: Prentice Hall.

Kaplan, Robert S., and David P. Norton. 1996. *The Balanced Scorecard: Translating Strategy Into Action.* Boston, Mass.: Harvard Business School Press.

Kassirer, Jerome P. 1994. "The Use and Abuse of Practice Profiles." *New England Journal of Medicine* 330(9): 634-36.

Katz, Martin R., et al. (Anna Miller-Tiedeman, Samuel H. Osipow, and David V. Tiedeman). 1977. *The Cross-Sectional Story of Early Career Development as Revealed by the National Assessment of Educational Progress.* The National Advisory Council for Career Education. Washington, D.C.: U.S. Government Printing Office, January (revised March).

Kelly, Fred J., et al. 1937. *Implications of Social-Economic Goals for Education.* National Education Association of the United States. Committee on Social-Economic Goals of America.

Kelman, Steven, and John N. Friedman. 2007. "Performance Improvement and Performance Dysfunction: An Empirical Examination of Impacts of the Emergency Room Wait-Time Target in the English National Health Service." Faculty Research Working Paper No. RWP07-034. Cambridge, Mass.: Kennedy School of Government, August.

Kerr, Steven. 1975. "On the Folly of Rewarding A While Hoping for B." *Academy of Management Journal* 18(4): 769-83.

Kingsbury, G. Gage, et al. (Allan Olson, John Cronin, Carl Hauser, and Ron Houser). 2003. *The State of State Standards: Research Investigating Proficiency Levels in Fourteen States.* Northwest Evaluation Association, November 21. http://www.nwea.org/research/national.asp

and http://www.nwea.org/assets/research/national/State%20of%20State%20standards%20-%20 complete%20report.pdf

Kirp, David L. 2007. *The Sandbox Investment.* Cambridge, Mass.: Harvard University Press.

Kirst, Michael W. 1991. "School Board: Evolution of an American Institution." *American School Board Journal.* November (Special Supplement).

Knudson, Eric I., et al. (James J. Heckman, Judy L. Cameron, and Jack P. Shonkoff). 2006. "Economic, Neurobiological, and Behavioral Perspectives on Building America's Future Workforce." *PNAS (Proceedings of the National Academy of Sciences)* 103(27): 10155-10162.

Koretz, Daniel M. 1991. "State Comparisons Using NAEP: Large Costs, Disappointing Benefits." *Educational Researcher* 20(3): 19-21.

Koretz, Daniel. 2007. "Inflation of Scores in Educational Accountability Systems: Empirical Findings and a Psychometric Framework" (Powerpoint). Prepared for the Eric M. Mindich Conference on Experimental Social Science: Biases From Behavioral Responses to Measurement: Perspectives From Theoretical Economics, Health Care, Education, and Social Services. Cambridge, Mass., May 4.

Koretz, Daniel M. 2008. *Measuring Up: What Educational Testing Really Tells Us.* Cambridge, Mass.: Harvard University Press.

Koretz, Daniel, et al. (Karen Mitchell, Sheila Barron, and Sarah Keith). 1996. *Final Report: The Perceived Effects of the Maryland School Performance Assessment Program.* CSE Technical Report No. 409. Los Angeles: National Center for Research on Evaluation, Standards, and Student Testing (CRESST), Graduate School of Education and Information Sciences, University of California.

Krumboltz, John D., et al. (Martin E. Ford, Charles W. Nichols, and Kathryn R. Wentzel). 1987. "The Goals of Education " In Robert Calfee, ed., *The Study of Stanford and the Schools: Views From the Inside. Part II. The Research.* Stanford, Calif.: School of Education.

Ladd, Helen F. 2007. "Holding Schools Accountable Revisited." 2007 Spencer Foundation Lecture in Education Policy and Management, Association for Public Policy Analysis and Management. http://www.appam.org/awards/pdf/2007Spencer-Ladd.pdf

Ladd, Helen F., and Arnaldo Zelli. 2002. "School-Based Accountability in North Carolina: The Responses of School Principals." *Educational Administration Quarterly* 38(4): 494-529.

Lapointe, Archie E., and Stephen L. Koffler. 1982. "Your Standards or Mine? The Case for the National Assessment of Educational Progress." *Educational Researcher* 11(10): 4-11.

Lee, Jaekyung. 2006. *Tracking Achievement Gaps and Assessing the Impact of NCLB on the Gaps: An In-Depth Look Into National and State Reading and Math Outcome Trends.* Cambridge, Mass.: Civil Rights Project at Harvard University. http://www.civilrightsproject.ucla.edu/ research/esea/nclb_naep_lee.pdf

Levy, Frank, and Peter Temin. 2007. "Inequality and Institutions in 20th Century America." Working Paper No. W13106. Cambridge, Mass.: National Bureau of Economic Research, May.

Linn, Robert L. 2000. "Assessments and Accountability." *Educational Researcher* 29(2): 4-16.

Linn, Robert L. 2006. *Educational Accountability Systems.* CSE Technical Report 687. Los Angeles, Calif.: National Center for Research on Evaluation, Standards, and Student Testing, June.

Liu, Goodwin. 2006. "Interstate Inequality in Educational Opportunity." *New York University Law Review* 81(6): 2044-128.

Liu, Goodwin. 2008. "Improving Title I Funding Equity Across States, Districts, and Schools." *Iowa Law Review* 93: 973-1013.

Livingston, Samuel A., and Michael J. Zieky. 1982. *Passing Scores. A Manual for Setting Standards of Performance on Educational and Occupational Tests.* Princeton, N.J.: Educational Testing Service.

Loomis, Susan Cooper, and Mary Lyn Bourque, eds. 2001a. *National Assessment of Educational Progress Achievement Levels, 1992-1998 for Mathematics.* Washington, D.C.: National Assessment Governing Board, July. http://www.nagb.org/pubs/mathbook.pdf

Loomis, Susan Cooper, and Mary Lyn Bourque, eds. 2001b. *National Assessment of Educational Progress Achievement Levels, 1992-1998 for Writing.* Washington, D.C.: National Assessment Governing Board, July. http://www.nagb.org/pubs/writingbook.pdf

Lu, Susan Feng. 2007. "Multitasking, Information Disclosure, and Product Quality: Evidence From Nursing Homes." Chicago, Ill.: Kellogg School of Management, Northwestern University, November 15. http://www.kellogg.northwestern.edu/faculty/lu/multitasking.pdf

Maeroff, Gene. 2003. "Universal Pre-Kindergarten: State of Play." New York, N.Y.: Foundation for Child Development. http://www.fcd-us.org/usr_doc/UPKStateofPlay-Maeroff.pdf

Mann, Horace. 1844. *Seventh Annual Report of the Board of Education Together With the Seventh Annual Report of the Secretary of the Board.* Boston, Mass:: Dutton and Wentworth, State Printers.

Mann, Horace. 1845. *Eighth Annual Report of the Board of Education Together With the Eighth Annual Report of the Secretary of the Board.* Boston, Mass.: Dutton and Wentworth, State Printers.

Mann, Horace. 1848. *Twelfth Annual Report of the Board of Education Together With the Twelfth Annual Report of the Secretary of the Board.* Boston, Mass.: Dutton and Wentworth, State Printers.

Marzano, Robert J., John S. Kendall, and Louis F. Cicchinelli. 1999. *What Americans Believe Students Should Know: A Survey of U.S. Adults.* Aurora, Colo.: Mid-Continent Regional Educational Laboratory.

Matthews, Peter, and Pam Sammons. 2004. *Improvement Through Inspection: An Evaluation of the Impact of Ofsted's Work.* London: Institute of Education, University of London, and Ofsted (Office for Standards in Education), July. http://www.ofsted.gov.uk/assets/3696.pdf

McAdams, Donald R., 2000. *Fighting to Save Our Urban Schools and Winning. Lessons From Houston.* New York, N.Y.: Teachers College, Columbia University.

McElroy, Neil. 1956. *A Report to the President. The Committee for the White House Conference on Education. Full Report.* Washington, D.C.: U.S. Government Printing Office, April.

McKee, Martin. 1996. "Discussion of the Paper by Goldstein and Spiegelhalter." In Harvey Goldstein and David J. Spiegelhalter. "League Tables and Their Limitations: Statistical Issues in Comparisons of Institutional Performance (with discussion)." *Journal of the Royal Statistical Society*, Series A 159: 385-443.

McKee, Martin, and Duncan Hunter. 1994. "What Can Comparisons of Hospital Death Rates Tell Us About the Quality of Care?" In T. Delamothe, ed., *Outcomes Into Clinical Practice.* London: British Medical Journal Press: 108-15.

McMurrer, Jennifer. 2007. *Choices, Changes, and Challenges: Curriculum and Instruction in the NCLB Era.* Washington, D.C.: Center on Education Policy, July (revised December). http://www.cep-dc.org/_data/n_0001/resources/live/07107%20Curriculum-WEB%20FINAL%207%2031%2007.pdf

McMurrer, Jennifer. 2008. *Instructional Time in Elementary Schools: A Closer Look at Changes in Specific Subjects.* Washington, D.C.: Center on Education Policy, February. http://www.cep-dc.org/document/docWindow.cfm?fuseaction=document.viewDocument&documentid=234&documentFormatId=3713

McNeil, Linda M. 2000. *Contradictions of School Reform. Educational Costs of Standardized Testing.* New York, N.Y.: Routledge.

McVey, William Estus. 1942. *Standards for the Accreditation of Secondary Schools.* Ph.D. Dissertation, Department of Education, University of Chicago.

Meier, Deborah. 2002. *In Schools We Trust: Creating Communities of Learning in an Era of Testing and Standardization.* Boston, Mass.: Beacon Press

Mendenhall, Edgar. 1929. *The City School Board Member and His Task.* Pittsburg, Kansas: College Inn Book Store.

Merwin, Jack C., and Frank B. Womer. 1969. "Evaluation in Assessing the Progress of Education to Provide Bases of Public Understanding and Public Policy." In Ralph W. Tyler, ed., *Educational Evaluation: New Roles, New Means.* National Society for the Study of Education. Committee on Educational Evaluation. Yearbook.

Messick, Samuel. 1985. "Response to Changing Assessment Needs: Redesign of the National Assessment of Educational Progress." *American Journal of Education* 94(1): 90-105.

Mishel, Lawrence, Jared Bernstein, and Heidi Shierholz. 2008. *The State of Working America, 2008-2009.* Washington, D.C.: Economic Policy Institute.

Mitchell, John (chairman, Joint Committee of the City and County of Philadelphia). 1830. "Public Education." *The Working Man's Advocate* (New York), March 6 (reprinted from the Philadelphia Mechanic's Free Press).

MMWR (Morbidity and Mortality Weekly Report). 2003. "Physical Activity Levels Among Children Aged 9-13 Years: United States 2002." *Morbidity and Mortality Weekly Report* 52 (33). http://www.cdc.gov/mmwr/PDF/wk/mm5233.pdf

Moore, Solomon. 2007. "In California, Deputies Held Competition on Arrests." New York Times, October 5.

Morgan, Alan D., et al. 1991. *Education Counts. An Indicator System to Monitor the Nation's Educational Health.* Washington, D.C.: U.S. Department of Education, National Center for Education Statistics, NCES 91-634, September.

Morrisett, Lloyd. 2004. "An Interview With Lloyd Morrisett." In Lyle V. Jones and Ingram Olkin, eds., *The Nation's Report Card. Evolution and Perspectives.* Bloomington, Ind.: Phi Delta Kappa Educational Foundation.

Morrissey, W. R. 1972. "Nixon Anti-Crime Plan Undermines Crime Statistics." *Justice Magazine* 5/6: 8-14.

Moses, Robert P., and Charles E. Cobb Jr. 2001. *Radical Equations. Math Literacy and Civil Rights.* Boston, Mass.: Beacon Press.

Mosher, Frederic A. 2004. "The Age of Innocence." In Lyle V. Jones and Ingram Olkin, eds., *The Nation's Report Card. Evolution and Perspectives.* Bloomington, Ind.: Phi Delta Kappa Educational Foundation.

Mullen, P.M. 1985. "Performance Indicators: Is Anything New?" *Hospital and Health Services* Review, July: 165-67.

Murray, Michael. 2005. "Why Arrest Quotas Are Wrong." *PBA Magazine*, Spring. http://www.nycpba.org/publications/mag-05-spring/murray.html

Murray, Sheila E., William N. Evans, and Robert M. Schwab. 1998. "Education-Finance Reform and the Distribution of Education Resources." *American Economic Review* 88(4): 789-812.

NAE (The Review Committee of the National Academy of Education). 1987. "Commentary by the National Academy of Education." In Lamar Alexander, chair. *The Nation's Report Card. Improving the Assessment of Student Achievement. Report of the Study Group. With a Review of the Report by a Committee of the National Academy of Education. Robert Glaser*, Chairman. Washington, D.C.: Office of Educational Research and Improvement, U.S. Department of Education, and the National Academy of Education.

NAE (National Academy of Education Panel on the Evaluation of the NAEP Trial State Assessments). 1993. *Setting Performance Standards for Student Achievement. A Report of the National Academy of Education Panel on the Evaluation of the NAEP Trial State Assessments: An Evaluation of the 1992 Achievement Levels.* Stanford, Calif.: National Academy of Education.

NAEP (National Assessment of Educational Progress). 1979. *Technical Information and Data From the 1977 Young Adult Assessment of Health, Energy, and Reading: Released Exercises, National and Group Results.* Denver, Colo.: Education Commission of the States, March.

NAGB (National Assessment Governing Board). 2003. "Background Information Framework for the National Assessment of Educational Progress." Review Draft. Washington, D.C.: NAGB, March 24.

Nation at Risk (The National Commission on Excellence in Education). 1983. *A Nation At Risk: The Imperative for Educational Reform. A Report to the Nation and the Secretary of Education.* Washington, D.C.: U.S. Government Printing Office, April.

NCEE (National Center on Education and the Economy). 1990. *America's Choice: High Skills or Low Wages.* Commission on the Skills of the American Workforce, Ira Magaziner, chair; William E. Brock and Ray Marshall, co-chairs. Washington, D.C.: NCEE, June. http://www.skillscommission.org/pdf/High_SkillsLow_Wages.pdf

NCEE (National Center on Education and the Economy). 2006. *Tough Choices, Tough Times.* The Report of the New Commission on the Skills of the American Workforce. Washington, D.C.: NCEE.

NCES (National Center for Education Statistics). 2004. *Digest of Education Statistics 2003.* NCES 2005-025. Washington, D.C.: U.S. Department of Education, Institute of Education Sciences.

NCES (National Center for Education Statistics). 2006. *NAEP Data Explorer.* Washington, D.C.: U.S. Department of Education, Institute of Education Sciences. http://www.nces.ed.gov/nationsreportcard/nde/criteria.asp. Accessed September 16, 2006.

NCES (National Center for Education Statistics). 2008. *Digest of Education Statistics 2007.* Washington, D.C.: U.S. Department of Education, Institute of Education Sciences. http://nces.ed.gov/programs/digest/d07/

NCLB (No Child Left Behind Act of 2001). 2002. Pub L. No. 107-110, 115 Stat. 1425.

Neal, Derek, and Diane Whitmore Schanzenbach. 2007. "Left Behind by Design: Proficiency Counts and Test-Based Accountability." Working Paper No. W13293. Cambridge, Mass.: National Bureau of Economic Research, August.

NEASC-CPSS (New England Association of Schools and Colleges, Commission on Public Secondary Schools). 2008. *Teaching and Learning Standards.* Bedford, Mass: NEASC. http://cpss.neasc.org/downloads/Getting_started/complete_standards.pdf

Neuman, Susan B. 2008a. *Changing the Odds for Children at Risk: Seven Essential Principles of Education Programs that Break the Cycle of Poverty.* Westport, Conn.: Praeger.

Neuman, Susan B. 2008b. "Education Should Lift All Children." Detroit Free Press, July 31. http://www.freep.com/apps/pbcs.dll/article?AID=/20080731/OPINION01/807310343.

Nichols, Sharon L., and David C. Berliner. 2007. *Collateral Damage: How High-Stakes Testing Corrupts America's Schools.* Cambridge, Mass.: Harvard Education Press.

Nixon, Richard. 1970. "Special Message to the Congress on Education Reform." In John T. Woolley and Gerhard Peters, *The American Presidency Project* [online]. Santa Barbara, Calif.: University of California, March 3, http://www.presidency.ucsb.edu/ws/?pid=2895

Nove, A. 1964. "Economic Irrationality and Irrational Statistics." Chapter 16 in A. Nove, ed., *Economic Rationality and Soviet Politics; or, Was Stalin Really Necessary?* London: George Allen & Unwin.

NSBA (National School Boards Association). 1967. "School Boards – A Proud Heritage." *Information Service Bulletin* 5(1).

Obama, Barack. 2008. "Education Plan." *Obama 08.* http://origin.barackobama.com/tv/education.php; text at http://www.commoncore.org/pressreleases.php

O'Day, Jennifer A. 2004. "Complexity, Accountability, and School Improvement." In Susan H. Fuhrman and Richard F. Elmore, eds., *Redesigning Accountability Systems for Education.* New York, N.Y.: Teachers College Press

OECD. 2007. "OECD Stat." Organization for Economic Cooperation and Development. On line tool. http://www.oecd.org/statsportal/0,3352,en_2825_293564_1_1_1_1_1,00.html

Ofsted (Office for Standards in Education). 2008. *Every Child Matters: Framework for the Inspection of Schools in England From September 2005.* London: Ofsted, April. http://www.ofsted. gov.uk/assets/Internet_Content/Shared_Content/IIFD/SchoolsFramework/Framework_For_Inspection_Of_Schools.doc

Ogden, Cynthia L., et al. (Margaret D. Carroll, Lester R. Curtin, Margaret A. McDowell, Carolyn J. Tabak, and Katherine M. Flegal). 2006. "Prevalence of Overweight and Obesity in the United States, 1999-2004." *Journal of the American Medical Association* 295(13): 1549-55.

Pangle, Lorraine Smith, and Thomas L. Pangle. 2000. "What the American Founders Have to Teach Us About Schooling for Democratic Citizenship." In Lorraine M. McDonnell, P. Michael Timpane, and Roger Benjamin, eds., *Rediscovering the Democratic Purposes of Education.* Lawrence: University Press of Kansas.
Pauley v. Kelly. 1979. 162 W. Va. 672; 255 S.E.2d 859.

Paulson, Henry. 2006. "Remarks Prepared for Delivery by Treasury Secretary Henry M. Paulson at Columbia University." HP-41, Press Room. Washington, D.C.: U.S. Department of the Treasury, August 1. ttp://www.ustreas.gov/press/releases/hp41.htm

Pelligrino, James W., Lee R. Jones, and Karen J. Mitchell, eds. 1999. *Grading the Nation's Report Card.* Washington, D.C.: National Academies Press.

Pence, Katharine. 2006. "The Accreditation Process: An Inside/Outside School Quality Review System." In Ken Jones, ed., *Democratic School Accountability*. Lanham, Md.: Rowman and Littlefield Education.

Perie, Marianne, W. Grigg, and G. Donahue. 2005. *The Nation's Report Card. Mathematics 2005.* Washington, D.C.: U.S. Department of Education, National Center for Education Statistics, October. http://nces.ed.gov/nationsreportcard/pdf/main2005/2006453.pdf

Persky, Hilary R., Brent A. Sandene, Janice M. Askew. 1998. *The NAEP 1997 Arts Report Card.* U.S. Department of Education, Office of Educational Research and Improvement, November. http://nces.ed.gov/pubsearch/pubsinfo.asp?pubid=1999486

Peternick, Lauri, et al. (Andrew Cullen, John Guarnera, Erin Massie, and Adrienne Siegendorf). 1999. "Developing a Dynamic Indicator System: Measuring the Input, Output, Outcome, and Efficiency of School Systems." Washington, D.C.: Pelavin Research Center, The American Institutes for Research. Draft, January.

Pfeffer, Jeffrey. 1998. "Six Dangerous Myths About Pay." *Harvard Business Review* 76(3): 108-19.

Phillips, Gary W. 2007. *Expressing International Educational Achievement in Terms of U.S. Performance Standards: Linking NAEP Achievement Levels to TIMSS.* Washington, D.C.: American Institutes for Research, April 24. http://www.air.org/news/documents/naep-timss.pdf

Pineau, Vicki, and J. Michael Dennis. 2004. "Methodology for Probability-Based Recruitment for a Web-Enabled Panel." San Francisco, Calif.: Knowledge Networks, November 21. www.knowledgenetworks.com/ganp/docs/Knowledge%20Networks%20Methodology.pdf

Popham, James. 2000. "Looking at Achievement Levels." In Mary Lyn Bourque and Sheila Byrd, eds., *Student Performance Standards on the National Assessment of Educational Progress: Affirmation and Improvements*. Washington, D.C.: National Assessment Governing Board. http://www.nagb.org/pubs/studentperfstandard.pdf

Project Appleseed (Project Appleseed, the National Campaign for Public School Improvement). 2006. "Frequently Asked Questions and Answers for Families and Communities." St. Louis, Mo.: Project Appleseed. http://www.projectappleseed.org/nclbtesting.html.

Raden, Anthony. 1999. *Universal Prekindergarten in Georgia. A Case Study of Georgia's Lottery-Funded Pre-K Program.* New York, N.Y.: Foundation for Child Development, August. http://www.fcd-us.org/usr_doc/UPKInGeorgiaACaseStudyNew.pdf

Ravitch, Diane, 1974. *The Great School Wars. New York City, 1805-1973. A History of the Public Schools as Battlefield of Social Change.* New York, N.Y.: Basic Books.

Ravitch, Diane, ed. 2003a. *Brookings Papers on Education Policy 2003.* Washington, D.C.: Brookings Institution.

Ravitch, Diane. 2003b. *The Language Police.* New York, N.Y.: Knopf

Ravitch, Diane, ed. 2004. *Brookings Papers on Education Policy 2004*. Washington, D.C.: Brookings Institution.

Ravitch, Diane (U.S. assistant secretary of education, 1991-93). 2008. Personal correspondence with author, July 26.

Reich, Robert B. 1991. *The Work of Nations: Preparing Ourselves for 21st-Century Capitalism.* New York, N.Y.: A.A. Knopf.

Reich, Robert. 2006. "The People Are Rising." October 18. http://robertreich.blogspot. com/2006_10_01_archive.html

RIDE (Rhode Island Department of Elementary and Secondary Education). 2008. "School Accountability for Learning and Teaching (SALT)." Providence, R.I.: RIDE. http://www.ride.ri.gov/ PSI/SALT/default.aspx

Ridley, Clarence E., and Herbert A. Simon. 1938, 1943. *Measuring Municipal Activities: A Survey of Suggested Criteria for Appraising Administration.* Chicago, Ill.: International City Managers' Association.

Rivas, Frank. 1974a. *The First Music Assessment: An Overview.* National Assessment of Educational Progress, Report 03-MU-00. Washington, D.C.: U.S. Government Printing Office, August.

Rivas, Frank. 1974b. *A Perspective on the First Music Assessment.* National Assessment of Educational Progress, Report 03-MU-02. Washington, D.C.: U.S. Government Printing Office, April.

Rivas, Frank. 1974c. *An Assessment of Attitudes Toward Music.* National Assessment of Educational Progress Report 03-MU-03. Washington, D.C.: U.S. Government Printing Office, September.

Robinson, Glen E. 1983. *The Educational Research Service on Its Tenth Anniversary: A Look at Its Past, Present, and Future.* Special Report to the Board of Directors of the Educational Research Service. Arlington, Va.: Educational Research Service.

Rockefeller Brothers Fund. 1958. *The Pursuit of Excellence: Education and the Future of America. The "Rockefeller Report" on Education.* Special Studies Project Report V. New York, N.Y.: Rockefeller Brothers Fund.

Ronalson, Peter. 1923. "A Budget of Advice for the New School Board Member." *American School Board Journal* 67(4): 35-36.

Rose, Lowell C., and Alec M. Gallup. 2005. "The 37th Annual Phi Delta Kappa/Gallup Poll of the Public's Attitudes Toward the Public Schools." *Phi Delta Kappan* 87(1): 41-54.

Rossi, Peter. 1964. *Letter to John Gardner.* February 3. New York, N.Y.: Carnegie Corporation of New York Archives, Columbia University Rare Book and Manuscript Library, Box 516.

Rothman, Robert. 1991. "NAEP Board Urged to Delay Standards-Setting Plan." *Education Week*, January 16.

Rothstein, Richard. 1998. *The Way We Were? The Myths and Realities of America's Student Achievement*. New York, N.Y.: Century Foundation.

Rothstein, Richard. 2000a. "Making a Case Against Performance Pay." *New York Times*, April 26.

Rothstein, Richard. 2000b. "Equalizing Education Resources on Behalf of Disadvantaged Children." In Richard D. Kahlenberg, ed., *A Notion at Risk: Preserving Public Education as an Engine of Social Mobility*. New York, N.Y.: Century Foundation Press.

Rothstein, Richard. 2002. "States Teeter When Balancing Standards With Tests." *New York Times*, May 1.

Rothstein, Richard. 2004. *Class and Schools: Using Social, Economic, and Educational Reform to Close the Black-White Achievement Gap*. New York, N.Y.: Teachers College Press.

Rothstein, Richard, and Rebecca Jacobsen. 2006. "The Goals of Education." *Phi Delta Kappan* 88(4): 264-72.

Rothstein, Richard, Rebecca Jacobsen, and Tamara Wilder. 2006. *Proficiency for All: An Oxymoron*. Paper prepared for the symposium, "Examining America's Commitment to Closing Achievement Gaps: NCLB and Its Alternatives," sponsored by the Campaign for Educational Equity, Teachers College, Columbia University, November 13-14. http://www.epi.org/webfeatures/viewpoints/rothstein_20061114.pdf

Rubin, Joel. 2004. "Are Schools Cheating Poor Learners? Officials Say Federal Rules Compel Them to Focus on Pupils More Likely to Raise Test Scores." *Los Angeles Times*, November 28.

Sandholtz, Judith Haymore, Rodney T. Ogawa, and Samantha Paredes Scribner. 2004. "Standards Gaps: Unintended Consequences of Local Standards-Based Reform." *Teachers College Record* 106(6): 1177-202.

Santora, Marc. 2005. "Cardiologists Say Rankings Sway Choices on Surgery." *New York Times*, January 11.

Schemo, Diana Jean. 2003. "U.S. Officials Pull Questions From Surveys About Children." *New York Times*, September 16.

Schick, Allen. 2001. "Getting Performance Measures to Measure Up." In D.W. Forsythe, ed., *Quicker; Better; Cheaper: Managing Performance in American Government*. Albany, N.Y.: Rockefeller Institute Press.

Schiesel, Seth. 2008. "Former Justice Promotes Web-Based Civics Lessons." *New York Times*, June 9.

Schiff, Michael. 1966. "Accounting Tactics and the Theory of the Firm." *Journal of Accounting Research* 4(1): 62-67.

Schlafly, Phyllis. 2001. "Leave No Child Behind." *Washington Times*, December 30.

Schonlau, Matthias, Ronald D. Fricker Jr., and Marc N. Elliott. 2002. *Conducting Research Surveys via Email and the Web*. Santa Monica, Calif.: RAND.

Schuman, Howard, and Stanley Presser. 1996. "Question and Answers in Attitude Surveys: Experiments on Question Form, Wording, and Context." London: Sage Publications.

Schwartz, Robert B. 2004. "Multiple Pathways – And How to Get There." In Richard Kazis, Joel Vargas, and Nancy Hoffman, eds., *Double the Numbers: Increasing Postsecondary Credentials for Underrepresented Youth*. Cambridge, Mass.: Harvard Education Press.

Seidman, David, and Michael Couzens. 1974. "Getting the Crime Rate Down: Political Pressure and Crime Reporting." *Law & Society Review* 8(3): 457-94.

Shonkoff, Jack P., and Deborah A. Phillips, eds. 2000. *From Neurons to Neighborhoods. The Science of Early Childhood Development*. Washington, D.C.: National Academy Press.

Simmons, Edward B. 1976. "The Emerging Trend Towards Elementary School Accreditation." Qualifying paper, Harvard University Graduate School of Education, July.

Simon, Herbert A. 1978. "Rational Decision-Making in Business Organizations." Nobel Memorial Lecture, December 8. http://nobelprize.org/nobel_prizes/economics/laureates/1978/simon-lecture.pdf

Skolnick, Jerome H. 1966. *Justice Without Trial: Law Enforcement in Democratic Society*. New York, N.Y.: Wiley.

Smith, Carl (executive director, Maryland Association of Boards of Education). 2008. Interview with author, May 28.

Smith, Marshall. 2006. "What's Next? Our Gains Have Been Substantial, Promising, But Not Enough." *Education Week* 25(17): 66-71.

Smith, Peter. 1990. "The Use of Performance Indicators in the Public Sector." *Journal of the Royal Statistical Society*, Series A 153: 53-72.

Smith, Peter. 1993. "Outcome-Related Performance Indicators and Organizational Control in the Public Sector." *British Journal of Management* 4(3): 135-51.

Smith, Peter. 1995. "On the Unintended Consequences of Publishing Performance Data in the Public Sector." *International Journal of Public Administration* 18(2 & 3): 277-310.

Smithers, Rebecca. 2001. "Punishment for Black Pupils Appears Harsher. Watchdog's Report Points to Inconsistency Over Exclusions." *Guardian*, March 1.

Snyder, Thomas D., Sally A. Dillow, and Charlene M. Hoffman. 2007. *Digest of Education Statistics-2006*. National Center for Education Statistics, Institute of Education Sciences, U.S. Department of Education. Washington, D.C.: U.S. Government Printing Office. http://eric.ed.gov/ER-

ICWebPortal/custom/portlets/recordDetails/detailmini.jsp?_nfpb=true&_&ERICExtSearch_Sea rchValue_0=ED497523&ERICExtSearch_SearchType_0=no&accno=ED497523

Spellings, Margaret. 2007. "Letter to George Miller. September 5. http://www.ed.gov/print/policy/elsec/guid/secletter/070905.html

SREB (Southern Regional Education Board). 2008. "About SREB." http://www.sreb.org/main/SREB/index.asp.

SSRC (Scripps Survey Research Center, Ohio University). 2005. Survey, July 5-July 19. http://newspolls.org/survey/php?survey_id=20

Stecher, Brian, and Sheila Nataraj Kirby, eds. 2004. *Organizational Improvement and Accountability:* Lessons for Education From Other Sectors. Santa Monica, Calif.: RAND. http://www.rand.org/pubs/monographs/2004/RAND_MG136.pdf

Steinbrook, Robert. 2006. "Public Report Cards: Cardiac Surgery and Beyond." *New England Journal of Medicine* 355(18): 1847-49.

Sum, Andrew, et al. (Tim Barnicle, Ishwar Khatiwada, Joseph McLaughlin, with the assistance of Sheila Palma). 2006. *Educational and Labor Market Outcomes for the Nation's Teens and Young Adults Since the Publication of America's Choice: A Critical Assessment.* Paper commissioned by the National Center on Education and the Economy for the New Commission on the Skills of the American Workforce, January. http://skillscommission.org/pdf/commissioned_papers/Education%20and%20Labor%20Market%20Outcomes.pdf

Taylor, Grace, et al. (Lorrie Shepard, Freya Kinner, and Justin Rosenthal). 2001. *A Survey of Teachers' Perspectives on High-Stakes Testing in Colorado: What Gets Taught, What Gets Lost.* Los Angeles, Calif.: National Center for Research on Evaluation, Standards, and Student Testing, University of California at Los Angeles, September. http://education.colorado.edu/cpic/EPIC%20Documents/COsurvey.pdf

TEA (Texas Education Agency) 2007. "Test Security Enhancements Planned." Austin: Texas Education Agency News, May 31.http://www.tea.state.tx.us/press/07securityenhancements.pdf

Thorndike, Robert L. 1964. *Draft of a Proposal for a Survey of Educational Attainment in the United States.* New York, N.Y.:Carnegie Corporation of New York Archives, Columbia University Rare Book and Manuscript Libraray, Box 516, January 10.

Thorpe, Francis Newton, ed. 1909. *The Federal and State Constitutions, Colonial Charters, and Other Organic Laws of the States, Territories, and Colonies, Now or Heretofore Forming the United States of America. Compiled and Edited Under the Act of Congress of June 30, 1906. Volumes 1-7.* Washington, D,C.: Government Printing Office.

Thurlow, Martha (director, National Center on Educational Outcomes). 2007. Personal correspondence with author, November 28ff.

Thurow, Lester C. 1992. *Head to Head: The Coming Economic Battle Among Japan, Europe, and America.* New York, N.Y.: Morrow.

Timmins, Nicholas. 2005. "Blair Bemused Over GP Waiting Times." *Financial Times*, April 30.

Toch, Thomas. 2006. *Margins of Error: The Education Testing Industry in the No Child Left Behind Era.* Washington, D.C.: Education Sector, January.

Tucker, Marc. 2007. "Making Tough Choices." *Phi Delta Kappan* 88(10): 728-32.

Twigg, R. 1972. "Downgrading of Crimes Verified in Baltimore." *Justice Magazine* 5/6: 1, 15-18.

Tyack, David, and Larry Cuban, 1995. *Tinkering Toward Utopia.* Cambridge, Mass.: Harvard University Press.

Tyler, Ralph W. 1936. "Defining and Measuring Objectives of Progressive Education." *Educational Research Bulletin* 15(3): 67-72.

Tyler, Ralph W. 1949. *Basic Principles of Curriculum and Instruction.* Chicago, Ill.: University of Chicago Press.

Tyler, Ralph W. 1972. "Why Evaluate Education?" *Compact* 6(1). Education Commission of the States.

UFT (United Federation of Teachers). 2007. "Report of the UFT Task Force on High Stakes Testing." New York, N.Y.: UFT, April 20. http://www.uft.org/news/issues/reports/taskforce/

Uhlig, Mark A. 1987. "Transit Police Remove Officer for Quota Plan." *New York Times*, December 21.

Urban, Wayne. 1998. *More Than the Facts: The Research Division of the National Education Association.* 1922-1997. Lanham, Md.: University Press of America.

Vail, Kathleen. 2006. "Mind and Body: New Research Ties Physical Activity and Fitness to Academic Success." *American School Board Journal* 193(3): 30-33.

Viadero, Debra. 2003a. "NAEP Board Wants to Reduce Background Queries." *Education Week*, May 14.

Viadero, Debra. 2003b. "'Report Card' Lacking Usual Background Data." Education Week, July 9.

Viadero, Debra. 2008. "Exercise Seen as Priming Pump for Students' Academic Strides." *Education Week*, February 13.

Villani, Joseph (deputy executive director, National School Boards Association). 2008. Personal correspondence with author, various dates.

Vinovskis, Maris. 1998. *Overseeing the Nation's Report Card: The Creation and Evolution of the National Assessment Governing Board (NAGB)*. Washington, D.C.: National Assessment Governing Board, U.S. Department of Education. http://www.nagb.org/pubs/95222.pdf

Viscusi, Margot. 1964. *A Report on the Second Conference on a National Assessment of Educational Attainment, January 27/28, 1964*. New York, N.Y.: Carnegie Corporation of New York Archives, Columbia University Rare Book and Manuscript Library, Box 516.

Von Zastrow, Claus, with Helen Janc. 2004. *Academic Atrophy: The Condition of the Liberal Arts in America's Public Schools*. Washington, D.C.: Council for Basic Education.

Von Zastrow, Claus. 2005. Personal correspondence with author, December 6, providing underlying data for von Zastrow with Janc 2004.

Wagoner, Jennings L., Jr., 1991. "Jefferson, Justice, and the Enlightened Society." In Deborah A. Verstegen and James Gordon Ward, eds., *The 1990 American Education Finance Association Yearbook: Spheres of Justice in Education*. New York, N.Y.: Harper-Collins.

Wagoner, Jennings L., Jr. 2004. *Jefferson and Education*. Charlottesville, Va.: Thomas Jefferson Foundation.

Washington, George. 1790. "First Annual Address," January 8. In Fred L. Israel, ed. 1966. *The State of the Union Messages of the Presidents*, Volume I, 1790-1860. New York, N.Y.: Chelsea House-Robert Hector Publishers.

Washington, George. 1796. "The Farewell Address," September 17. In Burton Ira Kaufman, ed. 1969. *Washington's Farewell Address. The View From the 20th Century*. Chicago, Ill.: Quadrangle Books.

WASC (Western Association of Schools and Colleges). 2008. "About WASC Accreditation: WASC Criteria." WASC Accrediting Commission for Schools. Burlingame, Calif.: WASC. http://www.acswasc.org/about_criteria.htm#FOLA

Weingarten, Randi. 2008. Keynote Address. 33rd Annual Conference of the American Education Finance Association, April 10, Denver, Colo.

West, Martin. 2007. "Testing, Learning, and Teaching: The Effects of Test-Based Accountability on Student Achievement and Instructional Time in Core Academic Subjects." In Chester E. Finn Jr., and Diane Ravitch, eds., *Beyond the Basics: Achieving a Liberal Education for All Children*. Washington, D.C.: Thomas B. Fordham Institute, pp. 45-62.

WGBH (PBS Kids 2008). "Between the Lions." Boston, Mass.: WGBH. http://pbskids.org/lions/parentsteachers/program/index.html

White, Alpheus L. 1962. *Local School Boards: Organization and Practices*. U.S. Department of Health, Education, and Welfare. Washington, D.C.: U.S. Government Printing Office.

Wilson, James Q. 1989. *Bureaucracy: What Government Agencies Do and Why They Do It.* New York, N.Y.: Basic Books.

Wilson, Thomas A. 1996. *Reaching for a Better Standard: English School Inspection and the Dilemma of Accountability for American Public Schools.* New York, N.Y.: Teachers College Press.

Wirtz, Willard, and Archie Lapointe. 1982. *Measuring the Quality of Education: A Report on Assessing Educational Progress.* Washington, D.C.: Wirtz and Lapointe.

Wiseman, Michael. 2007. "Performing for Prizes: The High Performance Bonus as an Instrument for Improving Management of American Social Assistance." Paper presented at the Ninth Public Management Research Conference, Public Management Research Association, Tucson, Ariz., October 25-27.

Womer, Frank B., and Marjorie M. Mastie. 1972. "Can National Assessment Change American Education?" *Compact* 6(1): 26-28. Education Commission of the States.

WOPI (State of Washington Office of Public Instruction). 2008. "Frequently Asked Questions About the WASL." Olympia: WOPI. http://www.k12.wa.us/assessment/WASL/FAQ.aspx

Zehr, Mary Ann. 2007. "Texas Plans New Test-Security Measures as Cheating Allegations Swirl." *Education Week*, June 13.

Zlatos, B. 1994. "Don't Test, Don't Tell: Is Academic Red-Shirting Skewing the Way We Rank Our Schools?" *American School Board Journal* 181(11), 24-28.

Acknowledgments

I am grateful to have had the opportunity to work on this project with creative and insightful collaborators. They began assisting me when they were graduate students; Rebecca Jacobsen is now an assistant professor of education at Michigan State University, and Tamara Wilder is a postdoctoral fellow at the University of Michigan. I cannot thank them enough.

And likewise, my deepest appreciation and gratitude go to Jessica Salute, a teacher at P.S. 161 in Manhattan, the Don Pedro Albizu Campos Elementary School, who conducted the interviews reported in Appendix 4.

I am fortunate to have benefited from careful critical reviews from several colleagues who have thought long and deeply about the issues discussed in this book. As always, Lawrence Mishel, president of the Economic Policy Institute, was my most important reviewer, not only by reading the manuscript but from our ongoing discussions about these issues over the course of the years in which this project has evolved. Diane Ravitch corrected several errors of historical interpretation in an earlier draft of this book, as well as contributing many helpful suggestions about improving the entire manuscript. Susan B. Neuman, who has been intimately involved in the development and implementation of many of the federal policies discussed in this book, took great care to help me understand how we have gotten to where we are in education accountability and how we should move forward. Nobody knows more about the development of educational policy over the last 30 years than Bella Rosenberg, who was at the center of it as assistant to American Federation of Teachers President Albert Shanker and his successor, Sandra Feldman. Reading her careful critique of an early draft of this manuscript made it obvious that we would all have benefited if Bella had written this book herself; I regret that her failure to do so forces readers to accept an inferior product. Monty Neill, the deputy director of FairTest, has applied his deep knowledge and insight to a careful critique of the manuscript, from which it has benefited. Helen F. Ladd, who has studied and written about the theory of accountability policy in education (see especially her superb 2007 lecture, anticipating some themes of this book, to the conference of the Association for Public Policy Analysis and Management [Ladd 2007]), likewise made careful suggestions that influenced the final draft. Three officials of regional accreditation bodies, Jacob Ludes and Pamela Gray-Bennett, executive director and director of the Commission on Public Secondary Schools, respectively, of the New England Association of Schools and Colleges, and Jill Hawley, executive vice president of AdvanceEd (the product of a merger of the North Central and Southern Associations) were generous in their willingness to help me improve a manuscript that may interpret their own organizational work differently than they would do so themselves. Each of these reviewers raised important objections to portions of the manuscript, and while I followed many of their suggestions, I rejected others. These are complex issues and, with regard to the suggestions I rejected, the reviewers may well be correct and I wrong. Therefore, the usual caveat that the author is responsible for any errors that remain has particular force in this case.

Indeed, some of these reviewers' suggestions, particularly with regard to the policy recommendations in Chapter 8, invite further discussion and debate that could lead to a revision of the views advanced here. In particular:

- Susan B. Neuman is concerned about the reliability of measures that this book suggests could assess the less easily standardized outcomes of the educational process. Her concern is consistent with an objection raised by Jacob Ludes, who noted that criticisms we make of the generality of standards used by the accreditation agencies might just as well apply to the standards used by English inspectors who assess outputs that are similar to our very broadly defined eight goal areas.

- As endnote 486 suggests, some analysts (e.g., Goodwin Liu) are skeptical of a proposal that the federal government subsidize states with low fiscal capacity and high need, without also demanding a minimum tax effort by states, to prevent states from supplanting their own tax dollars with federal ones. If, however, enforcing a "supplement not supplant" regime proves practically impossible, then some, including my reviewer Helen Ladd, argue that the federal government should instead increase its categorical grants for specific programs to benefit low-income children, such as the Title I program.

- Diane Ravitch is not as persuaded as I that a debate about content standards would be more ideological at the federal than at the state level. While acknowledging the unfortunate polarization that surrounded attempts to develop voluntary national standards in the early 1990s, she also recalls her experience as a member of the National Assessment Governing Board that demonstrated that it was possible, in NAEP, to develop highly regarded subject matter content frameworks for the NAEP assessment without this development being excessively politicized.

- This book recommends that states employ higher-quality standardized tests for assessment of academic goal areas, supplemented by other examination of student work and observations during the inspection process. Reviewing the manuscript, Monty Neill objected that we still may place too much faith in the relative value of standardized tests and too little in the relative importance of examination of student work. Perhaps he is right.

The preparation of this book was jointly sponsored by the Campaign for Educational Equity (CEE) at Teachers College, Columbia University and by the Economic Policy Institute (EPI). I mentioned above my appreciation for the on-going advice of Lawrence Mishel, president of EPI. Over the years during which I worked on this book, I also benefited from and have been grateful for the support and insights of Michael Rebell, executive director of CEE.

Support of CEE for this book was provided by the Lumina Foundation for Education. The foundation never once used the power of its purse to influence the content of this work. For this, I am grateful to Sam Cargile, senior director of grantmaking, and am hopeful that he will find the final product to have been deserving of his arms-length support.

In 2004, Arthur Levine, then president of Teachers College, together with the Teachers College Board of Trustees, asked me to develop a "Report Card" to describe the achievement gap between disadvantaged and middle-class youth. It soon became apparent that such a gap could not be meaningfully described unless the many outcomes of education for which we seek equity were more precisely defined. I am indebted to former President Levine and to the trustees for their willingness to support, with enthusiasm, what at first must have seemed a detour of defining the goals of education. Susan Fuhrman, the current president of Teachers College, was likewise supportive of the project that led to this book, and I thank her as well.

As the book describes, an early step in this project was a survey of representative samples of the national adult population, school board members, state legislators, and school superintendents regarding the relative priorities they placed on the eight goals of education we had specified. Anne Bryant, executive director of the National School Boards Association; David Shreve, committee director for education, labor, and job training of the National Conference of State Legislatures; and Bruce Hunter and C.J. Reid, associate executive directors of the American Association of School Administrators; were all enthusiastic about this survey. They not only provided membership lists from which a random sample could be drawn, but communicated with the sample participants to encourage their participation in the survey. The survey could not have been conducted without this assistance.

Chapter 4 draws in part on a paper, "'Proficiency for All' – An Oxymoron," I co-authored with Rebecca Jacobsen and Tamara Wilder for the symposium, "Examining America's Commitment to Closing Achievement Gaps: NCLB and Its Alternatives," sponsored by the Campaign for Educational Equity, Teachers College, Columbia University, November 13-14, 2006. That paper expressed gratitude for advice and assistance of scholars and policy experts (James Guthrie, Walt Haney, Daniel Koretz, Robert Linn, Lawrence Mishel, Senta Raizen, Michael Rebell, Bella Rosenberg, Jesse Rothstein, and Christopher Weiss) and government technical experts (Eugene Owen, Susan Loomis, Larry Feinberg, Gary Phillips, and Kelley Rhoney). As always, none were responsible for our failure to follow their advice or heed their cautions; the errors of fact or interpretation that remained were the sole responsibility of the authors.

Knowing of my interest in analogies between accountability in education and in other fields, Professor Daniel Koretz of the Harvard Graduate School of Education invited me to attend a seminar he organized in May 2007, the "Eric M. Mindich Conference on Experimental Social Science: Biases From Behavioral Responses to Measurement: Perspectives From Theoretical Economics, Health Care, Education, and Social Services." Several participants in that seminar, particularly George Baker of the Harvard Business School, Carolyn Heinrich of the Lafollette School of Public Affairs at the University of Wisconsin, and Meredith Rosenthal of the Harvard School of Public Health, were generous in introducing me to the literatures in their respective fields, answering my follow-up questions, and referring me to other experts. Much of Chapter 5 results from following sources initially identified by these experts.

Chapter 5 summarizes a paper prepared for presentation at the conference, "Performance Incentives: Their Growing Impact on American K-12 Education," sponsored by the National Center on Performance Incentives at Peabody College, Vanderbilt University, February 27-29, 2008. I am grateful to Matthew Springer, research assistant professor of public policy and education at Peabody College, for commissioning this paper. That paper itself benefited from critical reviews by Marcia Angell, Julie Berry Cullen, David Figlio, Carolyn Heinrich, Jeffrey Henig, Rebecca Jacobsen, Trent Kaufman, Ellen Condliffe Lagemann, Lawrence Mishel, Howard Nelson, Bella Rosenberg, Joydeep Roy, Brian Stecher, and Tamara Wilder. Thanks to all. None, of course, are responsible for errors of fact or judgment that remain.

I mentioned above that Jacob Ludes, Pamela Gray-Bennett, and Jill Hawley provided helpful reviews of an early manuscript of the book. Along with Janet Allison, deputy director of the Commission on Public Secondary Schools of NEASC, they invited my collaborators, Rebecca Jacobsen and Tamara Wilder, to be full members of school accreditation review teams in New England. And Mike Bugenski, Michigan director of the North Central Association Commission on Accreditation and School Improvement, invited Professor Jacobsen and her undergraduate research assistant, Sarah Winchell, to join accreditation teams in Michigan. Without this experience (including Ms. Winchell's careful notes), we could not have written the accreditation section of Chapter 7, and we thank them.

Fortuitously, two academic colleagues at American universities have fathers who either were or are professional inspectors of English schools as officials of, or contractors to, Ofsted. The colleagues, Harry Brighouse and Damon Clark, introduced me to their fathers, Tim Brighouse and Joe Clark, each of whom corresponded with me regarding the English school inspection system. Thank you, Harry and Damon, and your fathers! In addition, Peter Earley, head of the leadership and management faculty at the Institute of Education at the University of London, was kind enough to review and comment on portions of the manuscript concerning Ofsted.

Other colleagues assisted with other aspects. Nobody but James W. Guthrie would have remembered, and been able to point me to, the investigation of the goals of education that Lawrence Downey undertook with his graduate students at the University of Chicago a half century ago. Myron Lieberman called my attention to a 1970 issue of *Phi Delta Kappan* on accountability, of which he had been the guest editor, and which included important contributions upon which Chapter 1 relies. Guido Stempel, a professor at the Scripps School of Journalism at Ohio University, and Thomas Hargrove, of the Scripps Howard News Service, were willing to explore, at our request, weighting the goals of education in their regular public opinion poll; their results, described in Chapter 2, helped us to understand the benefits and limits of such polling. The staff of Knowledge Networks, the firm that conducted our constant sum poll to weight the goals of education, also described in Chapter 2, took great interest in this project, for which we are grateful: in particular, Knowledge Networks Vice Presidents Bill McCready and J. Michael Dennis, and Project Director Stefan Subias, who paid careful attention to the details. Professor Robert Shapiro at Columbia University assisted Rebecca Jacobsen in evaluating the Knowledge Networks methodology; Sharif Shakrani, co-director of the Education Policy Center at Michigan State University and formerly the deputy executive director of the National Assessment Governing Board, helped her to estimate the cost of expanding NAEP in the ways we have proposed. Joel Packer, director of education policy and practice at the National Education Association, identified several of the teachers whom we contacted for interviews for Appendix 4.

Patrick Watson had edited two previous books of mine, *Class and Schools* and *The Charter School Dust-Up*, and so I was confident that this manuscript would be immeasurably improved by his hand. My faith was not misplaced. Thanks, Patrick.

We thank Valerie Echavarria, a student at the University of New Hampshire, who checked all the websites in the bibliography and made sure that references and endnotes were consistent in style.

There are undoubtedly others who, during the four years that Rebecca Jacobsen, Tamara Wilder, and I worked on this and related projects, gave us important assistance, and whom we have carelessly neglected to thank. To them, both our gratitude and apologies.

– Richard Rothstein
September 2, 2008

Index

About the authors

RICHARD ROTHSTEIN is a research associate of the Economic Policy Institute. From 1999 to 2002 he was the national education columnist of *The New York Times*, and he was a member of the national task force that drafted the statement, "A Broader, Bolder Approach to Education" (www.boldapproach.org). He is also the author of *Class and Schools: Using Social, Economic, and Educational Reform to Close the Black-White Achievement Gap* (EPI & Teachers College 2004) and *The Way We Were? Myths and Realities of America's Student Achievement* (1998). Rothstein was a co-author of the books *The Charter School Dust-Up: Examining the Evidence on Enrollment and Achievement* (2005) and *All Else Equal: Are Public and Private Schools Different?* (2003). A full listing of Rothstein's publications on education and other economic policy issues, including links, can be found at www.epi.org/author_publications. cfm?author_id=271. He can be contacted at riroth@epi.org.

REBECCA JACOBSEN is an assistant professor of teacher education and education policy at Michigan State University. She was a 2006-07 Spencer Foundation Dissertation Fellow, and received her Ph.D. in politics and education from Columbia University. Her research focuses on the achievement gap, the democratic purposes of education, and public opinion and representation; she was a co-author of *The Charter School Dust-Up: Examining the Evidence on Enrollment and Achievement* (2005). Jacobsen was also a Teach for America corps member, and taught for eight years in New York City and Connecticut public schools. She can be contacted at rjacobs@msu.edu.

TAMARA WILDER is a postdoctoral fellow at the Ford School of Public Policy at the University of Michigan and was a 2007-08 Spencer Foundation Dissertation Fellow. Her research focuses on equity issues, accountability, school choice, and parent and community involvement in schools. She received her M.A. in quantitative methods in the social sciences and her Ph.D. in politics and education from Columbia University. Wilder can be contacted at wildert@umich.edu.

About EPI

THE ECONOMIC POLICY INSTITUTE was founded in 1986 to widen the debate about policies to achieve healthy economic growth, prosperity, and opportunity. Today, despite rapid growth in the U.S. economy in the latter part of the 1990s, inequality in wealth, wages, and income remains historically high. Expanding global competition, changes in the nature of work, and rapid technological advances are altering economic reality. Yet many of our policies, attitudes, and institutions are based on assumptions that no longer reflect real world conditions.

With the support of leaders from labor, business, and the foundation world, the Institute has sponsored research and public discussion of a wide variety of topics: globalization; fiscal policy; trends in wages, incomes, and prices; education; the causes of the productivity slowdown; labor market problems; rural and urban policies; inflation; state-level economic development strategies; comparative international economic performance; and studies of the overall health of the U.S. manufacturing sector and of specific key industries.

The Institute works with a growing network of innovative economists and other social-science researchers in universities and research centers all over the country who are willing to go beyond the conventional wisdom in considering strategies for public policy. Founding scholars of the Institute include Jeff Faux, former EPI president; Lester Thurow, Sloan School of Management, MIT; Ray Marshall, former U.S. secretary of labor, professor at the LBJ School of Public Affairs, University of Texas; Barry Bluestone, Northeastern University; Robert Reich, former U.S. secretary of labor; and Robert Kuttner, author, editor of *The American Prospect*, and columnist for *Business Week* and the *Washington Post* Writers Group.

For additional information about the Institute, contact EPI at 1333 H St. NW, Suite 300, Washington, D.C. 20005, (202) 775-8810, or visit www.epi. org.

About Teachers College Press

For over a century, TEACHERS COLLEGE PRESS has been committed to addressing the ideas that matter most to educators. Today, its publishing program carries on this tradition and seeks to open and expand the dialogue between theory and practice by looking at education, learning, and teaching in diverse ways; exploring the tension between the academy and the public school; challenging assumptions that devalue the quality of the educational experience at all levels of schooling; and providing substantive resources for all of the participants in the education process (teachers, teacher educators, researchers, academics, administrators, school board members, policy makers, parents, and students).

Teachers College Press publications include books and materials of interest in all areas of education, from infant/toddler to adult learning. It also publishes works in related subjects like psychology, sociology and culture, history, philosophy, and women's studies. Its authors include seasoned practitioners and scholars as well as fresh new talent from around the world.

Many Teachers College Press books cross disciplinary boundaries in ways that are always of interest and frequently provocative. Though sometimes controversial, the Press's publishing decisions are supported by grounded research and reviewed by authorities in the field. Through its series editors, editorial advisory boards, and peer reviewers, Teachers College Press strives to ensure that what it publishes deserves its readers' attention and contributes to deepening the understanding and improvement of the practice of education.

OTHER BOOKS FROM
THE ECONOMIC POLICY INSTITUTE

THE STATE OF WORKING AMERICA 2008/2009
by Lawrence Mishel, Jared Bernstein, and Heidi Shierholz

Prepared biennially since 1988, EPI's flagship publication sums up the problems and challenges facing American working families, presenting a wide variety of data on family incomes, taxes, wages, unemployment, wealth, and poverty—data that enables the book's authors to closely examine the impact of the economy on the living standards of the American people. *The State of Working America 2008/2009* is an exhaustive reference work that will be welcomed by anyone eager for a comprehensive portrait of the economic well-being of the nation.

From Cornell University Press, January 2009. For more information, visit StateofWorkingAmerica.org.

ISBN: 1-932066-34-9(paperback) $ 24.95   SBN: 1-932066-35-7(cloth) $ 59.95

THE CASE FOR COLLABORATIVE SCHOOL REFORM
THE TOLEDO EXPERIENCE
by Ray Marshall

The Case for Collaborative School Reform argues that the most successful school reforms will be undertaken collaboratively between teachers, school district officials, and union leaders. The study focuses on the superior results of the reform efforts of the Toledo School District and the Toledo Federation of Teachers, an innovative and collaborative teachers union in a representative urban school district. Toledo's experience not only demonstrates the value of union-management collaboration to focus the parties' attention and efforts on school reform, but also illustrates the evolution of school policies toward a greater focus on student achievement.

ISBN: 1-93-2066-31-4, 6" x 9", paper, 112 pages, July 2008, $13.50

THE CHARTER SCHOOL DUST-UP
THE EVIDENCE ON ENROLLMENT AND ACHIEVEMENT
by Martin Carnoy, Rebecca Jacobsen, Lawrence Mishel, and Richard Rothstein

When federal statistics showed test scores lower in charter than in regular schools, some charter school supporters insisted this must result from charter schools enrolling harder-to-teach minority students. Data show, however, that typical charter school students are not more disadvantaged, yet their average achievement is not higher. EPI's latest book, *The Charter School Dust-Up: Examining the Evidence on Enrollment and Achievement*, reviews the existing research on charter schools and suggests how such debates could be improved: by carefully accounting for the difficulty of educating particular groups of students before interpreting test scores, and by focusing on student gains, not their level of achievement at any particular time.

ISBN: 0-8077-4615-0, 192 pages, paperback, 6" x 9", March 2005, $16.95

THE TEACHING PENALTY
TEACHER PAY LOSING GROUND
by Sylvia Allegretto, Sean P. Corcoran, and Lawrence Mishel

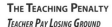

For decades, researchers have asked whether teacher compensation has kept pace without side job opportunities, and whether compensation is sufficiently competitive to attract the quality of instructors desired. While the popular view is that teacher pay is relatively low and has not kept up with comparable professions over time, new claims suggest that teachers are actually well compensated when work hours, weeks of work, or benefits packages are taken into account.

The Teaching Penalty reviews recent analyses of relative teacher compensation and provides a detailed analysis of trends in the relative weekly pay of elementary and secondary school teachers. It finds that teacher compensation lags that of workers with similar education and experience, as well as that of workers with comparable skill requirements, like accountants, reporters, registered nurses, computer programmers, clergy, personnel officers, and vocational counselors and inspectors. Incorporating benefits into the analysis does not alter the general picture of teachers having a substantial wage/pay disadvantage that eroded considerably over the last 10 years.

ISBN 1-93-206630-6, 6"x 9", paperback, 76 pages, March 2008, $12.50

CLASS AND SCHOOLS
USING SOCIAL, ECONOMIC, AND EDUCATIONAL REFORM TO CLOSE THE BLACK-WHITE ACHIEVEMENT GAP
by Richard Rothstein

At the 50th anniversary of the U.S. Supreme Court's landmark Brown v. Board of Education ruling, the stubborn achievement gap between black and white students is a key measure of our country's failure to achieve true equality. Federal and state officials are currently pursuing tougher accountability and other reforms at the school level to address this problem. In making schools their sole focus, however, these policy makers are neglecting an area that is vital to narrowing the achievement gap: social class differences that affect learning. The new book Class and Schools — co-published by the Economic Policy Institute and Teachers College, Columbia University — shows that social class differences in health care quality and access, nutrition, childrearing styles, housing quality and stability, parental occupation and aspirations, and even exposure to environmental toxins, play a significant part in how well children learn and ultimately succeed.

ISBN: 1-932066-09-8, 210 pages, 6" x 9", paperback, May 2004, $17.95

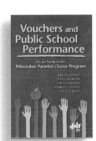

VOUCHERS AND PUBLIC SCHOOL PERFORMANCE
A CASE STUDY OF THE MILWAUKEE PARENTAL CHOICE PROGRAM
by Frank Adamson, Amita Chudgar, Thomas F. Laschei, and John F. Witte

School choice and vouchers have become an increasingly important part of that educational reform policy debate. The debate is rooted in ideological differences between market proponents, who attach greater importance to individual choice, and supporters of a publicly run educational system, who place greater importance on equity, commonality, and public accountability. In a new book, *Vouchers and Public School Performance*, authors Martin Carnoy, Frank Adamson, Amita Chudgar, Thomas Luschei, and John Witte ask whether there is evidence that increased competition among schools introduced by a large-scale voucher plan in an urban school district, Milwaukee, resulted in improved student performance in public elementary schools. The study uses data from an extensive choice reform in Milwaukee's Public School District, a district with the typical educational problems of an American urban center, but unusual in that it has had a voucher plan targeted at low-income students since 1990—the Milwaukee Parental Choice Program.

ISBN: 1-932066-29-2, 6"x 9", paperback, 82 pages, October 2007, $ 11.95

ENRICHING CHILDREN, ENRICHING THE NATION
Public Investment in High-Quality Prekindergarten
by Robert G. Lynch

Research is increasingly demonstrating that the policy of investing in high-quality prekindergarten programs provides a wide array of significant benefits to children, families, and society as a whole, including job creation, inequality reduction, education and health care improvement, and reduced crime rates. In a new EPI book, *Enriching Children, Enriching the Nation: Public Investment in High-Quality Prekindergarten*, Robert G. Lynch examines the costs and benefits of both a targeted and a universal prekindergarten program and shows the positive impact of these programs on the economy, federal and state budgets, crime, and the educational achievement and earnings of children and adults.

ISBN: 1-932066-28-4, 6"x 9", paperback, 135 pages, May 2007, $14.95

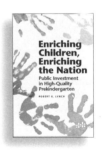

RETHINKING HIGH SCHOOL GRADUATION RATES AND TRENDS
by Lawrence Mishel and Joydeep Roy

In a knowledge-driven economy, those without at least a high school diploma will be far more limited in their work prospects than those with one. But scholars and educators disagree on the rate of graduation in U.S. high schools. Some new statistics seriously understate minority graduation rates and fail to reflect the tremendous progress in the last few decades in closing the black-white and the Hispanic-white graduation gaps. *Rethinking High School Graduation Rates and Trends* analyzes the current sources of available data on high school completion and dropout rates and finds that, while graduation rates need much improvement, they are higher, and getting better.

ISBN 1-932066-24-1, 6"x 9", paperback, 99 pages, April 2006, $13.50

OTHER BOOKS FROM
TEACHERS COLLEGE PRESS

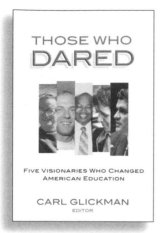

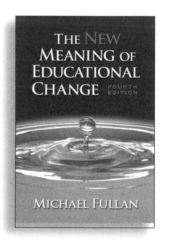

CITY SCHOOLS AND THE AMERICAN DREAM
RECLAIMING THE PROMISE OF PUBLIC EDUCATION
by Pedro Noguera

"Will prove useful to anyone interested in and perplexed by how to reform urban public schools in this country." —Harvard Educational Review

In this bestselling book, Pedro Noguera gives politicians, policymakers, and the public its own standard to achieve—provide the basic economic and social support so that teachers and students can get the job done! Drawing on extensive research performed in San Francisco, Oakland, Berkeley, and Richmond, Noguera demonstrates how school and student achievement is influenced by social forces such as demographic change, poverty, drug trafficking, violence, and social inequity. Readers get a detailed glimpse into the lives of teachers and students working "against the odds" to succeed.

MOVING EVERY CHILD AHEAD
FROM NCLB HYPE TO MEANINGFUL EDUCATIONAL OPPORTUNITY
by Michael A. Rebell and Jessica R. Wolff
Foreword by Susan H. Fuhrman

"Rebell and Wolff set forth compelling reasons for their recommendations and suggest specific steps that should be taken by local, state and federal education officials." —**Richard Riley**, Former U.S. Secretary of Education

Acting as a counterbalance to the current unworkable law, this book proposes a more realistic way to achieve NCLB's inspiring vision by ensuring the right to "meaningful educational opportunity" for all students. This timely volume tackles specific provisions in NCLB head-on, such as the popular, but impossible, goal of 100% student proficiency by 2014.

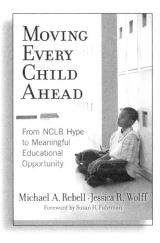

FROGS INTO PRINCES
WRITINGS ON SCHOOL REFORM
by Larry Cuban

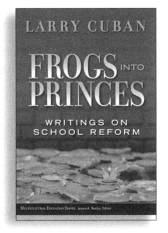

"A fascinating review of Larry Cuban's 45-year-long quest for urban school reform." —**Jack Jennings**, Center on Education Policy, Washington, D.C.

Here is the essential collection of Larry Cuban's writings on urban school reform. These carefully selected studies and articles examine instructional, curricular, organizational, and governance reform in mostly poor and minority districts and schools. The volume includes an Introduction and Epilogue that frames the book, giving readers a sense of Cuban's career as teacher, administrator, and researcher, and how those experiences were intimately tied to the writings presented here. Cuban's deep compassion for students and educators is evident in every page of this stunning collection.